THE
DYNAMICS
OF
PERSONALITY

THE
DYNAMICS
OF
PERSONALITY

LEWIS R. WOLBERG, M.D.

*Dean and Medical Director, Postgraduate Center for Mental
Health; Clinical Professor of Psychiatry, New York Medical
College*

JOHN P. KILDAHL, Ph.D.

*Faculty, Postgraduate Center for Mental Health; Director of
Program in Pastoral Psychology, New York Theological Seminary*

GRUNE & STRATTON, INC.   **NEW YORK · LONDON**

© 1970 by Grune & Stratton, Inc.
757 Third Avenue, New York, N.Y. 10017

Library of Congress Catalog Card Number 75-91600

Printed in the United States of America
(GL-B)

To Samuel Rubin,
whose direction and support precipitated the found-
ing of the Postgraduate Center for Mental Health,
under whose auspices this volume was inspired.

Preface

Following the assassination of Senator Robert Kennedy, a panel of experts—a sociologist, a psychoanalyst, and a minister—was convened by a television network to discuss the reasons behind the unrest and violence that were tearing America's cities apart.

The sociologist insisted that people are pawns on the chessboard of time, implacably moved by contemporary social forces over which they have no control. The psychoanalyst considered this answer too superficial, and he credited man's brutality to an envenomed instinctual nature that dragoons him against his will and best interests to acts of violence and destruction. The minister disagreed with both and, charging society with a disgraceful loss of faith in God, petitioned his listeners to return peacefully to the bountiful graces of the Heavenly Being.

What each of the three panelists was obviously doing was viewing the phenomena of a troubled world through the limited lens of his personal perspective. This is not extraordinary, since we all perceive reality within the subjective bounds of our special experience. And thus, in presenting this book we must qualify our point of view. Since we are in the mental health field, we regard what is happening in the world today as a collective manifestation of intricate human needs and foibles.

Our point of view is a comprehensive one. It looks on social phenomena as the instrumentalities that design human nature, and sees the intrapsychic and spiritual forces that activate mankind as the tools that mold contemporary social structures. Perhaps idealistically, we regard society as a vigorous organism that is constantly changing its form and evolving toward the ultimate goal of gratifying the needs of all of humanity. Our slant is thus optimistic: we believe that despite wars, racial prejudices, and other destructive anomalies, man is moving steadfastly toward a more peaceful social order. We believe that self-knowledge is the key to helping man to liberate himself from the violent instinctual background that he shares with other animals.

This book is written with the objective of providing an understanding of the troubled world within man, in order that he may fashion a better world without.

LEWIS R. WOLBERG, M.D.
JOHN P. KILDAHL, PH.D.

Contents

Part One

xi

Part Two

PART ONE

Introduction

An elder statesman, reviewing his life, remarked: "I am living in a house and I know I built it. I work in a workshop which was constructed by me. I speak a language which I developed. And I know I shape my life according to my desires by my own ability. I feel I am safe. I can defend myself. I am not afraid. This is the greatest happiness a man can feel—that he could be a partner in creation. This is the real happiness of man—creative life, conquest of nature, and a great purpose."

The essential marks of a personality capable of making a healthy adaptation encompass that life-affirming summation. Who would not soar inwardly if he knew that this described himself? The truth is that such an affirmation is indeed accurate for many people. And it can become true for many, many more. The ingredients and the conditions for evolving such a healthy structure are not shrouded in mystery. In our society, if our young persons can be given optimum conditions, there can be the kind of human development that leads to "creative life, conquest of nature, and a great purpose."

It is the goal of this book to present a comprehensive view of man's development and adaptation. But perhaps not of *Everyman*, since we know best that kind of man who lives in the western world. It is he whom we have most intimately studied, through the microcosm of psychological science.

We acknowledge the necessity of focusing on western and, perhaps, American man, because we have not entered into both the private and public world of *Everyman*.

1

We acknowledge the limitations also of our historical perspective. Surely the long hair of Mozart and of George Washington reflected a different era of personality style than does the long hair worn by some of the male sex today. And whatever it meant to Isaiah when he described seeing a six-winged seraphim flying about and speaking in a temple, surely it would have a different meaning if someone presently reported a similar sight. We write therefore of the adaptational capacities of late twentieth century western man. And when we speak of man's adaptation we refer essentially to his behavior and personality.

What are the identifying characteristics of western man's behavior and personality? Behavior has always been considered an inchoate substance dealing as it does with the totality of human experience. It embraces complex biochemical transactions, elaborate neurophysiological reverberations, puzzling intrapsychic phenomena, shifting interpersonal relationships, and entangling liaisons with the environment and the culture. When one speaks of personality, he refers to the interconnecting organization of all those functions combined to form a congruent balance.

For the understanding of man's behavior, i.e., his total internal and external interactions, there are at least a half dozen popular models, corresponding to those above-mentioned functions. Each model stresses a particular axiom as the crucial element in personality determinations. Here are the six: 1. A *hereditary constitutional model* that conceptualizes man's potentials and liabilities, and even specific modes of symbolization, in terms of genetic and prenatal residues. 2. A *physiological model* that regards behavior as the product of complex transactions in different parts of the brain, such as inhibitory and excitatory cortical phenomena or reverberations of the limbic and reticular activating systems. 3. An *internal environmental model* that deals with the biochemical interchanges in the brain and neural apparatus. 4. A *learn-

ing model that conceives of processes in terms of how people acquire knowledge and establish patterns of behavior. 5. A *cultural-social model* that fashions man's morals and manners from vectors in the milieu. 6. A *developmental, motivational model* that deals with interpersonal and intrapsychic dimensions in the light of a "dynamic" psychological conception in its formation and movement.

A vital question that challenges behavioral scientists is whether it is possible to weave out of factual fibers from each of the models a tapestry that can lead to a better understanding of human personality.

Fragmentary attempts have been made in this direction in the form of a so-called "eclectic" orientation, in which there are borrowed from different systems aspects that may be fused into a composite structure. Unfortunately the end product generally has been a potpourri of constituents, which, though facile, have easily revealed their illogic. It is as though in an effort to construct a perfect animal we were to join individual parts of the host of varieties, species, genera, and phyla that populate the earth.

We must avoid the historical pitfall of attempting to provide one convenient explanation for all things. Having abandoned the syncretic objective of reconciling diverse viewpoints, and having forsaken the search for an Absolute Principle, we may then apply ourselves to the critical selection of postulates from the varied systems that have scientific merit.

This epistemological diversion is most relevant to the thesis of this book which deals with the formulation of an integrated theory of behavior.

Our task is thus before us: to determine the distinguishing landmarks of personality development, but within the limitations of our time and our society.

3

1

Man's Machinery of Adaptation

What makes men good is held by some to be nature, by others habit or training, by others instruction.   ARISTOTLE

A seventeen year old girl is brought by her parents to see a psychiatrist. The reason, the parents say, is that "Debbie just doesn't seem happy. She just sits around and eats and gets fat. She doesn't seem to have much confidence. She feels that everything she does is no good. We have tried to urge her to get out and do things, but maybe we are too easy on her. She only plays with younger girls, although she gets along quite well with much older women. We don't know what is going to become of her. She doesn't have any serious interests, and she has no idea what she wants for herself."

The many faces of behavior are revealed in the parents' remarks. We propose, with Debbie serving as our negative example, that:

1. *Man is a biological creature.* ("She just . . . eats and gets fat.") Man's hereditary and constitutional make-up fashion the ingredients of his nature. His biochemistry and neurophysiology are subject to orderly processes that are specific to

his physical operations. The global term "behavior" is too circumscribed to embrace all the rich complexities that constitute the total functioning of the human organism.*

2. *Man is a psychological creature.* ("Everything she does is no good.") Man possesses a psychic organization, a blend of maturational and experiential forces, which has stimulated a special vocabulary to aid the explanation of how man functions. Thus behavior may be described as being fashioned by dynamic, structural, and economic laws of the psyche, a portrayal that is limited to man's internal psychological (i.e., intrapsychic) functioning.

3. *Man is a creature of his conditionings.* ("We have tried to urge her...") Man is subject to laws of learning and evolves patterns in his social exposures. Statements employed in learning theories make possible an understanding of this dimension but do not necessarily apply to other dimensions, particularly the biological one.

4. *Man is an interpersonal creature.* ("She only plays with younger girls.") Man can survive only in relationship with other human beings. His maneuverings are particularized by special expressions that do not lend themselves to being understood in any way but the interpersonal.

5. *Man is a spiritual creature.* ("She has no idea what she wants.") Man is motivated by moral and ethical values and by artistic and creative promptings that can only be conceptualized in a philosophic idiom.

Using these five propositions about human behavior as a base, let us contrast the melancholy description of Debbie with the positive philosophy of our statesman quoted in the introduction. 1. Biological: "I am living ... I work ... I speak."

---

* Freud (1954) made some early attempts at a neurodynamic formulation of psychology, and he contended that it might be possible to substitute physiological terminology for psychological terms. However, he soon abandoned these efforts and restricted himself to purely psychological characterizations.

2. Psychological: "I am not afraid." 3. His conditionings: "a workshop constructed by me . . . a language which I developed." 4. Interpersonal: "a partner . . . " 5. Spiritual: "a great purpose."

With these two brief examples as a background, we will attempt to develop a unifying structure around which to synchronize these propositions relating to man. Such a structure is the concept of "personality."

The Structure of Personality

An examination of the dominions of personality has occupied the interest of many of those who deal with the problems of human beings. However, the investigation of the boundaries of personality by the various disciplines has resulted in findings that cannot readily be amalgamated. This is partly because each discipline has viewed personality from its own point of view, reflecting its special interests and needs. To add to the confusion, a kind of sectarianism has developed among the disciplines that has tended to isolate them from each other, interfering with healthy conceptual "cross-fertilization."

Amidst this chaos some attempt has been made to bring objectivity to the data on personality structure by studying material from a number of different sources. These include observations by trained workers of newborn babies at hospitals, institutions, and day-care centers; experiences of teachers with children at nursery schools, kindergartens, and grade schools; reports of parents describing the behavior of their offspring; studies of recordings of plays, art productions, dreams, phantasies, and spontaneous verbalizations of presumably normal children; psychological tests of children,

7

especially projective tests; investigations by social workers, correctional workers, and psychologists of the socio-economic environment, family relationships, and other areas of potential conflict among maladjusted, delinquent, and criminal young-sters and adults; scrutiny of case records of children with severe emotional problems who have been hospitalized in mental institutions; observations of psychotherapists treating children in their private practices or in out-patient clinics; exploration of memories, dreams, and transference phe-nomena that reflect childhood experiences of adult patients receiving psychoanalysis; field studies of anthropologists re-porting on the customs, folkways, creative artistic expres-sions, modes of child rearing, and family structure of various cultural groups; demographic surveys by various social scientists of the incidence and prevalence of emotional prob-lems in different parts of the world; analysis of reactions of individuals to psychotropic drugs; accounts by ethologists of animal behavior in a natural setting; and research findings of animal experimenters who have subjected higher mammals to artifacts in upbringing or to motivational conflicts.

Objective appraisal of this data requires a more or less precise application of the scientific method. Unfortunately, investigators in the field of personality research are handi-capped by formidable methodological problems in attempting to subject their observations to clinical research. Moreover, current theories of human behavior are so complex, their inherent terms so operationally indefinable, their derivations so diffuse, their implications so widespread that we are un-able to expose them readily to scientific experiment.*

In spite of these obstacles, it has been possible to scrutinize many of the events associated with the development of per-sonality and to examine and analyze this data, making ap-

---

* Of the more than 1400 empirical studies on children reported in re-sponsible publications since 1890, one 110 or 8 percent meet accepted criteria of observational child study. (Wright, 1960)

propriate connections, discerning combinations, and otherwise synthesizing the material in a constructive way. Out of this synthesis, a number of propositions have emerged, the most important of which are the eight that follow.

1. The task of human development is to transform an amorphous creature, this animated digestive tract that we call an infant, into a civilized adult capable of living adaptively in a complex social framework. Toward this end the child cultivates restraints on his biological impulses, acquires skills in interpersonal relationships, evolves values that are consonant with the society in which he lives, and perfects techniques that allow him to fulfill himself creatively within the bounds of his potentials. This process is not without incident. Someone has said, for example, that the main virtue of a two year old is that some day he will be three.

2. Growth is governed by a number of developmental laws—laws of maturation common to the entire species, laws peculiar to the cultural and subcultural group of which the individual is a part, and finally, laws unique to himself, parcels of his personal experience that will make his development unlike that of any other individual. Even as every fingerprint is unique, how much more so is every personality.

3. While growth is broadly similar in all human infants and children, there is great difference in individual styles and rates of growth. Thus it is that a three month age difference between two five year olds can have great significance for each child's reading readiness.

4. Development may conveniently be divided into a number of stages of growth corresponding roughly with certain age levels. While there is some variation in timing and rate, the average individual appears to follow these stages with surprising sequential regularity. Parents often can safely reassure each other with the words "It's only a passing stage."

5. The various stages are characterized by specific needs that must be propitiated, common stresses that must be re-

solved, and special skills that must be developed. A healthy personality structure develops on the basis of the adequacy with which these needs are supplied, stresses mastered, and skills learned at progressive age levels. To say to a two year old "You are acting like a two-year old" is a high compliment.

6. Difficulties may arise at each stage of growth that engender a partial or complete failure in the satisfaction of needs, the solution of current conflicts, and the learning of skills. Such failures handicap the individual in adapting to the more elaborate demands and requirements that constitute the succeeding stages of growth. To use an analogy, an individual will suffer in advanced mathematics courses if he failed to master some earlier fundamental procedure.

7. Where essential personality qualities characteristic of maturity are not evolved, the individual will be burdened with residual childhood needs, attitudes, and ways of handling stress. These anachronisms tend to clash with the demands of a healthy biological and social adjustment. Plutarch attributed to Caesar this same insight about the burden of residual needs when he wrote: "It is not," said Caesar, "these well-fed long-haired men that I fear. But the pale and hungry-looking" (Brutus and Cassius, by whose conspiracy he later fell). Primitive strivings and conceptions of the world, early fears and guilt feelings, and defenses against these usually survive in their pristine form though they are not always manifest. They tend to contaminate an adult type of integration.

8. Personality, evolving as it does from a blend of heredity and experience, is not merely a repository of special abilities, attitudes, and beliefs. It is a broad fabric that covers every facet of man's internal and external adjustment. Through the medium of personality operations, the individual satisfies even the most elemental of his needs.

Summary

There are five faces, then, to personality development: biological, psychological, conditioned, interpersonal, and spiritual. In addition, there are eight propositions that synthesize the nature of this development: the amorphous infant must be transformed into a civilized adult; growth is governed by developmental laws; there are, however, wide individual differences in styles and rate of growth; there are several discernible stages of growth; each stage is characterized by specific needs; the attempt to satisfy these needs may result in partial or complete failure; such failure results in a backlog of unfulfilled demands which then clash with more mature needs; and finally, this broad composite of man's internal and external adjustment is what is called personality, and through its operation all of his needs are satisfied or frustrated.

The study of personality is thus the study of mankind. No human experience is outside its bounds. There is not a single thought, word, or deed that does not issue from these personality operations. In understanding personality we attempt to understand the parts, i.e., the complexities of behavior which flow predictably from the whole. Through discerning the elements that prompt the evolution of a healthy personality we can shed light on the making of a healthy society. And in retrospect, as we understand the difficulties of the individual child and adult in our society, we can reduce the unfortunate ingredients in family life, cultural patterns, and societal values that have wrought these symptoms of ill health. This is our task in the chapters that follow.

2

Eleven Measures of a Healthy Personality

The formative period for building character for eternity is in the nursery. The mother is the queen of that realm and sways a scepter more potent than that of kings and priests.

Jeff Parker, a "normal" person, comes from one of the leading families in town. He is well-liked and a respected member of the community who plays a pretty good game of golf. He and a few friends formed a barbershop quartet that now sings at Kiwanis Club and PTA meetings, he is the treasurer of the Boy Scout troop; he has a son in medical school; and is considered by those who know him to be an adjusted, normal person.

But Jeff is not a well man. He gets periodically depressed, and he drinks too much. He also has periodic attacks of colitis that his physician considers nervous in origin. He usually has a good idea where the closest bathroom is. He will sometimes become terribly frightened when he has to make a business trip out of town. Actually, he doesn't have much in common with his wife, and their life together in

12

recent years has been characterized by an effort to stay out of each other's way, although it isn't terribly noticeable when they are out together. When his wife aggravates him, he becomes withdrawn and sullen. By no means can we qualify Jeff Parker as a good example of psychological balance.

There are some simple criteria for mental health that prevail in the community. If a man is married, has one or more children, holds a good job, goes to church occasionally, and keeps out of trouble with his neighbors and the law, he is accepted as a stable citizen. From a utilitarian standpoint, such criteria may be respected. From a scientific viewpoint, they leave much to be desired. There are many emotionally sick people who marry, procreate, work steadily, support their churches, and avoid destructive entanglements with other individuals and with the law.

Criteria for Mental Health

What, then, are appropriate criteria for mental health? If these could be identified they would be of significant help to those who deal with the educational, vocational, marital, legal, medical, religious, social, and correctional problems of human beings.

It is obvious that mental health must be judged by criteria other than those mentioned above, but what the "other criteria" are has puzzled behavioral scientists for many years. Marie Jahoda, under the auspices of the Joint Commission on Mental Illness and Health, conducted a review of the pertinent literature and held an interdisciplinary seminar "for the purpose of evaluating the theoretical, experimental, and empirical evidence of the psychological nature of mental health" (Jahoda, 1958). Sifting through a bulk of published

13

materials, she was able to compile and classify a great many opinions, but was not able to delineate specifically the criteria for a mentally healthy individual.

There are some authorities who insist that the task is an impossible one, because the standards that apply to one group of people do not necessarily apply to another. By this token the ingredients of mental health in a taxi driver are different from those of a bank president; an adjusted Ubangi native cannot possibly be compared with a well-functioning Anglo-Saxon. Even if we confined ourselves to one country, who would we in the United States, for instance, use as a baseline for determining behavioral norms and deviations? The financiers of Wall Street? The fishermen of Gloucester? The workers in the garment district of New York? The potato farmers of Idaho? The actors in Hollywood? The clergymen of the Episcopal Church? Holy Rollers? Ethical Culturists? Statesmen? Each group would show attitudes, goals, and values that would set them apart from the others. We could not in all honesty classify one as "superior" or "typical."

Should we then try to reduce the special patterns and characteristics of people the world over to basic common denominators? Our most pessimistic scholars insist that the resulting abstractions could only lead to nothing. It would, however, be an act of scientific nihilism to subscribe completely to such defeatist notions.

What is lacking is a pertinent yardstick. Mental health is a relative term, and it is necessary to deal with its gradations. We are much in the position of the man who responded to the question "How is your wife?" by saying, "Compared to what?" With what do we compare the various items that constitute human adjustment?

One idea that has been advanced is that we contrast mental health to mental illness. By this standard we would say that a mentally healthy person is one who is not mentally ill. This immediately imposes upon us the responsibility of defining the phrase "mentally ill." Do we mean by mental illness a condition specifically characterized by distortion of reality, with such symptoms as disorientation, hallucinations, and delusions? If so, we are permitting a host of maladjusted mortals to wave the banner of mental health. If we extend the concept of mental illness to include neurotic and behavioral aberrations, there is scarcely an individual left who is unblemished. Understandably we have to employ some kind of practical gauge.

Mental health has been considered synonymous with happiness, well-being, and contentment. When we examine these criteria we find that they are not too satisfactory in giving us a clinically valid picture of mental health. They certainly apply, for example, to the patient in a manic state of manic-depressive psychosis, who, while subjectively happy and exuding contentment and well-being, cannot be considered mentally healthy. While we may say that the mentally healthy individual has a capacity for happiness, well-being, and contentment under propitious circumstances, we must also say that he must demonstrate a capacity for unhappiness, noncontentment, and ill-being. Otherwise, he would not be able to make an adequate adjustment for his difficulties or to take steps towards modifying disturbances in his environment.

If we turn to the apparently less complicated field of physical health for a lead, we find that there is no such thing as absolute physical health. We deal constantly with relative measures. No skin is free from moles, blackheads, or pimples. There is scarcely a joint in which some arthritic change may not be found. In the vast network of blood vessels some sclerotic changes are the rule, even in youth. Yet we would not consider these imperfections reasons for classifying the individual as physically ill. Nor should we designate as mental illness the universal flurries of emotional distress, the random tensions, anxieties, fears, and somatic upsets that are a parcel of everyday transactions in life.

Our dilemma might be solved if we could establish some kind of standard around which to orient ourselves. Toward this end we may, following the precedent of physical medicine, examine large groups of people and set up measurements of normality that apply to the various dimensions of adjustment. We would then take as a cue the homespun notion that, by and large, the average citizen is a reasonably contented and well-balanced individual. Were this not so, we should constitute an unhappy society indeed. For out of the "average" citizens are drawn our scientists and clergymen and lawmakers and law enforcers and even psychotherapists. Why not, then, take a sampling of traits of the total population in a representative community? We may then contrast the characteristics of the small group of manifestly neurotic and disturbed persons with those of the better adjusted minority. This would serve as a starting point for a reasonably sound assay of criteria of mental health.

Precisely such a study was done. Leo Sroll, Marvin Opler, and Thomas Langner (1962) describe an epidemiological investigation conducted by an interdisciplinary research team that discovered that only 18.5 percent of persons interviewed between the ages of 20-59, residing in a 190 block residential area in Manhattan could be classified as being without some degree of mental disturbance. The great majority of individuals (81.5 percent) possessed symptoms and displayed patterns that classified them as maladjusted and neurotic.

This is not an insignia of human nature. This is a sorrowful tribute to the way people are brought up, to the value systems of contemporary society. It would be absurd to say that because the average individual is emotionally ill, that his characteristics should be established as criteria of mental health.

Despite these complex obstacles, a number of the constituents of "normal" personality can be described. But what is a normal personality? Normality, as has been indicated, is more or less a cultural concept varying with the mores of the group with which the person is identified. Society prescribes special norms for individuals belonging to different strata of class, age, and sex. What is normal for one group may not be acceptable for another. Yet within the wide range of assorted social groupings general principles of adjustment must apply to healthy individuals possessing certain traits in common irrespective of widely divergent modes of expression.

It would be better then to speak of a "healthy" rather than a "normal" personality structure, since the "normal" individual living in a society with many neurotic values may be emotionally unhealthy and even sick. What are the characteristics that make for a good adjustment in most societies? We may classify these in the following categories:

1. *Adequate security feelings. The individual possesses a solid sense of belonging and of being accepted without fears of rejection or expectations of injury.*

Beginning as a helpless infant, the individual needs to experience a consistently responsive world that he can rely on. As the infant cries, and bountiful milk and dry pants materialize, he develops faith that all is well. As he re-experiences these events dozens and hundreds of times, he develops a firm belief that his own impulses and the world he lives in can cooperate happily. This trust forms the basis for his all-inclusive view of life.

But as adults, of course, our sense of security is not bound up only in milk and dry pants. We can become anxious about events that take place 6,000 miles away, over which we have no control, no matter how loudly we cry. A beloved leader is assassinated, another nation develops a hydrogen bomb, we wake up some morning to hear that two more nations are at war—and we all can cry out that we do not like the treatment that our world offers us. The evidence around us is that both children and adults in our society feel too unsafe. But the evidence is that in the face of untoward events of either a personal or global nature, those persons with the early, firm experiences of consistent emotional support can respond the most productively.

The *unsafeness* of our adult world places upon every adult the imperative necessity of providing for infants and youngsters the safety and predictableness upon which a reasonable sense of security may be built.

2. *A good measure of self-esteem. The good self-image does not require fortification by such devices as perfectionism, narcissism, and compulsive ambition, nor is it depreciated by inferiority feelings. Self-confidence, self-acceptance, self-reliance, self-respect, and assertive aggressiveness are blended with a tolerance of one's shortcomings.*

A child's view of himself is formed, first of all, through the esteem that he is accorded by other people. It is more caught than taught. There is an atmosphere in every home which a child experiences, and which tells him that he is or is not welcomed when he walks into a room. He perceives whether his mother takes delight in him, from the time he nurses at her breast and on through thousands of other experiences, including arriving at the dinner table with a dirty face and grimy hands.

And secondly, the young person's view of himself is developed through thousands of minor and major challenges met and mastered with a reasonable percentage of success—again ranging from finding his mouth with his thumb during his first months to not being all thumbs when he tries to repair the flat tire on his bike some ten years later.

Through being accorded respect, and through undergoing successful life experience, one develops a good measure of self-esteem.

3. *An adequate sense of personal identity. While patterning himself after models in his environment in response to a need for "belongingness," the individual retains a distinguishing uniqueness. The self-image reflects an identification with*

members of the same sex, with acceptance of one's own "male-ness" or "femaleness."

"Know thyself," said Socrates. Shakespeare said "To thine own self be true, and it must follow, as the night the day, thou canst not then be false to any man." And Jesus indicated his developing sense of identity at age 12 when he said "Know ye not that I must be about my father's business?"

But consider some of the difficulties in establishing and maintaining a healthy sense of identity in this generation:

First, consider the immense complexity of the demands on every person now—what one is called upon to know and do. Would you believe that there actually appears in President George Washington's diary these words, "There being no business for the government for the summer, I decided to go to New England for three months"? Indeed, there have been days when demands on a person were simpler.

Second, consider the conflicting pulls of advertising: Page through the *New York Times* some Sunday. In a few pages a man will be informed that he should be well-dressed, well-travelled, good-looking, athletic, learned, handy with tools, poised, a leader, a follower, an individualist, gregarious, thoughtful, a good husband, a good provider, a good father. But by then, our reader may feel so inadequate that he would not want to read any further!

Third, consider the competitiveness of life, which often does not allow for the intimate relationships where a man is honestly respected for what he is, and is told as much by his colleagues and superiors. Walk on Wall Street during a lunch hour, and there you will see thousands and thousands of bright, well-educated young men, eager and ambitious—and how often also competing against each other for the next step up. What does this do to one's need for the intimacy of sharing, out of which one's identity may be defined?

4. *Capacity to gratify basic needs. The individual is able to recognize his important needs, to marshal his personal resources, to execute them, to find environmental opportunities*

19

for their consummation, and to enjoy their fulfillment without fear or guilt. He has the ability to control and to provide socially approved outlets for such impulses as sexuality, aggression, and assertiveness.

The sheer delight in one's body that can be observed in an infant may often be subverted in later years, but the price is then a partially unlived life. Most Americans would profit far more from a half hour of exercise than from another half hour of sleep. There is often a middle class denial of the exhilaration that can come from luxuriating in the gratification of oral, excretory, and genital needs.

5. *Congenial and productive relationships with people. Interpersonal relationships are not contaminated by undue dependency, hostility, or detachment, irrespective of whether such relationships are with peers or with those in a subordinate or superior status.* Toward authority, the individual is able to assume, if necessary, a subordinate role without seeking to dominate or to control. There is an ability to accept essential dependencies on others without feelings of being exploited and enslaved, and while maintaining a good measure of assertiveness and independence. There is a capacity to respect, trust, communicate, and empathize with people and to consider their rights and needs. Aggressive and competitive behavior are adjusted to attitudes of cooperation and sympathy. There are desires to help those less fortunate than oneself and to work humanistically for the social good.

6. *A rich emotional life. There are capacities to feel pleasure as an eloquent affirmation of the goodness of life; to love and to tolerate being loved; to emote spontaneously and yet, when essential, to exercise restraint over emotion, with a minimum of ensuing tension, anxiety, and depression.*

To some persons it could truly be said "One feeling is worth a thousand thoughts." Middle class culture has, in the past, been captive to an obsessive, compulsive style of life. By that is meant a preoccupation with words and thoughts and ideas, which are often repetitive, and which frequently exist for their own sake, rather than leading on to action. There is a danger that those who love the academic life will tend to treasure every jot and tittle of intellectual nuance, while the capacity to *feel* may decline through disuse. The new and younger generation is surely hoping to reverse this trend.

7. *Appropriate and constructive life goals. Personal ambitions and goals are within the scope of the individual's existing competencies.* Success, when experienced, is well tolerated. There is an ability to align potentialities with presenting opportunities, to accept failure when inevitable, to reconcile oneself to environmental limitations, and to fulfill oneself creatively within the bounds of such limitations.

The words of Reinhold Niebuhr apply here: "Grant me serenity to accept the things I cannot change; courage to change the things I can; and wisdom to know the difference."

8. *An appropriate system of inner defenses. There is present a coordination of intellect, emotion, and behavior, as well as harmonization of needs, coping mechanisms, and controls.* This implies the capacity to employ reasoning and judgment in the interest of decision making and problem solving. Defenses are sufficiently flexible so that self-defeating tendencies may be discarded, substituting for them others of productive promise. There are abilities: to withstand average environmental stresses and hardships; to resolve remediable conditions with adjustment to irremediable ones; to endure deprivation and frustration when necessary; to adjust to conflict and tension in a resolute manner, without recourse to infantile modes of management; to inhibit at will those drives that are injurious to one's welfare, while developing adequate compensations and sublimations; and to profit from experience.

9. *Adequate self-understanding. Sufficient insight exists into one's personal problems, deficiencies, assets, and defenses*

to enable the individual to perceive reality correctly and to plan his life effectively. There is a facility to face feelings of guilt and failure related to the past and to isolate these from the present reality situation. This requires some recognition of important distortions in one's upbringing with proficiency to control childish impulses and fears.

To see ourselves as others see us, but not only in that way; to have a dream, but not to rely on that dream alone; to face guilt, but also to begin another day afresh; these constitute the balance between understanding one's experience, but not being stereotyped by it.

10. *Group membership and identification. Belonging to a group and functioning in it as a participating member are vital to a good adjustment.* Associated are acceptance by the group, a consonance of personal standards with group values, an ability to contribute to the group, and an assumption of interpersonal and community responsibilities that are approved by the group. There is a capacity to suppress without undue anxiety or hostility individual demands and satisfactions when necessary for the group welfare while retaining the option of opposing standards destructive to society even though condoned by the group.

The cheerful optimism that once resulted from seeing oneself as an American, or a Rotarian, or a Girl Scout is gone. The naïveté of the simplistic view that "I am on the side of what is right and good" is now a haven only for those who are unreflective and unaware of the ironies of our history. But to be crippled with caution and dependent upon utter certainty before taking action is also self-defeating. Healthy group membership should be heuristic, i.e., while absolute certainty is impossible, there is a conviction about one's group values that is sufficient for one to dare to take the next step.

11. *An adequate personal philosophy. It is important to possess values and spiritual promptings that lend meaning to*

one's existence and that sponsor feelings for one's fellow men.
Creative self-fulfillment is preserved with actualization of
intellectual, artistic, and ethical concerns.

In all of life, a focus is necessary in order to have meaning.
A vastly perceptive college professor would cordially greet
a student with these words, "What does your life revolve
around today?" This modern day Socrates, with his skillful
questioning, would draw out the often unrecognized personal
philosophy that was prompting his student.

One of the marks of a good jazz musician is the ability to
be absolutely free in giving musical flight to his fancy, but
at the end of 32 bars to be exactly on target. Dave Brubeck
may sound completely at liberty, but the musician will count
the beat and discover a precise and complicated nine-eight
structure around which the freedom is focused.

About John F. Kennedy at age 35, Arthur Schlesinger, Jr.
wrote: "He was still rather an unformed man . . . He was
bright and quick, but he had not resolved the problem of his
own style . . . Then came a series of operations . . . He nearly
died . . . Kennedy's near fatal sickness of 1955 no doubt accelerated his private crisis of identity . . . he emerged more
focused, more purposeful, more formidable. He began to
convey an impression of personal weight and authority. His
intelligence now had a goal. For the first time it swung into
full action" (Schlesinger, 1960). This quality of having a
philosophy, a direction, a commitment, is a factor that lends
coherence to all the other qualities of the healthy personality.

Summary

Obviously, no human being possesses all of the qualities
and traits that are ideal for health. We hope for a reasonable
balance of healthy personality characteristics that are amal-

23

gamated, even in the most adjusted individual, with some unhealthy qualities. Accordingly, the average person in our culture will suffer from mild psychological troubles as a consequence of residual personality defects. These need not incapacitate him too much if distortions are not present in extreme. However, where the personality contains many unhealthy attributes, he may be unable to make an appropriate adjustment even when the demands on him are not too great.

Disturbed or neurotic behavior represents a collapse in the individual's capacities for adjustment. This collapse is sponsored by a personality structure that cannot sustain the individual in the face of his inner conflicts and the external demands. Inherent in every neurosis is an attempt at adaptation that strives to restore the person to some kind of balance (homeostasis). Unfortunately, the experiences that are exploited, while arresting anxiety for the moment and temporarily resolving stress, are ultimately destructive to adjustment, crippling the individual in his dealing with the world. On the other hand, the person who has characteristically had a happy cooperation between his own needs and the needs of the world around him will exhibit the necessary flexibility that we call a good adjustment.

3

Building Blocks of Personality Structure

Perhaps a child who is fussed over gets a feeling of destiny; he thinks he is in the world for something important and it gives him drive and confidence.   DR. BENJAMIN SPOCK

The experience of watching 20 newborn infants in a hospital nursery is a powerful lesson in convincing one of the genetic and biological influences on personality. All men are created equal? Not so. Even on the first day of life, some are twice the size of others. Some take life easily, others fret and fume. Some accept the ministrations of the nurse passively, while others protest. At that age, it is unlikely that the postnatal environment is producing these individual differences.

The essential ingredients of personality are probably genetically determined, being rooted in the biological heritage of the individual. Moreover, the fetus during the intrauterine life is exposed to stimuli that probably fashion, in some measure, his psychic organization. The infant, therefore, at the time of birth already possesses potentialities and handicaps that tend to shape his future. Yet evidence is overwhelming to the effect that prenatal influences may be significantly modified by the environment.

The first few years of life are the most crucial in personality development, laying down thinking, feeling, and behavioral patterns that will influence the individual the remainder of his life. Where experiences with the parent and with the early environment are harmonious, the child is encouraged to evolve a system of security that regards the world as a bountiful place and to develop a self-esteem that promotes assertiveness and self-confidence. He will be convinced of his capacities to love and to be loved, and this will form the foundation of a healthy personality. On the other hand, where the child has been deprived of proper stimulation and care, or where he has been over-protected, improperly disciplined, or unduly intimidated, the world will constitute for him a place of menace. A personality organization structured on the bedrock of such unwholesome conditionings is bound to be unsubstantial and shaky.

Heredity and Personality

The post-Darwinian emphasis on biology presented man as essentially a creature of instinct dragooned toward stereotyped actions to preserve himself and the species. Genetically inherited patterns were considered to be the mainspring of behavior. At one time it was thought that man had an "instinct" for almost everything he did. This concept was challenged by social scientists who insisted that social customs rather than innate drives fashioned human behavior in all of its dimensions. Contended was the fact that while instinct provided some motivational force for behavior, cultural influences contributed even more significantly to its manifold forms. This gave rise to a trend that promulgated a complete elimination of instinct as a significant factor in behavior and promoted society as the exclusive determining agency.

New data from biology, genetics, and ethology have, however, pointed to the relative stability of certain behavioral patterns that do not depend on learning or social acquisition, but rather are affected by the general course of development for survival (Eiduson, 1958). While instinctual promptings in man are materially tamed by environmental conditionings, the biological heritage does in all probability set the limit for the influences of experience. Gradually a viewpoint has been evolving that considers man as an integrate of hereditary-instinctual and social components, each interacting with the other (Dobzhansky, 1962). While there is abundant evidence that all forms of behavior may be modified by experience, there is evidence also that man, like other animals, is endowed with innate impulses which cause him to respond differentially to distinctive cues in his environment (Lorenz, 1952, 1965; Tinbergen, 1951, 1953, 1954, 1959, 1961; Harlow, 1960, 1962). The stimuli to which man reacts are many, and it is probable that responses to them are in terms of diffuse pleasure and pain rather than in specific fixed forms of behavior (McClelland, 1951, 1955, 1961, 1964).

Clinical studies of human infants indicate that innate characteristics determine individual differences at birth and lay down the basis for variations in sensitivity to stimuli, perception, motility, discrimination, anxiety, and memory (Benjamin, 1961; Bergman and Escalona, 1949). These variables will undoubtedly influence the manner in which the infant is affected by his environment. For example, the intensity with which the infant experiences stress and the forcefulness of the protests by which he signals his needs are probably related to genetic factors, e.g., does he scream vociferously or weakly? Where the child is unable to respond to hunger, pain, and discomfort appropriately, he may not give proper clues to his needs. Weak, indistinct, and contradictory clues will not invoke the proper mothering responses, particularly from a mother who is emotionally disturbed and preoccupied with her own problems (Bruch, 1964). The failure of the mother to provide proper help will deprive the child of the essential feeling of trustingness and of proper identification and separation experiences that make it possible to differentiate the "me" from the "not-me." This is but one instance of how nature and nurture interact. Differential protective barriers against stimuli as well as corrective stress-response patterns exist at birth which appear to coordinate with personality, cognitive style, interpersonal relations, defense mechanisms, and other psychologic functions (Roche Report, June 1, 1964). Important to consider also is the fact that a mother will respond uniquely to the type of baby with whom she has to deal, for instance, to an irritable crying baby as compared with a placid and easily manageable one.

Intrauterine and Postnatal Physiology

Of vital significance are the experiences of the fetus in utero. The placement of the placenta on the uterine wall, the quality of diet and the physical health of the mother will determine the nutritive integrity of the developing embryo. Noxious drugs, alcohol, and products of infectious disease permeate the placental membrane and undoubtedly have an effect on brain and other cells. The position of the infant in the uterine cavity may exert untoward pressure on vital organs, interfering with essential circulation and impairing growth. This is perhaps why identical twins, occupying different places in the womb may be favored or unfavored in the freedom of circulation. At birth the twins who have the same basic physical heredity may evidence distinctive sensitivity and motor reactive patterns that sponsor vast differences in personality make-up, differences that may continue the remainder of their lives.

The Environmental Impact

Innate patterns manifest themselves not only at birth, but also in chronological sequence following birth in line with what seem to be set laws of maturation. Some patterns are related to the development of the central nervous system and to the progressive maturing (myelinization) of nerve tracts. Others follow upon the ripening of certain organs, such as the hormonal glands. Throughout the life of the individual, physical changes appear to sponsor special psychological activities.

It takes 12 years for a child to develop the adult electro-encephalograph (brain wave) pattern (which is 250 times longer than it takes a rabbit). This means that the human brain is not fully formed physiologically until the twelfth year. There must necessarily be a correspondingly slow personality development.

More precise knowledge of the developmental sequence gives rise to possibilities that are as fascinating as science fiction. There are critical periods when the time is physiologically ripe for acquiring certain intellectual and emotional functions. Going back further in time, it is conceivable that interventions in the maternal physiology may positively influence characteristics in the unborn fetus. We have definite knowledge of certain harmful influences on the fetus (x-ray, measles, thalidomide), and it is a small step to conceive of the corollary of beneficial influences.

And suppose that there are critical periods in the physiological development of a child when certain psychological functions are optimally acquired, such functions as thinking, planning, perceiving, verbalizing, and motor responding. The discovery of the critical periods when the nerve tissues reach their full capacity for the development of these functions—plus the understanding of the psychological factors which optimally accentuate this learning—could remodel the process of the evolution of all living things including humans.

A finding suggested by animal studies, which has profound implications for personality development, is that the neural system becomes susceptible to the imprinting of certain stimuli for only limited periods during the life cycle. Beyond this period the necessary imprinting does not take place even upon exposure to identical stimulation. Thus, among monkeys it has been shown that separation of an infant from the mother during the first few weeks in life, and isolation from other monkeys, may produce damage from which the animal never recovers, even though he is returned to the mother following the limited separation span. Disturbances such as withdrawal, fear, and rage, will persist (Harlow, 1960, 1962). Among dogs the optimal imprinting period for the development of social bonds is from six to eight weeks of age. Contact with a handler during this period establishes a capacity for a relationship with humans and a ready breaking to the leash. If contact occurs later than eight weeks, the dogs tend to become fearful and resist training. Such phenomena are probably organically determined since specific biochemical changes in the brain have been reported during imprinting periods that are not present thereafter.

A reasonable assumption is that a human child may also never recover from essential need deprivations or the absence of important growth experiences if they are sustained at crucial phases in development. The sabotage to the evolving personality may be drastic. No amount of therapy in later life can restore that which never existed. For example, if a child is severely neglected or abandoned during the first year and therefore has never been supplied with a consistent mothering experience, it is probable that emotional apathy and a lack of trust in people may pursue him throughout his life irrespective of how benevolent his environment may be afterward.

Interacting with genetic factors are life experiences that vitally influence the lines along which the personality will be organized. How the child becomes programmed to respond needs some further elaboration. We know that various events in childhood can have an oppressive effect on both the immediate and later well-being of the individual. Early separation from a mother; experiences of extreme rejection or deprivation; excesses of coerciveness or indulgence; an abusing, psychotic, or alcoholic adult in the home; improper discipline; exposure to maladjusted, defective, or handicapped siblings; inadequate moral standards and values in the home; victimization and discrimination—all these are known to wield unfortunate influences on the growing child. But exactly how they register their effects is not entirely clear. Unclear also is what promptings and characteristics in some children enable them to compensate for severe deprivations and to construct out of a few healthy elements remaining in their environment materials that permit them to work through a satisfactory adjustment, while other children, exposed to what to all outward appearances seems like a bountiful milieu, develop a *weltanschauung* of misery.

Surely there must be forces both within the individual and in his milieu that influence the lines along which he will develop, determine his susceptibility to inimical external factors, and fashion the repertoire of his defenses. It has been difficult to identify these forces with any degree of scientific

31

PERSONALITY DEVELOPMENT
(Constitutional Factors: Sensitivity and Activity)

Year	Principal Tasks to be Achieved	Basic Difficulties	Consequences of Developmental Failure	Principal Manifestations of Breakdown in Adaptation	Degree of Repression
1	Feeling of security; attitudes of trust	Rejection; abandonment	Pervasive insecurity feelings; mistrust	Disturbed physiological reactions (esp. gastro-intestinal); depression	Great
2–3	Feeling of autonomy; incorporation of discipline; self-control; tolerance of frustration	Too lax or too severe disciplines	Lack of self-confidence; inability to control self (impulse, emotions, etc.)	Rageful, defiant, withdrawal reactions; habit disorders; bowel and bladder disorders	Great
3–5	Proper sexual identification; oedipal resolution; beginning of socialization	Overprotection; seduction; improper identification	Persisting oedipal conflicts; inability to identify with persons of own sex	Phobic reactions; conversion reactions; exaggerated sexual interests	Moderate to Great
5–11	Group identification	School problem; neighborhood problem	Inability to accept a proper social role; disturbed relations with others	Behavior disorders; compulsive reactions	Little to Great
11–15	Social control over sexuality and aggression; resolution of ambivalence toward parents	Environmental encouragement of aggression and sexuality	Sexual acting-out; excessively hostile attitudes toward authority	All of above plus childhood schizophrenia	Little to Moderate
15–21	Resolution of dependency; establishment of heterosexual relatedness	Parental conflicts; economic stress	Excessive dependence	All of above	Little to Moderate

accuracy, although many attempts to do so have been made. To consolidate such efforts, the methods of empirical research are increasingly being applied to problems of human development. Fruitful dividends have already accrued from these applications (Piaget, 1952; Escalona and Latch, 1953). Perhaps the most important finding is that the first few years are the most crucial in personality development, establishing thinking, emotional, and behavioral patterns that will influence the individual throughout his life in terms of security, trust, autonomy, self-control, confidence, assertiveness, self-esteem, proper sexual identification and maturity of sexuality, social command of rage and aggression, tolerance of stress and frustration, problem solving competencies, capacities for self-realization, and the ability to relate to people. (See "Personality Development" chart which outlines essential stages of growth and the consequences of good as well as bad development).

Mothering Patterns

The womb of personality conditioning is the mother-child relationship. Many mothering patterns may be observed, some of which are conducive to and others detrimental to the welfare of the child. For example, an *insecure mother* will be fearful of depriving her child and will be unable, more or less, to stand his screaming protests at any kind of frustration. She will, therefore, tend to yield to his needs on demand and deny him the opportunity of learning to tolerate gradually increasing quantities of deprivation. As a consequence the child may fail to acquire essential self-restraints and to accept disappointment. He may tyrannize the household with his manipulations as he grows older, having learned to receive gratification through coercion.

The *over-protective mother* will be frightened lest harm befall her helpless child. This may be a denial reaction for her rejection of the child or may constitute a means of maintaining control, essential to her own personal needs. Whatever the reason, over-protective mothers hasten to do for their child what he should learn to do for himself. In this way the child, robbed of the opportunity to acquire essential skills, is thwarted in the development of self-reliance, initiative, and enterprise.

The *apathetic, distinterested, or hostile mother* may openly neglect her child, failing to provide the essential care, stimulation, and love that he requires. Or she may manifest such tension in holding and feeding the child that she is unable to participate in the affectionate feedback that constitutes the proper mother-child relationship. A child so managed will often become colicky, allergic, sensitive to colds and illness. More insidiously, he will develop distrust of, suspicion toward, and lack of feeling for people.

Sometimes mothering patterns are inconsistent, shifting from one type of approach to another, as when a rejecting and insecure mother sporadically responds to her guilt feelings with bouts of over-protection and over-indulgence. Under such circumstances the child will become particularly insecure and upset, since he is unable to evolve consistent coping mechanisms.

A study of the variables involved in mother-infant interactions shows that most mothers have areas of competence and areas of weakness in their handling of their infants (Yarrow and Goodwin 1965). Mothers are never consistently "good" or "bad," great variation occurring in the adequacy or inadequacy with which they fulfill their mothering role. They may be delinquent in satisfying some aspects of a child's needs, while they may be interested in and capable of gratifying other aspects. For example, a mother may supply the child with food on demand, but she may shy away from holding him closely. She may be capable of satisfying a need on one occasion, but be incapable of doing so on another occasion. How mothers respond to their children will depend on their own tension and anxiety levels which will alter from time to time. Thus when a mother is irritated by the press of household duties she will tend to be more punitive, detached, indifferent, and rejecting than when she is happy and relaxed. Mothers will also project onto their children feelings and attitudes harbored toward their own parents, siblings, or mate with whom a child is unconsciously identified. These projections may be consistent, the mother favoring certain of her offspring, and rejecting and punishing others; or they may shift with fluctuating inner needs, with an inconsistency of responses toward the same child. Maternal reactions also vary with the behavior of the child. Aggressive, screaming infants will bring forth different responses from passive and compliant infants. The interaction of the child's needs with the mother's needs, the child's disposition with that of the mother, the child's sensitivities with the mother's neurotic qualities makes for variegated and sometimes unpredictable responses.

Important to consider also is the developmental phase at which improper handling occurs. Thus, during the first weeks of infancy skin and movement stimulation is most important, the child needing physical contact in the form of being held and carried. Deprived of such stimulation at this stage, or handled too roughly, he will probably react more catastrophically than when robbed of kinesthetic stimulation later on.

Let us turn now to some specific factors in the mother-infant interaction which are thought to affect personality development. Recent research projects have been thoroughly detailed by Martin and Lois Hoffman (1966): 1. The necessity for thorough mouth gratification is a well-established fact. 2. On the other hand, 19 well-done studies related to the three factors of (a) source of nourishment (breast or bottle), (b) schedule of feedings, and (c) technique of weaning have established nothing definitive in relation to personality development. One can only conclude that it is the infant's *reaction* to the various aspects of the feeding situation as presented to him by the mothering person that influences his later characteristic responses to life. 3. Infants who had a rooming-in arrangement with their mothers have accelerated motor and mental development. But does this only reflect the attitude of those mothers who choose this arrangement? 4. Moving the infant about, rather than constricting him to one position, speeds maturation. 5. The more fondling the child receives (within reasonable limits) the less crying and frustration he exhibits during feeding. 6. A number of factors relating to an infant's separation from his mother have been discerned through research: (a) Separation from the mother is the most damaging between the ages of 6 months and 24 months. Before this age a focused relationship with the mother is not yet established. (b) The immediate trauma is greater but the long term damage is less when the infant has had a close relationship before being separated from the mother. (c) All studies indicate that permanent damage can be avoided if the substitute mother establishes a nurturing relationship. (d) It has been demonstrated that it is better if the mother can see the baby intermittently during the separation. (e) The severity of the impact is related to the length of the separation. (f) The more traumatic the separation, the more traumatic will be subsequent separations. (g) Constitutional factors play a role in the sensitivities of different infants to the separation experience.

The research on correlations between mothering patterns and later personality development has brought disappointingly few fruitful results. This is perhaps because mothering patterns change somewhat with each passing decade, which makes longitudinal studies impossible. Furthermore the subtle variables in human interaction lend themselves neither to precise description nor to calculation. There are some 80 known factors that determine whether a laboratory white rat turns left or right in a simple T-maze. It is understandable then that human responses to more complex choices are based on an infinitely larger number of factors, making definitive research exceedingly difficult.

The successful outcome of proper mothering is registered in the establishment of an emotional security system and the acceptance of reality, the evolution of patterns of social control over bodily functions, and the expansion of assertiveness and self-confidence. This prepares the child for extra-familial relationships; social modification and resolution of ambivalent (hostile-loving) feelings toward the parents; identification with persons of one's own sex; acceptance of the group and group identification; social control over sexuality and hostility; expansion of independence and resolution of dependency ties; and the capacity to fulfill himself creatively and adaptively through satisfactory interpersonal relationships. Unhealthy mothering makes for a personality structure that is riddled with insecurity, with an undermining of self-esteem, with distorted interpersonal relationships, and with spurious life goals and values.

Fathering Patterns

Sorely neglected is the consideration of the vital role played by fathers in providing for the male child an identification object and for the female child a means through which sexual feelings become channeled toward acceptance of her femininity. An overly harsh or stern father, a detached and

37

neglectful father, a passive and ineffectual father may be responsible for blocks in the child's maturation from which the individual may never recover. Important to consider is that compensations may be available to the child for both mothering and fathering deficiencies through relationships with accepting and stable relatives or older siblings who make themselves available to the child.

While mothering patterns have been blamed for most children's later psychological difficulties, it is vitally significant that an emotionally generous father can counteract the impact of a neglectful or overwhelming mother. Even if the mother is seductive and over-protective, the father who is supportive and nurturant toward the son will be able to neutralize to a considerable degree the mother's deleterious influence in the boy's sexual area. It is unlikely that there is any homosexual who ever had a good relationship with his father. On the other hand, positive heterosexual attitudes develop when a boy is able to experience a male model in a father or father substitute whom he admires and wants to emulate. Interestingly the temporary absence of the fathering person, or the death of the father, need not be seriously harmful so long as the boy remembers the warmth of the father, and if these positive memories are not undercut by the mother.

To save a son from the possibility of becoming a homosexual, there need be a fondness on the part of the father for the son, coupled with some activity in the direction of reaching out to understand what a boy is experiencing. When this relationship is present in actuality or in memory, a boy will see himself as similar to his father, will begin to adopt the typical behavior of a male, and have the confidence that others will also regard him as having masculine characteristics.

Summary

Structures are built through combining individual parts into a whole. The significance of one part of a structure can scarcely be understood apart from the other parts. In so complex a structure as personality this is especially true. Each building block noted in this chapter has little meaning apart from the others. This chapter has been an overview of five of the major building blocks of personality: heredity, intrauterine and postnatal factors, the overall impact of the environment, and the influence of mothering and fathering patterns.

4

Cultural and Social Molds

The true test of a civilization is not the census, nor the size of cities, nor the crops—no, but the kind of man the country turns out.   RALPH WALDO EMERSON

The idols of a nation will put a premium on certain aspects of life that may be overdeveloped at the expense of others. Thus industrial nations, with their emphasis on efficiency, productiveness, and industriousness will sponsor traits in the individual that reflect these ideals—very possibly at the expense of personal relationships.

The sense of security may be organized around financial mobility, the possession of wealth serving as a symbol of security.

There is a definite relationship between the socio-cultural constellations to which the child is exposed and the kind of person he becomes. Cultural pressures establish patterns of response, values, ideals, and goals by offering incentives and rewards for culturally approved reactions and by threatening punishment or condemnation for culturally disapproved reactions. Conformity with cultural demands results in group acceptance. Nonconformity brings an elimination from participation in group life.

A surviving society is one which recognizes the physical and emotional needs of its citizens and provides opportunities for them to satisfy their needs with security and dignity. Its mores and institutions are those that are consonant with the demands of the individual as well as the group. Its modes of child training build patterns and attitudes that enable the person, as an adult, to fulfill a participating role in the social framework. Disciplines and incentives to which the child is exposed reflect the kinds of values and attitudes that exist in the culture.

The social organization in which the individual is reared cannot help but influence his personality structure. Where the child is raised in an authoritarian framework at home and at school, where he is crushed and subordinated, he will develop a fealty to pomp and power, and he will find value in subordinating himself to dictatorship, while harboring arrogant ambitions to crush and to destroy in order to make himself the dictator. He will feel contempt for democratic values, and he will want to erect a social edifice in which power is the deity that he can worship.

On the other hand the democratic home and the democratic school will create a different kind of human being— one who esteems cooperative and democratic relationships with his colleagues. He will respect authority but neither worship nor be in awe of authority. He will respect himself and thus create the foundation for personal happiness. These are conditions under which a democratic society perpetuates itself and brings security to its citizens.

The mature individual has a responsibility to himself and to society in surveying the elements in his environment that are hurtful to his needs and to the needs of the group.

Any social order that fails to provide for its citizens opportunities to fulfill their basic biologic needs, that does not recognize the dignity of each individual irrespective of socio-economic status, and avoids giving him some means for self-expression, self-development, and living up to his creative potentials, is bound to mobilize resentment, aggression, and perhaps eventual coercive action toward environmental change.

The late 1960's have seen just this trend in action in the United States, where the values of the culture in the direction of political-military aggrandizement in the Far East outreached the tolerance of the populace for the loss of human life in behalf of such a cause. There has also been expression, especially on the part of the young, against the conventional forms of cultural competitiveness and success. There has been a swing of the pendulum toward romanticism, a quest for wide experience, self-expression, a free life, and against the assumed hypocrisy and self-interestedness of the previous generation.

Such a reaction can be anticipated through the examination of the trends in a culture. When the cultural idols have grown out of touch with basic human need, then it can be predicted that the idols will be toppled—most usually by the student and young adult generation.

Values, Meaning Systems, and Personality

Is it true that a good Irishman gets drunk, a good Pole beats his wife, and a good Scotchman pinches pennies when each confronts a tough problem? An Oriental authority steeped in Buddhism would probably consider strivings for self-contemplation and passivity more desirable than aggesiveness and concern with material essences which constitute important indices in Western Society.

The value systems of the society in which one is reared fashion the dimensions and overtones of personality. These values eventually become incorporated within the individual and act as filters through which all of life is experienced.

One will react to a panhandler's request for a dime with a certain revulsion, while smiling graciously at a member of a religious order who makes the same request. The differing reaction is the result of the value which we put on one kind of begging but not on the other. A person in the United States will regard a ring through an African native's nose as disgusting, while a ring through a fellow American's ear is seen as chic. The aesthetic reaction to each is prompted by the value systems of the society.

When the values of a society blend with one's basic needs, adjustment will be enhanced; should they obstruct and conflict with his needs, inner turmoil will ensue. For example, a society which suppresses the need for a reasonable degree of freedom will eventually produce an angry and bitter populace and perhaps in time reap a revolutionary movement that shouts, as did the American colonists, "no taxation without representation." Fortunately, every surviving society provides institutionalized outlets for important needs. For example, most societies support certain standards of sexual abstinence before marriage, yet considerable tolerance is shown toward individuals whose needs are executed within the bounds of reasonable discretion. Taboos exist also against the expression of violence and aggression, but outlets for those urges are encouraged in combative sports and in the competition of school and business.

Values constitute a form of symbolization through which a person codes his experiences and gives them special meaning. Of all the animals, man alone possesses this refined and elaborate capacity to symbolize and thereby to respond to the events of life solely in accordance with the meaning he imparts to them. Values constitute the measure of how he reacts to his total existence, from the biological instinctual imprints which are his genetic heritage to the commonplace everyday burdens of his daily chores.

For example, a 12 year old boy would surely prefer to stay in bed at 5 a.m. on a dismally wet and cold Saturday morning in October. But if it is duck hunting season, and "all the boys" are going out with their fathers that morning to hunt ducks, this 12 year old boy will leave his warm bed before daybreak. One reason is that hunting for him is fun. But deeper than this, in all likelihood, is the *meaning* of the act which represents manliness, and the boy will respond to the duck hunting ritual in accord with the meaning that the act imparts to him.

To state this more formally: High in the hierarchy of a person's thought processes are meaning systems and values that weight the individual's past and present experiences according to an appraisal formula that is part of his culture. Gleaned from interactions with significant parental and other authority figures, from old and more recent group identifications, from exposure to cultural and social injunctions, this standardizing body acts as a filtering device to screen perceptions, sensations, attitudes, feelings, and actions, lending to them a distinctive pleasurable or unpleasurable flavor.

Just as the taste for coffee usually has to be acquired, many experiences in life may have a very neutral taste until a young person is "taught" that they are either delightful or loathesome. All the agencies of society in this case are the teachers. Some agencies are more prestigious than others, as for example, the advertising in *The Reader's Digest* in contrast to the advertising in *The Police Gazette*. The divorce of Nelson Rockefeller, the suicide of Marilyn Monroe, the remarriage of the former Mrs. John F. Kennedy all make an impact on untold millions of others who look to celebrities for cues on how they should feel and act. There is no one standardizing body that sets the tone for how to regard the people and events of life. But we are sophisticated enough to be able, at least in the long run, to use the many institutions of society as checks and balances against each other so that we can have a reasonable assurance that we are able to discern whether the emperor has no clothes on.

Meaning systems are by no means fixed. They are constantly shifting, being modified by newly incorporated values that superimpose themselves on the old. These changes are brought about through contacts with respected agencies and authorities, through gratifying and painful personal experiences, through group pressure and identification, and through self-knowledge and understanding. Some early values may be difficult to alter, since they are deeply imbedded in the subsoil of one's early existence and involve conditionings firmly set prior to the era of critical reasoning. Other values are more easily displaced, having been formulated during less crucial stages of personality development. As a general rule values are more easily replaced where the individual has little investment in them and where they do not satisfy important current needs.

Philosophical and religious credos are often incorporated into value systems and may serve as a means of regulating one's life. Through forced mental set it may even be possible to convert painful and humiliating circumstances into those through which gratification is derived. For instance, if the individual can accept the premise that suffering is a cleansing atonement for past personal indiscretion or for humanity as a whole, and that future rewards for self-castigation accrue and will be available in the hereafter, he may be able to endure untold misery and even learn to enjoy suffering. In this conversion of pain into pleasure he may hasten to demonstrate his martydom.

On the other hand, specific happenings may in their value processing acquire a signification of imminent catastrophe.

To these the individual will respond with alarm. They will then act as stress stimuli. Thus a man might say, "If I couldn't work, I would rather be dead." He is then identifying the meaning of life with productive work. Someone else might say "The unreflective life is not worth living," or "I would rather be dead than Red." One person will say "Sticks and stones may break my bones, but words will never hurt me," while Shakespeare thought "Who steals my purse steals trash . . . but he that filches from me my good name, Robs me of that which not enriches him, And makes me poor indeed." The point is this: it is not the deed itself, but the meaning of the deed that gives the deed significance.

The values through which events are viewed as having meaning—or a lack of meaning—at this time and place in history are *social status, economic status, educational achievement, vocational adjustment, conventional standards of behavior, standards of success and failure,* together with certain *mores* and *customs.*

Life is viewed as being significant by most people when it can be weighed against those values and found to be "making it." A parent transmits his feelings to his child according to how the child is meeting those standards whether it be his choice of friends, leisure activities, school grades, or haircuts. Both parent and child feel some anguish when there is a conflict of values, interpersonally or intrapersonally. What if a young man chooses to live in a shabby apartment, without furniture, and with his girl griend whom he chooses not to marry? And what if a girl from a nonreligious home chooses to marry a missionary whose prospects for social and economic advancement are nil, and where the children of such a union might not even have access to decent schools?

The values inherent in society serve to pressure its citizens in the direction of conformity to those values. This is largely unwitting and automatic. When a citizen accepts the group that sponsors the system of attitudes or code of behavior, then the group becomes identified with the superego or conscience. Philosophical or religious precepts are seen as authoritative when there is large scale espousal of the group itself. The acceptance of the group prompts feelings of authoritative approval which leads to a sense of security. On the other hand, rejection leads to feelings of disapproval, abandonment, punishment, and anxiety.

In order to set at rest the experience of conflict and anxiety, the individual will tend to accept emotionally the injunctions of the group and, in fact, even elevate those injunctions to the level of a categorical imperative. If, for example, one's psychological or physical life depends on it, one may begin to believe all kinds of things in order to survive. Thus, in wartime, we do begin to believe that the enemy are really bad people, thereby making killing a tolerable act.

Where the specific rules of conduct or values proposed by a movement satisfy certain basic inner needs, normal or neurotic, the individual will be most likely to accept them and to promote the movement or authority into a powerful position that he must accept, and not reject.

Fortunately, meaning systems *can* be changed or modified. In contrast to earlier historical epochs, the signs of the times can now often be ascertained. And what is perhaps even more significant, the errors of a culture can now be communicated to those agencies and institutions which are the carriers of meaning systems. Precepts from the field of the behavioral sciences, for example, are making substantial impacts on our values and mores, altering certain fundamental conceptions of human nature and changing traditional ideas about child-rearing, sexual education, minority problems, and attitudes toward delinquents, alcoholics, recidivists, sex offenders, and drug addicts. The shift from punishment toward rehabilitation reflects more optimistic expectations of what can be done about what have been considered the most hopeless elements of humanity.

Other examples of how meaning systems can be changed may be cited: Supreme Court decisions, public alarm over the mistreatment and killing of civil rights workers and the assassination of public figures, and the television reporting of poverty and war have all wrought a questioning of what we believe to be the "good life."

There are three primary ways of changing or modifying meaning systems. First, through group identification and pressure. Since there is a need for group approval there will be a heightened suggestibility in group experience. While the Supreme Court decision of 1954 on segregated education did not change anyone's attitudes toward the negro, soon there were many groups that became convinced that it was their duty to pursue the implications of that decision into other spheres of life. As this "righteous cause" became the daily fare of great numbers of civic and religious groups, individual attitudes changed, and one dared not express discriminatory attitudes for fear of being deprived of group acceptance.

Second, meaning systems are changed through authoritative identification and pressure. Here the need is for one person to feel that he is like another person—particularly an authoritative figure. In history there are certain individuals who define an era. The contribution of President John F. Kennedy for example, was not so much in the legislation that was passed during his tenure, but more in his personal style with which young persons particularly identified. And when a singing group on television wears long hair and beads as a mark of their individuality, countless other young persons will declare their emancipation by the same means.

Third, meaning systems are changed through self-knowledge and self-understanding. The pursuit of knowing one's inner self and listening for that inner drummer who beats the cadence to which one feels compelled to march, is the path followed by many great cultural revolutionaries. Every innovator must bear the anguish of exposing something new to the world and be willing to face the consequences. Consider the torment that Freud knew as he discovered that his inner life had a meaning which he felt he must share, but which he was literally spat upon for daring to expose. But as Kierkegaard wrote: "To venture is to cause anxiety, but not to venture is to lose all." It is this venturing in response to a new self-knowledge that constitutes a most significant means for making a new, and perhaps better world.

Summary

While many human strivings are rooted in biological needs, the mode of satisfaction of those needs is significantly affected by the cultural values of the society. Values act like codes, which enable persons intuitively to sense the meaning of an experience. When the values of a culture have grown out of touch with basic human need, the culture will eventually be subjected to changes of a reforming or revolutionary character.

5

Some Denominators of Personality

Of this, at least I feel assured, that there is no such thing as forgetting possible to mankind; a thousand accidents may and will interpose a veil between our present consciousness and the secret inscriptions on the mind; accidents of the same sort will also rend away this veil; but alike, whether veiled or unveiled, the inscription remains forever, just as the stars seem to withdraw before the common light of day, whereas, in fact, we all know that it is the light which is drawn over them as a veil, and that they are waiting to be revealed when the obscuring daylight shall be withdrawn.

THOMAS DE QUINCEY

Unresolved Childhood Promptings

William is a man of 40 who enjoys working with his hands, but cannot stay in his workroom more than an hour by himself because he gets a painful feeling of emptiness. He attends sandlot baseball games, and although he knows nothing about the teams, he enjoys himself because he feels

50

somewhat better sitting in the bleachers in the midst of people. He likes music and has a good stereo set, but he cannot tolerate being home alone listening to the music. When he is with friends, he invariably overstays his welcome. He eats hamburgers, but does not like to chew steak. Rice pudding and white cake are favorites with him. His greatest sexual pleasures involve being physically close to a woman, while genital experiences are of only minor significance to him. He keeps a rather large sum of money hidden in his apartment, and each night after returning from work proceeds at once to see if the money has been stolen.

The question is: what is William's personality structure? What is the unity that makes sense out of William's behavior and gives consistence to otherwise seemingly contradictory traits and behavior? But before we focus on William, let us examine the scaffolding of personality. Where and how is it erected for the good and bad?

Where experiences with life are harmonious, the child is best able to evolve a foundation of security which regards the world as a bountiful place and to develop self-esteem which encourages assertiveness and self-confidence. This is that firm understructure on which the scaffolding will rest. The child will be convinced of his capacities to love and to be loved. He most probably will develop character strivings that permit him to relate constructively to other persons and to express, through culturally condoned outlets, his important needs. On the other hand, where the child has been rejected, over-protected, or unduly intimidated, the world will probably constitute for him a place of menace. He will be devastated by fears and tensions. His self-esteem will be warped to a point where he is overwhelmed by feelings of helplessness and loss of self-confidence. His relationships with people will be disturbed, and he may harbor destructive attitudes, while remaining passively clinging, and invoking or coercing help.

51

Longitudinal developmental studies indicate that personality strength or weakness is more or less developed by the experiences during childhood. If, in the first few years of life, the individual has developed a feeling of security, a sense of reality, a good measure of assertiveness, positive self-esteem, and capacities for self-control, he will probably be able to endure considerable environmental hardships thereafter and still evolve a healthy adult. On the other hand, early unfavorable development handicaps the child in managing even the usual vicissitudes that are common to growing up. This does not mean that all children with a good personal substructure will inevitably emerge as healthy adults, since an overly harsh environment can inhibit development at any phase in the growth process. Nor does it imply that a child with an inadequate personality structure may not in the face of favorable circumstances overcome severe early impediments in growth and mature to satisfactory adulthood. Were we to subscribe to the pessimistic philosophy that all early psychic damage is irreparably permanent, we would blind ourselves to the efficacy of psychotherapy which is predicated on the assumption that it is possible through the emotionally corrective experience provided by treatment to overcome many childhood personality distortions.

Much misunderstanding surrounds the notion that one's personality is fixed in childhood, that it becomes immutably hardened in those formative years, and that it is subsequently impervious to any meaningful alteration. There are several considerations that should be noted: Occasionally undue emphasis is put on childhood factors as a result of the need of "television psychiatry" to be dramatic within the space of 30 minutes, not counting the time out for a few commercials. In order to present the problem and effect the cure in a half hour, or perhaps in one chapter of a book, it is necessary to telescope the formative experiences of life. There will often be the presentation of one significant trauma of life that is revealed in a "Eureka" experience, and the patient is promptly cured. The tacit implication is that if this trauma had gone undiscovered, the patient would have continued to be bound to his misery. Such oversimplifications have made their way into the folklore about personality development. The truth is, however, that only rarely does any one event significantly set the course of one's personality. It is more cogent to observe that there are common denominators in the thousands of events of childhood, and that these oft-repeated patterns are the stimuli that slowly pattern a child's personality. It may be observed that the way parents discipline a child of 18 months is the way that those same parents discipline that same child when he is 18 years.

It is true that the law of primacy operates in personality development. The law of primacy states, for example, that the first pancake always tastes best to a hungry man. That is, later mouthfuls are somehow less memorable than the first bite, and can always be judged as over against the impact of the first taste. But this fact must be weighed against the total significance of all later mouthfuls of pancakes. Thus, while early experiences are formative, they constitute only a percentage of the events of life. There are many factors in personality development, as noted in the previous chapter, and while the patterns of childhood are the most significant, the rich diversity of life gives us hope that the purveyors of childhood determinism have seen only part of the picture. When it does appear in psychological writings that a determinism based on childhood events is being espoused, it must be understood that these (usually unwholesome) childhood influences continue to be the pattern throughout the later years, and that these noxious events were unrelieved by reparative experiences. Only when the damage was severe, consistent, and unrelieved can it be unequivocally stated that early experiences imprison one to stereotypy.

53

Personality traits in adult life are never an exact reduplication of childhood strivings. Early conditionings are tempered by experiences in later life that tend to modify, neutralize, or reinforce them. Moreover, though behavior is influenced by patterns rooted in the past, responses vary widely in different situations in accordance with their symbolic significance and the prevailing social role played by the person at the time. The sundry variations of personality strivings in operation are infinite. Incorporated are attitudes, values, and patterns of behavior that issue out of a defective security system, distorted conceptions of reality, imperfect social control over bodily functions, vitiated sense of assertiveness, stunted independence, impaired self-esteem, inadequate frustration tolerance, improper mastery of sexual and hostile impulses, incomplete identification with members of one's own sex, deficient group identification, faulty integration of prevailing social values, and impaired acceptance of one's social role. Pressure of early unsatisfied needs, anticipation of the same kinds of turmoil that existed in childhood, or the actual setting up of conditions that prevailed in one's early life, and survival of anachronistic defenses, symptoms, and their symbolic extensions are incorporated into the personality structure. Compulsive in nature, they permeate every phase of thought, feeling, and action; they govern the random and purposeful activities of the individual, forcing him to conform with them in a merciless way..

Nuclear Conflicts

Common to all mankind are certain conflicts from which there is no escape. Some aspects of these conflicts are part of man's biological heritage mingled with the inevitable painful experiences of growing up. The "Nuclear Conflicts" chart summarizes the chief conflicts imbedded in the psyche of each person, products of the inevitable clash of personal needs and reality restrictions, the mastery of which constitutes one of the primary tasks of psycho-social development. It must be emphasized that these conflicts are universal qualitatively, though quantitatively differing in all persons as a result of constitutional-conditioning variations and the integrity of the developing defenses.

The earliest nuclear conflicts are organized in relationship to the parents. For instance, the infant's association of the presence of mother with satisfaction of his need (hunger, thirst, discomfort, pain, demand for stimulation) results in her becoming affiliated with gratification of these needs, with pleasure, and with the relief of tension. At the same time the absence of mother becomes linked to discomfort, distress, and pain. During the last part of the first year the child reacts with what is probably a primordial type of anxiety to separation from the mother and with rage at her turning away from him toward anybody else, child or adult. This blended gratification-deprivation image of mother is probably the precursor of later ambivalencies, powering sibling rivalry and the rivalries during the oedipal period. It also gives rise to motivations to control, appease, and win favors from mother and mother-figures, to vanquish, eliminate, or destroy competitors for her interest and attention, and to punish mother and mother-figures for actual or fancied deprivations. The mother symbol becomes associatively linked to later sources of gratification or deprivation. Moreover, if a disruption of the emotional equilibrium occurs at any time later on in life, or if for any reason anxiety erupts with a shattering of the sense of mastery, the imprints of primordial anxiety may be revived, activating separation fears and mother-invoking tendencies along lines similar to those pursued by the individual as an infant.

NUCLEAR CONFLICTS

Ages	Conflictual Elements	Legend	Residual Manifestations (repressed or suppressed)
0–3 mo.	Constant freedom from distress and pain *opposed* by realistic environmental restrictions.	"I must be everlastingly happy and comfortable; instead I suffer."	Search for Nirvana. Demand for magic.
4 mo.–1 yr.	Need for oral, sensory and affectionate gratification *opposed* by realistic deprivations.	"I want to be fed, loved, stimulated and kept free from pain at all times; but mother denies me this gratification."	Ambivalence toward mother figures. Separation anxiety.
1–2 yrs.	Self-actualization *opposed* by essential restrictive disciplines.	"I want to do what I want to do when I want to do it; but I will be punished and told I am bad."	Impulsive aggresiveness. Guilt feelings.
3–5	Power impulses *opposed* by sense of helplessness. Oedipal desires *opposed* by retaliatory fears.	"I want to be big and strong, but I know I am weak and little." "I want to possess my mother (father) for myself, but I cannot compete with my father (mother)."	Inferiority feelings. Castration fears. Compulsive strivings for masculinity.
6–11	Demand for total group acceptance *opposed* by manifestations of aloofness and unfriendliness.	"I want everybody to like, admire and accept me, but there are some people who are against me and reject me."	Fear of rejection by the group.
12–15	Sexual impulses *opposed* by guilt and fear of punishment.	"I feel a need for sexual stimulation, but this is wrong and not acceptable."	Fear of lack of "maleness" in men and "femaleness" in women.
16–21	Independence strivings *opposed* by dependency.	"I need to be a grown, independent person, but I don't want the responsibility. I would like to be a child, but this would make me feel like a nothing."	Continuing dependency.

56

The gratification-deprivation, separation-anxiety constellations, laid down during phases of development prior to the period of conceptualization, will tend to operate outside the zone of conscious awareness. Whenever habitual coping mechanisms fail the individual and he experiences anxiety, he may feel the helplessness and manifest the behavior of an infant, and he may seek out, against all logic, a mother figure or her symbolic substitute (such as food in compulsive eating activities). It is little wonder that mothers, and their representatives (protectors, authorities) come to possess symbolic reward (pleasure) values along with symbolic abandonment (pain, anxiety) potentials. This conflict, deeply imbedded in the unconscious, acts as compost for the fertilization of a host of derivative attitudes, impulses, and drives that remain with the individual throughout his existence. Other conflicts develop in the child's relationships with the world that are superimposed on the conflicts associated with the demand for magic and for the constant presence of the mother figure. (See Nuclear Conflicts chart.)

The actual experiences of the infant during the first years of life, the degree of need gratifications he achieves, the relative freedom from deprivation, his learning to tolerate some frustration and to accept temporary separation from his mother, provide him with coping devices to control his nuclear conflicts, which, irrespective of how satisfying and wholesome his upbringing may have been, are still operative, albeit successfully repressed, waiting to break out in later life should his psychological balances collapse.

Nuclear conflicts, to repeat, are inherent in the growing up process irrespective of the character of the environment. This is not to say that a depriving or destructive environment will not exaggerate the effect of conflict or keep it alive beyond that time when it should have subsided; while a wholesome environment will tend to keep in check operations of conflict helping to resolve it satisfactorily. Nuclear conflicts are partially ordained by biological elements and in part are aspects of the culture. We should expect their appearance in some degree in all persons. Their importance is contained in the fact that they give rise to reaction tendencies that, welded into the personality structure, may later interfere with a proper adaptation. Of clinical consequence, too, is their tendency to stir from dormancy into open expression when anxiety breaks down the ramparts of the existent defensive fortifications.

The operation of a nuclear conflict may be observed in a person who habitually relies on alcohol as his means of escaping the anxiety of his life. Feelings about the deprivations of life are avoided through the tranquilizing effects of alcohol, and at the same time he reassures himself, at least so long as he drinks, that a nurturing agent is available to him which will keep him free of pain.

Another example of a later nuclear conflict is evidenced in a teen-ager who establishes a pseudo-independence through invariably doing the opposite of what his parents ask. A request to wear the green shirt immediately establishes in him an intensely felt desire to wear the red shirt. His own fears that he will succumb to his desire to be dependent on his parents drive him to exert his independence, little realizing that he is still not free because he is now imprisoned by his own needs to be oppositional. And much later in life, when a supervisor says "do it this way," he may still be bound up in his need to resist, irrespective of the merits of doing a task one way or another.

The current inability of many persons "to get involved" may be a manifestation of several nuclear conflicts. To remain one step removed from participation in a cause or to be a spectator rather than a player, may be skillfully rationalized by saying that one does not have the time, or that the cause does not justify the effort, or the candidate is all too human, or the political platform is just so much window-dressing. But behind these reasons that sound good, the real reason may be one's sense of helplessness and the subsequent despair about finding magical solutions. Or one may not become involved because one will not be totally accepted by any group or party that one joins, so it may be less painful not to expose oneself to such a possible rejection. The nuclear conflict is handled by avoidance.

The exposure of repressed nuclear conflicts constitutes a prime task of dynamically oriented psychoanalytic therapy, the object being to determine the distortions they produce in the character structure, their affiliation with current conflicts and the subversive role they play in symptom formation. We shall return later to examine the circumstances under which nuclear conflicts are revived to the point of seriously interfering with adult adaptation.

Summary

While the personality structure is tremendously complex and is understandably different in every human being by virtue of his special constitutional make-up and unique conditionings, certain common ingredients may be observed in all persons in our culture. Among these are interacting manifestations of unresolved childish promptings, aspects of nuclear conflicts that accrue in the course of personality development, and reverberations of character drives, such as excessive dependency, aggression, compulsive independence, detachment, and manifestations of a devalued self-image.

6

Indelible Imprints of the First Year of Life

Cause and effect, means and ends, seed and fruit, cannot be severed; for the effect already blooms in the cause, the end pre-exists in the means, the fruit in the seed.

RALPH WALDO EMERSON

From the moment of birth, the journey through life is accompanied by an accumulation of traits that will ease or augment the joys and burdens of existence. Many such traits, developed during early childhood can be predicted to last the individual's lifetime even though the formative experiences and conflicts they nurture have been repressed. Among these, according to a study done by Escalona and Heider (1959), are ways of doing things (motor habits and activity patterns); thinking methods (intellectual abilities and modes of reasoning); responsiveness to one's surroundings (sensitivity to perceptions); intensity and variety of feelings (volatility and complexity of affect); the ability to choose a task and diligently to immerse oneself in it (levels of decisiveness, concentration and goal striving); the tendency to derive satisfaction from one's own thoughts (fullness of fantasy life

60

and imagination); the pattern of how one regards himself as a sexual being (the acceptance of a sexual role and the nature of one's sexual conflicts); and the style that one intuitively uses for interacting with peers (patterns of relationships with siblings). Patterns of reaction to strange situations, attitudes toward the self and the world, intrapsychic mechanisms precipitated by frustration, needs for achievement, and competitiveness are not so easily predicted.

In his developmental journey the helpless, dependent infant passes through a number of substations (beautifully described by Erikson, 1959, and approximately categorized under age levels in the chart *Personality Development*) toward mature, independent self-fulfillment. A number of generalizations have been made about child development in relation to age levels, for example the work of Scammon, 1938, on physical growth and Gesell, 1945, on motor behavior. It is posited that distinctive behavioral patterns become manifest at certain epochs. These premises may not be entirely justified since unique modes of child rearing may nurture some traits as parcels of an existing culture (Kardiner, 1939; B. Whiting, 1963). Variables other than age interfere with maturational expectancies. Cross cultural studies are needed to verify assumptions that may apply only to one society. Only then will it be possible to approach a fundamental taxonomy of behavior. Interruptions in transit, generally caused by failure to fulfill important needs, register themselves as anachronisms that burden an adult adjustment. (Greenacre, 1958; Hartmann, Kris, and Lowenstein, 1946; Hartmann, 1950; E. Jacobson, 1964; Knight, 1940; Mahler, 1958; Piaget, 1955; Reich, 1960; Schur, 1960; Winnicott, 1960).

A study of the most important components of the growth process is helpful in understanding how and why childish promptings survive. Many casual accounts about child development may be found in the literature. Until recently these have been mostly descriptive, reflecting the biases of the observers. Applications of empirical research are, however increasingly being applied to the field of child development (Hoffman and Hoffman, 1964, 1966). These studies have not only given us new insights into dynamic aspects of human growth, but are contributing to the building of a scientific theory of behavior.

It is for this reason that behavioral scientists urge the expenditure of funds at that point where infants and children can be vitally helped through exposure to mature mothering and fathering experiences. The qualities that constitute healthy personality structure are most readily learned early in life. It is difficult, and sometimes impossible, to accomplish in five years of thrice-weekly psychoanalytic psychotherapy that which mature and loving mothering could have done more effectively at an earlier age. Since prevention is easier than cure, and since the most fruitful preventive mental health measure known is to provide a child with a secure first five years, those measures which promote a secure family structure should have high priority.

The First Year of Life: The Infant

Let us look at the little fellow as he lies there during his first months. In the first year he triples his weight and adds 50 percent to his length. What makes him tick? He wants, above all else, to be comfortable. That means nice warm milk, lots of cuddling, immediate relief of tension and discomfort, and a great deal of benevolent attention. It is our educated guess that he feels that he controls the universe during those early months, and when all goes well for him, he is blissfully content. All he asks is that Nirvana be his perpetual state. Since the infant is unable to communicate his thoughts we can only make assumptions about the psychological processes going on within him during the evolution of his personality.

A great deal of speculation is current in writings on psychological aspects of prenatal, infantile, and early childhood experiences. Actually there is no way of validating what the fetus or infant must think or feel since he has, prior to the development of language, no way of communicating the exact nature of his tribulations. Deduction from observations of infantile behavior are often contaminated with the biases of the observer and must be regarded with scientific skepticism. Memories of prenatal or infantile experiences after the development of language are too unreliable to possess credibility, even though they are "revived" during psychoanalysis, hypnosis, or psychotomimetic drug administration. Among the most common suppositions are these: 1. The process of birth is a traumatic situation for the child that determines many of his later reactions. 2. The infant is permeated with narcissism that makes him assume that he is the center of the universe. 3. Feelings of omnipotence rule the child.

While some or all of these premises may be correct, we cannot dogmatically say that they are true. There is, of course, some reasonableness in assumptions that are supported by clinical data and scientific experiments. Spitz (1946) observed a large number of babies in a foundling home who, after separation from their mothers, were receiving proper physical care but insufficient mothering, reported marasmus and death in 37.5 percent, and cachexia, severe depression, and underdevelopment in a good number of survivors. We may tenably conclude, therefore, that the physical and psychological well-being of an infant during the first year of his life is contingent on a close relationship with a "mothering" individual who supplies him with adequate gratifications; satisfies his hunger, thirst, and sucking needs; holds, strokes, and rocks him; sings, coos, and talks to him; and protects him from coldness, dampness, and pain. It is generally hypothesized that a "mother instinct" exists in mammals, including human females, which is mobilized on the first contacts with the infant. This instinct, expressed in tenderness and caring, is said to guarantee the survival of the infant. The need for mothering is probably an aspect of a more general biological need for companionship and body closeness which in animals have been experimentally supplied by contacts with agemates, and even by inanimate, artificial "mothers" (Science News Letter, 1959).

Profound changes in the physical-psychological organization take place during the first year. Patterns are laid down that determine nutritive, perceptual, motor, coordinative, ambulatory, reality-testing, communicative, and interpersonal facilities. Patterns of eating develop: is it a relaxed, pleasurable process, or is it surrounded by coercion and conflicts? Perceptual facilities develop: are the five senses agreeably stimulated, or are they harshly assaulted? Motor coordination and bodily movement develop, attended by fear because of the dangers involved, or with confidence because the baby is encouraged to enjoy his increasing skills. Reality testing develops as the infant tries new behavior to see if he can accomplish something, e.g., putting his toe in his mouth or smiling in order to gain a smile from others. Communication develops: does it commence in a way that will encourage him to keep trying, or is it safer to turn one's head to the wall and keep to oneself?

The foundations of the security and self-systems are established during this stage which serve as the substructure on which is built the scaffolding of trust, autonomy, self-control, confidence, assertiveness, and self-esteem; social control of rage and aggression; tolerance of stress and frustration; problem solving competencies; capacities for self-realization; and the ability to relate to people, to cooperate, and to love.

For example, security develops as the child experiences and re-experiences an environment which meets his needs in a loving manner. He develops self-esteem on the basis of the esteem that is accorded him and by sensing that he is able to initiate acts which modify the world around him. As he becomes frustrated and angry, he can cry out; if his efforts bring improvement in his situation, he learns the value of effective aggression; but if he can accomplish little, the result is a sense of impotent rage. A most significant aspect of his world is the atmosphere of his personal relationships—here are experienced love or the lack of it, warmth or detachment, and mutuality or isolation.

The kinds of coping mechanisms the child establishes in managing the nuclear conflicts at this period (see "Nuclear Conflicts" chart) will influence how he will react to stress and to the resolution of conflict at later stages of development. Certain reactions to stress can even persist through adulthood. For example, bodily responses such as breathing difficulties, circulatory troubles, and stomach disorders may all begin in infancy as reactions to tension and may persist with a characteristic pattern throughout life.

More positively, Lois Murphy (1962) has demonstrated experimentally that early infant oral gratification corresponds positively with the later "coping capacity of the ego." She noted that sensitive, nurturant gratification during the first six months of life enables the infant to be generally tension free, and therefore able to devote himself to observing and perceiving his environment, and to facilitate a positive self-concept. When an infant could take for granted that he would be well cared for, he was not preoccupied with those most elemental needs. Somewhat analogously, a chronically hungry man is preoccupied with his next meal, and cannot devote himself to building a brave new world. Preschool behavior, according to Murphy, was significantly more mature in those children whose feelings had been respected in the feeding process, i.e., who had been allowed to succeed in rejecting a certain food. Allowance for the independence of a child, even at six months, had beneficial results.

It is not remarkable that the rudiments of trust and self-esteem are laid down during the first year of life when the helplessness of the infant is greatest. The ability to associate gratification of needs with ministrations from another human being establishes the core of pleasurable expectations in contacts with people. Concepts of the world as bountiful or depriving, of people as loving or rejecting, and of life as good or menacing, are rooted in such early experiences. Where adequate feelings of security are present, primitive emotions of fear and rage evoked by frustration tend to become socially channeled, and there is a sense of assuredness in the child, the beginnings of wanting to do things for himself. Feelings of security and trust give the child the courage to grow and to adapt to change.

On the other hand, the child who does not develop so fortunately is vulnerable to change later on. He seems precariously perched on the brink of disaster no matter how stable his situation may become. Slight adversity will tend to plunge him into despair, while he reacts temporarily to happy conditions with a crescendo-like elation. He is apt constantly to anticipate rejection, and he will be suspicious of those who attempt to lend to him a helping hand. He will remain skeptical of any lasting satisfactions in life. At the same time, refusing to accept necessary restrictions on his pleasure impulses, he will be in a constant state of tension and rage. He will insist on immediate and complete gratification of his whims. Even minor deprivations and frustrations may incite him to acts of violence.

How vulnerable children are during the first year of life has been vividly described by Bowlby (1952) who has shown that children separated from their mothers from six to twelve months of age exhibit withdrawal tendencies, unresponsiveness to people, inertness, insomnia, loss of appetite, loss of weight—manifestations of a depressive, apprehensive reaction that may reach the proportion of a dazed stupor. It is as if the child's faith in people is shattered. Should the mother return and adequately care for the child, the depressive reaction may disappear. Where she does not return, dullness of affect, listlessness, unresponsiveness to stimuli, undernourishment, gastrointestinal upsets, and insomnia may persist. These responses will act as a basis for later depressive reactions (psychoneurotic, manic-depressive, involutional). More severe disturbances may also result, in which an infant turns away from contact with a depriving or punishing parent and establishes patterns of thinking that are autistic and actually distortions of reality. Such reactions may also be observed where the mother does not actually abandon her child physically, but does so only in spirit, bestowing upon the child inadequate stimulation, attention, and love.

Primitive mechanisms postulated in the growth of personality during the first year of life are the dynamisms of *projection* and *introjection*. One of the tasks in growing up is to distinguish between what others are feeling, and what one's own feelings are. It is hypothesized that an infant generally attributes to the world those same feelings that he has. In this mechanism of *projection,* inner feelings and attitudes are repudiated and attached to outside individuals and situations crediting them with the evil that burdens one within. Another primitive form of thinking that infants engage in is imputing to oneself the same characteristics as exist in others about him. Through this *introjection* there are incorporated as parts of the self the qualities and attributes of significant persons with whom one is related. These mechanisms ultimately become subdued as intellectual maturity proceeds. Their residues may nevertheless persist and press for expression; they may invade and pervert reason, whenever homeostasis becomes unbalanced in even mature and adjusted adults. For example, when an individual is under a strain or greatly fatigued, "childish" fears or superstitions may intrude on his adult thinking. Some of these ways of thinking may be the kind of distortions of reality that characterize the thinking of an infant. Children who do not establish a good base for reality testing or who display an inadequate separation of feelings of "self" from "nonself" because of the markedly inconsistent nurturing patterns to which they were exposed, will be more prone to have trouble in understanding themselves and their relationships with others.

By the same token, symptoms of adaptive breakdown during the first year of life may become the established patterns to any stress stimulus in later life. Thus an infant who develops diffuse anxiety-like reactions, psychosomatic responses (anorexia, vomiting, colic, diarrhea, breathing, and circulatory disorders), rage reactions (screaming and crying), and withdrawal tendencies (dullness, listlessness, apathy, stupor) may continue to display the same reactions throughout life should things not go too well. Since the origin of these patterns is not remembered, the adult may be unable to explain why he has cramps and diarrhea, asthma, and other symptoms whenever he becomes tense and upset.

The past thus casts a shadow over the present. The physically mature adult may still search for satisfactions that he should have left behind in childhood. This holds true in persons whose early needs were seriously frustrated, as well as in those who were too well satisfied but never trained to discipline themselves. The infant screams when he does not get what he wants when he wants it. He needs to develop restraints and to learn to tolerate deprivations, because as an adult he will very often have to go without immediate satisfactions. But where the proper disciplines were never instilled, he will, when he wants something, still insist on getting it, perhaps not through screams, but by round-about, stealthy cajoling or coercive methods and a continuous focus-ing on personal interests with an inability to "give" to others. This may be associated with an inflation of one's importance sometimes to the point of grandiosity. Associated with such drives are a low frustration tolerance, emotional instability expressed in a demand to be babied, and feelings of profound helplessness. At times of great stress, strange feelings of be-ing so close to a mother figure may occur that one may imag-ine a merging with her. Or there may be odd thoughts about rebirth, fear of starvation, fear of the dark, fear of abandonment, fear of poisoning, cannabalistic phantasies, and fear of being eaten and swallowed. These thoughts probably stem from very early, infantile "oral" notions about a child's relationship to his mother, and normally do not re-cur except under unusual circumstances such as drug use, hypnosis, or dreams. When the usual equilibrium of living is upset, there may be a return to other of the wishes that pre-dominated during the first year of life and that center around a search for Nirvana, a demand for magic, accompanied by fears that one will be alone and separated from the help that is so desperately craved.

The Oral Stage

The first year of life is often referred to as the "oral stage," probably because the chief source of stimulation is the mouth, which unlike other sensory organs is functionally mature at birth. The mouth not only serves as an avenue of nutritional intake, but it also is a chief means employed to make contact with the world. Soon after birth adequate sucking gratifications seem to be essential for proper physical and psychic development, sucking activities producing an increase and regularity of respiration and a general improve-ment of muscle tone (Ribble 1939, 1941). Tactile sensations in the tongue have a stimulating effect on all the vital activities of the organism. The evolution of the security system is apparently rooted in the supply of adequate mouth gratifications, difficulties in feeding, or unwise or traumatic handling during feeding, exerting a deleterious influence on the establishing of feelings of trust.

Where the child does not obtain sufficient stimulation, some reparative efforts may come into play. Thus the infant may compensate by sucking on his fingers or on the bed-clothes. He may cling to finger sucking as a tension-alleviating mechanism even after he has made a transition to the juvenile period. Where stimulation in being fondled and played with is inadequate, the child may find methods of stimulating himself, as by excessive body or head rolling, by intent peering, and by playing with various parts of his person. Genital tumescence may accompany tension, and the child toward the end of the first year will often chance upon genital stimulation. This may become an established means of overcoming tension.

A Case Study

The case of William noted in Chapter Five illustrates many of the unresolved childish promptings that originate in the first year of life. Further, the pattern of William's deprivation begun then was essentially unrelieved in later years. William was born three months after his father had died. He was the only child of this marriage, and soon after he was born it was necessary for his mother to seek work as a domestic. William was brought along by his mother in a bassinet. To the mother, the child represented the basis for her imprisonment, making it necessary for her to work only in those places where William could accompany her, and also denying her the opportunity to be free to seek new companionship.

Filled with this ambivalence, William's mother alternately neglected and over-protected him. Her guilt could cause her to over-indulge him, and often she dared not let him out of her sight. William developed many fears when he was away from his mother, and later in life he clung to others as he had clung to his mother. When at the age of 40 he began to date seriously, his girl friend told him she would not see him any more unless he sought psychotherapy, saying that she could not tolerate his cloying helplessness. When asked what his difficulties were he responded: "I have a great need for companionship, but it is not easy for me to make friends. I am very timid. I cannot do anything new or different. Security is very important to me. I have no sense of accomplishment. I have no sense of direction in life. I can't make up my mind. I can't drive a car; I get so anxious, and I can't judge distances at all. I have no ability to follow through on anything. I have no temper, but I can get upset by trivialities. I am overly careful and cautious, yet I have literally thrown away money on friends. I don't know what is normal—I don't know what other people are like. If I knew what others were able to do, then maybe I could evaluate myself. Others expect too much of me. But for myself, I am always easily satisfied. If I could find another girl friend now, I would probably be satisfied with her. My feeling about myself rises and falls so easily with the circumstances around me. I can find a dime and feel good. I am a sick man, and a sick man is really a little boy."

William typically dreamed of being in a cafeteria where he would see good looking pieces of cake, but he would be unable to bring himself to buy any. What he was seeking in his dreams was to fill up the void of love, closeness, and tenderness which he never had as a child and which he aim-

71

lessly sought as an adult with the conviction that his search would be in vain.

The consistency of William's life reflects the severity of his early deprivation and bears eloquent testimony to the residual effects of early neglect by his mother and her resulting ambivalent and guilt- ridden over-protectiveness.

Summary

The primary need during the first year of life is for tender, loving care, abundantly bestowed in an ungrudging manner by parents who are responsive first to the child's needs, and second to the demands of society that begin to call for certain necessary restrictions. An infant has two major needs, for affection and attention. If those needs are met, the infant will feel loved and secure in an interesting and beneficent world.

7

The Toddler Confronts the World

The capacity of indignation makes an essential part of the outfit of every honest man.   JAMES RUSSELL LOWELL

Picture the mighty two year old: He has learned to stagger about on his two legs. He has little or no common sense. He has hardly any fear of those things that adults fear. Heights, depths, broken bottles, moving traffic, deep water, dirt, germs, and contamination—all these hold no terrors for the child who is becoming a two year old.

The objectives to be achieved during the second year are the establishing of patterns of social control over bodily functions, hostility, and aggression; the evolution of a sense of mastery; the establishing of habits and toilet training; the acceptance of society; the beginnings of self-discipline; and the establishing of frustration tolerance.

Parent-Child Relationships

As a child passes his second birthday he has mastered the fundamentals of balance, coordination, purposeful movement, ambulation, and symbolization. His universe, greatly expanded with his conquest of space through crawling and toddling propulsions, offers him untold opportunities for exploration. His new found freedom is accompanied by the release of aggressiveness that taxes the forebearance if not the fortitude of his parents. He will tug and pull and tear and bang and break; he will squeeze himself into every available nook and cranny; he will turn knobs, open doors, uncork bottles, remove lids of containers, and pop into his mouth any object he can find. He will brook no interference with the freedom of his movements, and he will bitterly protest the tiniest restraint. Parents, hitherto prompted by tender instincts that have been awakened by the helpless passivity of their newborn gift from heaven, are, by the time he has become a yearling, suddenly brought to the realization that they have brought into the world a creature with a will of his own, who makes importunate demands on them and menaces their freedom and patience.

The liberated aggressiveness of the child and his rummaging of the limits of his environment, mobilizes the parents to apply restraint and disapproval which are essential for the disciplining of the child. Without discipline the child will be handicapped in developing inner controls that can protect him from the dangerous reaches of his impulses. The directives of frustrating parental agencies are "incorporated" within the child's psyche forming the rudiments of his conscience. Such incorporative tendencies continue during childhood as part of the socialization process, the parents serving as the doctrinal agency. An important mechanism essential to personality development which is refined during the early disciplinary period is *repression*. By inhibiting and sealing off from awareness aspects of his psyche, the child is enabled to cope with inner impulses that provoke admonition and punishment from outside authority, and from their incorporated images as they precipitate in his developing conscience. At the same time the child's capacities for realistic communication become enhanced, and he learns a verbal "shorthand" so that he can properly interpret the meaning of a frown, a tone of voice, or even the feeling of a prolonged silence. He learns that one word can sometimes speak a volume or that one feeling can guide his behavior for a long time. And he discovers that he can also misinterpret some of these signs, even as he is sometimes misinterpreted.

Through imitation and conditioning the child continues to learn, his intellectual growth being fostered by a thirst for knowledge and an insatiable curiosity. His strivings for mastery are legion, yet he manifests a massive need for approval and affection. Consistency in the employment of discipline is vital at this period. The application of reward and punishment, restriction and encouragement, must convey to the child a reasonable purpose. The child will be able to tolerate considerable deprivation and frustration if he feels that he is loved and wanted and that there is some meaning behind the prohibitions.

The child who feels loved and secure will condition his emotions to the demands imposed upon him by the loving parents. In doing this, he will not feel that he is sacrificing an essential part of himself. On the other hand, the child who is insecure in his relationship with his parents will undergo a great deal of conflict and trauma as the result of prohibitions that are put on him.

The child at this period becomes victimized by powerful feelings of rage and hostility and has to learn how to channel these in a socially approved manner. Rage may be the product of feelings that parents are not ministering sufficiently or quickly enough to satisfy the child's whims. It is also the product of interference with the child's sense of mastery, as well as a consequence of disciplines and frustrations that are imposed on him in the process of socialization. Obviously the child is unreasonable. But he has to learn reasonableness

75

from the guiding authorities who administer his life with firm lovingness.

A period of negativism normally develops during this period. The child here is inclined to say "no" to everything. If this resistance is met by counter-resistance, great hostility will come out, affecting the parent-child relationship. The consequences of this may persist for a long period afterward. The period of negativism lasts for approximately six months and apparently is a biological means of fostering the child's independence. He tends to be extremely quarrelsome, as a means of establishing his independent existence. Negativism, stubbornness, and acquisitiveness become coordinate strivings. The negativistic period should be regarded as a temporary phase of growth. *If it is not handled properly, it may persist for years.* Unwise handling may turn the period into a chronic rebellion that may persist throughout the individual's life.

Early genital manipulation of an exploratory nature is common around this period of life. The management of the child's genital curiosity can lay down the foundations of his attitudes toward his genitals and toward sexuality as an experience. Where the parents, acting out of their own fears and inhibitions, attempt to correct too drastically and call the child's attention to his exploratory activity, a child may invest too great value in this portion of the anatomy.

Toilet training may or may not have a significant effect upon the child when it is mishandled. When too harsh there may be an interference with the child's sense of independence and mastery, a tendency to over-value excretory products, and a projection onto these of qualities that may lay the foundation of certain character traits. Thus tidiness and untidiness may represent to the child a means of appeasing or defying authority. Constipation is a way of holding onto things of value to him, particularly being equated with his own sense of control and independence. Soiling may be a

76

way of punishing, hurting, and destroying authority. In this way, toilet activities become confused with modes of expressing aggression. A refusal to control excretory functions becomes a means of retaining independence.

Thus involved in a struggle for autonomy, the child mobilizes defiance and aggression in an effort to assert himself as an individual. Attempts to bridle the recalcitrant youngster result in open conflict between the parent and child. The ability on the part of the child to develop a sense of independence while retaining the good will of the parents is the first step in the resolution of the dependence-independence struggle that will continue well into adolescence.

The proper management of this stage enables the child to develop freedom of mobility and emotional expression without fear of retaliatory punishment. He will then be helped to develop initiative and independence and appropriate modes of dealing with problem situations. A basis is established for self-assertion, self-confidence, self-control. The child learns to react constructively to challenges and threats with ability to compete and to protect himself. Capacities are evolved to substitute a nonfulfilling or risky activity for another more likely to succeed, to change roles, to accept limitations, and to utilize flexibly his skills and resources. He learns to plan, to make choices, to execute actions, to tolerate restrictions, to understand what he can and what he cannot do, and to function within limited boundaries. The development of adequate reality testing results in an avoidance of excessive inhibition, negativism, and withdrawal. A sense of dignity and worth evolves.

Repeated observation demonstrates that it is unnecessary to bludgeon the average child into conformity with society as if he were a savage creature fighting with all his tiny might to cling to the gratifications of a primitive. Secure children want to grow up, and there is a forward moving tendency to assimilate experience and to develop into independent biologic beings. This tendency is reinforced by a positive desire to conform to the demands of the parents out of need for their love and approval. The love and admiration that the child has for his parents are produced by pleasurable conditionings that are fostered while he is being fed, clothed, carried, and stimulated by the adult who looks after his needs. To win the parents' love and support the child will willingly renounce other pleasure goals, pursuit of which might put him in disfavor with the adult.

The child who feels rejected, on the other hand, finds it more difficult to master the frustrations that come from the abandonment of infantile modes of gratification. The world that envelops him seems so hostile that he reacts catastrophically to the inevitable frustrations of being two years old. As a result he may be handicapped in the development of a personality that can adjust him to civilized living.

It becomes increasingly apparent that what is significant in the phenomenon of discipline is not so much the specific reward or punishment but rather the cues that the child divines in relation to the parental emotion *behind* the discipline.

To summarize: *A primary need of the two year old is that he might be able to experience an environment which does not punish him for having a will of his own. His relationship with the disciplining authority figure at that age should do two things: he should be protected against the inadequacies of his own judgment, but at the same time, he should be supported in his wish to stand on his own two feet. As he strives for mastery and autonomy, the wise parent aids him in his quest.*

Residues reflecting themselves in personality distortions that accrue from this stage of life show up in the form of lack of self-confidence, stubbornness, and inability to control impulses and emotions. Frustration may give rise to excessive aggression. Where the struggle with parents is related to toilet training, a preoccupation with anal activities may result. Rudiments of guilt and needs for self-punishment may be detected. The child may evolve a number of coping mechanisms during this stormy period of life that enable him to express his feelings of autonomy and assertiveness through the vehicle of violence. Where the child has learned that he can intimidate the parent by a show of force and aggression and thereby get his own way, where temper tantrums compel the parent to give in to him, the mobilization of aggression as a means of expressing assertiveness may become a pattern that displays itself in later life whenever the individual needs to assert himself. On the other hand, where there has been excessive punishment and unreasonable discipline, the child will be overcontrolled and will be unable to express his assertiveness or his aggression. This will eventuate in excessive restraints and the pursuance of a course of passivity. Crushed assertiveness may display itself in a need to seek permission and approval before any kind of self-assertion.

Patterns of Discipline

It would now be illuminating to apply these principles to our cultural scene. Six observable patterns of inadequate parental discipline are apparent in American families.

The *first type* is in the family which enforces an early, strict, consistent discipline in which the emphasis is on being neat, clean and dutiful; where there is an outward observance of convention and a considerable preoccupation with being polite, proper, and careful. It could be described as a Puritan or perhaps Victorian home. The house is generally neat, the children drink their orange juice only from small juice glasses, and certainly would not presume to drink orange juice from the larger water glass. A child is instructed to refuse a piece of cake at least once or twice before accepting when visiting outside his own home. Guests are entertained only under very carefully prepared for occasions. When a child like this goes to a party, he is not given a final instruction of "have a good time" but rather "be a nice boy."

Under this kind of discipline, young persons emerge who are outwardly meticulous, obstinate, and perhaps a bit stingy. They often make good, cautious students. They tend to be neatly dressed in a fairly conservative manner, and are dependable and steady. They are intellectual rather than emotional. They tend to be quiet rather than noisy. In communication, it is difficult to know whether or not they're being "reached." Many of the things they say tend to be somewhat in the manner of a platitude. They will not expose themselves very much. Often they become overly modest, because they have a great fear of saying anything that could be interpreted as a mistake. They often work hard later in life, although most usually alone. They typically tend to be somewhat rigid and may even lack a normal capacity for relaxation. There are not now as many homes where this kind of discipline is practised as there once were.

A *second kind of family discipline* is exemplified by inconsistent authority patterns, where each parent may vacillate, or where there may be an inconsistency between the mother's and the father's discipline. Many possible combinations may be observed. The father may be away from home frequently, and the mother may run things. While the father may be larger, he may appear to be psychologically weaker. The father may appear to be only the mouthpiece for the mother who instructs the father what to tell the children. Sometimes parents alternate between being strict and lenient. This produces a child whose expectations are never certain. In a home like this a child may grow up with a magical idea that relief from stress and worry is just around the corner. He may feel that the discipline is only temporary and that the other parent will soon be along to rescue him, or the parent will change his mind. Life then often becomes a source of conflict and turmoil because of the uncertain nature of the attitudes to which the child is exposed. Many American homes are blighted by such inconsistent disciplining, and the children are apt to develop into worried, fretful, obsessive adults, unsure of themselves and whether what they are doing is the right or wrong thing.

The *third kind of discipline* is characterized by extreme laxity on the part of both parents, where little or nothing is expected of the child. This develops a child who feels that he is not responsible for his actions, one who has little opportunity to learn the relationship between cause and effect and between his own actions and subsequent reward or punishment. Because such children are never expected to act with a sense of responsibility, they become ill-suited for the adult world. The brilliant portrait of Elmer Gantry by Sinclair Lewis clearly illustrates the development of this kind of personality. Try as he might to stop himself, Elmer Gantry was a person whose every appetite had to be satisfied immediately, and he continued to be the victim of his every urge. He could not postpone gratifications, and he used the world to satisfy his own personal needs. It could be said about him that he had the gift of grab, that he was polished, in a slippery sort of way, and that he stood for everything he felt other people would fall for.

Persons who have been subjected to very little discipline often leave school because they find it monotonous, they change jobs because too much is demanded of them, they get along with their teachers only so long as the teachers are being nice in giving them something. But any exercise of responsible authority sends such a person running away.

81

They are often very friendly and pleasant people, but only until something is expected of them.

The *fourth kind of parental discipline* exists in those families where both parents are excessively harsh and unbending. The flavor of such a home is exemplified in a remark by a father to a seven year old boy: "I only expect one thing of you, and that is 100 percent honesty." Such children develop a perpetual sense of defeat as a result of the excessive demands upon them. Because a young child has a hazy notion of truth and falesehood, or of right and wrong, he is perpetually beaten down by the parents' impossible standards. He acquires little feeling that he can measure up, and his feeling of failure leads to further failure.

Such persons are great at confessing their faults. But if they are complimented, they tend not to believe that they are being told the truth. They often underestimate their capacities and will assume only menial roles in society because they are not confident enough to risk leadership.

On the other hand, some children will respond with a violent defiance in the face of tyrannical parents, subverting every disciplinary attempt. Enormously outraged at the constant assaults of the parents, they have a great storehouse of hostility which becomes more and more difficult to manage, resulting in a variety of erratic struggles with the parents.

A *fifth style of discipline* is exemplified by the parent who is competing with his child and unable to tolerate his success. While the parent may say that he wants his child to have good grades or good looks or athletic achievements, such a parent may be unable to let a child have the last word in an argument, or to win at badminton, or to acknowledge undefensively the originality of the child's idea. While a parent may say that he wants his child to win, that same parent may mercilessly ridicule the child who corrects his parent on a point of grammar.

Such a child may tense up when the parent approaches, hit the ball more clumsily in a baseball game when the father is present, and become more awkward even when trying to tie his shoe lace. These signs indicate the presence of a disciplinary attitude in which the child is intuitively learning that he should take second place in life. Such young people may be able some day to become adequate servants, but they may be relatively incapable of leadership.

In the *sixth place,* is a pattern of discipline that is difficult to detect, and even difficult to describe: the pattern is one in which the child is somehow encouraged to act out the unconscious wishes of the parent. For example, the father will say one thing, but take a secret delight that his child does the opposite. The father who has grown up himself in a very rigid home, and who tended not to misbehave outwardly, often can take a secret delight in his own son who is able to be rebellious in a way the father could not have been. If the father has not resolved his own conflict about rebellion, he may find himself bragging that "my son is the worst kid in the whole Sunday School. Did you ever see a boy who would run around and make so much commotion in a church basement as Billy does?" And a careful observer may detect that the father has something of a prideful smile on his face as he describes his wild son. The son will surely be catching the message from his father that he takes delight in the rebelliousness, regardless of how much he tells him to behave and to sit quietly.

A teacher who has trouble disciplining her class, may secretly envy the troublemaker. The way in which a person emphasizes things in giving instructions to others, may convey an ambivalence about those instructions, so that the students will be receiving a double message. A father's strict admonition to a daughter about sex may be such that the daughter gets the impression that he is preoccupied with sex, and she then also might become similarly preoccupied. The mother who is constantly warning her daughter that to kiss a boy is to invite pregnancy, and threatening to disown her if her daughter comes home pregnant, is generally reflecting her own secret fears and wishes which will, more than not, be acted out by her offspring.

It can be readily seen that in the exercise of authority, it is important for parents to speak with a single-minded purpose. The overall marks of healthy discipline are noted at the end of this chapter.

Now, of course, all these inadequate modes of discipline and authority do not evidence themselves in the interaction of a parent with his two year old. But the two year old is extremely sensitive to the attitudes and the feelings of the disciplinarian. Further, the feelings of the parent may continue unchanged for many years as the child strives for autonomy through various stages of his life.

When a child's needs for the optimum combination of mature guidance and loving support continue to be imperfectly realized, then residual childish promptings threaten his pursuit of freedom with responsibility.

A Case Study

The case of George illustates several aspects of the residual effects of early, harsh training, coupled with a number of strikingly inconsistent patterns. George today is a young adult who trembles at the approach of a police officer; he feels that all physicians are butchers, that God continually is punishing people and especially him, that elected government officials are nothing more than tyrants, and that the internal revenue service is one vast agency that exists for the purpose of denying him pleasure. In contrast, he feels that a female clerk in a store will give him a better deal than would a male, and that female teachers will give him better grades. And even when the weather girl on TV predicts rain for the forthcoming holiday, George feels it is the weather *man* behind the scenes who is telling her to say the thing that will deny him the joy of a good day at the beach.

It can be surmised that George feels that his life with his mother was sheer bliss—and in this case simply because he had such nice blue eyes and pretty curls. George's mother reinforced his feelings that his father and men in general were ogres and beasts. To exert himself did not bring rewards. She gave to him if he was passive. She stunted his aspirations by reinforcing his dependency. She threatened him with all manner of terrors if he tried to enter the masculine world. And George's father, at times actively annoyed with his son, and at other times simply detached from him, left the boy with the two year old stage largely unresolved.

Summary

How can the tasks of the disciplining parent be summarized? The first task is to set a correct example. High standards do not develop in a moral vacuum. The parent who is consistently loving and faithful to his tasks provides the example that will be copied.

The second guideline, often neglected in recent years, is that strict, firm parental discipline produces a child with self-esteem and a relaxed, confident approach to life. Through loving and firm discipline a child gradually makes sense out of his world, experiencing that there is an orderly, dependable scheme of things on which he can rely. As he plays by the rules, he is able to learn how to be successful within a uniformly stable framework. Success, and the resultant self-confidence, is made easier for a child within the firm disciplinary structure where a child knows what is expected of him.

8

Preoccupations of the Preschool Child: Sex and Rivalry

When I get big, I'm going to marry my daddy.

ANY LITTLE GIRL

We are now able to picture a two year old. But what about the three and four and five year old? Our relative amnesia for those years may have its own meaning. It was Freud's insistence that the four year old was sexually preoccupied that brought down on his head the scorn of his own Victorian age. While his era was able to accept the presence of oral promptings in infancy, and the temper of the two year old, it balked at accepting the insight that a preschool boy or girl has a tremendous interest in sex and genital differences, and that he or she longs for some sort of possession with sexual overtones of his mother or her father.

Since Freud wrote, ample evidence has accumulated to warrant the assumption that the child between the ages of three and five is working on 1. the acceptance and satisfactory resolution of sexual impulses and curiosities; 2.

identification with members of his own sex; 3. resolution of exclusive attachment to parents, with beginnings of establishment of extra-familial contacts; and 4. social control over his hostile-loving (ambivalent) feelings toward his parents.

Strivings and Stresses

The preschool child is motivated by two sets of strivings: first, the impulse to be babied and to be cared for, particularly by the mother who has served in this role for so many years; second, the desire to be independent, strong, and assertive. The first set of strivings are perpetuations of impulses operating during the period of helplessness ensuing after birth. These show themselves in drives for dependency and passivity, and in our culture such drives are often equated with femininity. The second group of strivings occur in response to the biological need for mastery and independent growth. They manifest themselves in drives for activity and aggressiveness and are usually equated in our culture with masculinity.

Conflict often develops in relation to the desire for dependency, passivity, and femininity on the one hand, and for independence, activity, and masculinity on the other. The child, male or female, seeks to satisfy both sets of impulses, and his or her capacity to do so will be contingent on the achievement of a proper dependence-independence balance, and the ability to dissociate activity and passivity from the kind of genitals possessed.

Both the boy and the girl require the presence of a strong male individual. The boy needs such a person with whom to identify in order to develop patterns associated with a masculine role in life. The girl requires a good relationship with a strong father figure in order to free herself from dependent ties to her mother, to overcome her fears of male authority, and to develop capacities for companionship and affectionate relationships with men. Weak, brutal, destructive, or irresponsible and absent (physically or psychologically) fathers prevent the development of these essential attitudes.

The exploration and stimulation of the sexual organs in early childhood are essential elements in the growth of a healthy identity. The experience of deriving pleasure through one's own manipulative efforts tends to liberate the child from the parent as an exclusive agency for gratification. The dependency drive may even undergo some deflation. Where there is no interference with sexual exploratory activities, the child's concentration on the genital region remains casual, being replaced by other areas of interest, as the attention of the child becomes focused on the many things happening in his environment. On the other hand, undue parental excitement about the child's genital curiosity may frighten, intimidate, or infuriate the child, filling him with tension and rage. The placing of an extraordinary emphasis on the sexual region will cause the child to associate with it emotions and attitudes that may distort its function as a pleasure zone.

In all children, penal or clitoral and vaginal sensations lead to genital exploration and manipulation. Where the child is rejected, or where he is denied other sources of stimulation, such exploratory activities may become a chief tension-relieving mechanism. Sexual intimidation and punishment for masturbation in such children may be severely traumatic, since the child is threatened with the loss of a main sense of pleasure and stimulation. The genital organs and their activity may consequently become overvalued, either in a positive or negative sense. Focusing the child's attention on the genital region as a forbidden zone causes the child to regard it as an unwholesome part of himself.

Other factors may reinforce an overevaluation of the sexual function. Among these are early traumatic sexual experiences and seductions, the witnessing of unrestrained or perverse adult sexual play, and an extraordinarily repressive upbringing which shrouds all sexuality in secrecy and fear.

What has traditionally been described as the *oedipus complex* is a tremendous oversimplification of the complex relationship and conflict the child experiences with his parents. What Freud discovered, in his analysis of adult patients, was that memories were revived of intense sexual desires toward the parent of the opposite sex. Such desires, he believed, had been forgotten and repressed, principally because they were associated with fear of, and murderous attitudes toward, the parent of the same sex. In the instance of the male child, the fear of injury inflicted by the father reinforced a renunciation of the sexual desire for the mother. Conflict with the father was ended when the child allied and identified himself with the father, incorporating the father's attitudes and behavior. With this renunciation of the mother as a sexual object, the fear of injury was allayed, and the boy developed a warm, affectionate friendship toward the mother, rather than an intense desire for her. In the case of the girl, Freud believed that she went through the same phase of attachment to the mother as did the boy, even with sexual feelings. But as the girl became cognizant of the fact that she lacked a male organ, and, due to her overvaluation of this organ, she mobilized hostility toward the mother, blaming her for having robbed her of the privilege of masculinity. She then turned to the father and developed an emotional interest in him which was coordinate with her resentment toward her mother, Freud's contention was that the interest toward the father was essentially of a sexual variety.

Disagreement with Freud's suppositions has been widespread. Many do not accept the universality of sexual attraction toward the parents and contend that this attraction is an abnormal manifestation, developing only when the child feels insecure and rejected. In the latter circumstance, the child then will attempt to reassure himself of parental love by a desperate and compulsive craving for stimulation. An additional cause for the sexual impulse toward parents would be the result of open or covert seduction by the parent who overfondles the child as an outlet for his or her own frustrated sexual needs. Those who challenge the sexual emphasis also insist that hostility toward the parent of the same sex is the product, not of sexual rivalry for the parent of the opposite sex, but of resentment of the latter's authority.

Nearly all observers agree that the child is fired by tremendous competitiveness, as well as power impulses. How much these are products of maturation and how much they reflect the values of a competitive society, is difficult to say. Nevertheless, the child strives to possess things in his environment that are of value to him. Particularly he seeks the exclusive ownership of the parent with whom he has been in closest contact. This is usually the mother. Interfering with ownership are siblings and the other parent. The latter especially poses an insurmountable problem, since the child realizes that priority is not his, that mother prefers the father or is obliged to accept the father. Frustration, despair, and rage are common, and often there are phantasies of disposing of the father, with great fear of retaliatory injury by this more powerful adversary. Fears may be displaced to other objects or animals, with development of phobias toward such objects. Phantasies of being retaliated against may mobilize intense anxiety. Whether or not this struggle is essentially sexual, or whether it is more broadly interpersonal in nature need not be decided here. In either case, the happy outcome for a child is assured in those circumstances where a loving father or mother, who is able to accept his or her psychological and sexual role, provides the child with the opportunity for the psychological and sexual identification that is appropriate for the child's biological endowment.

Another source of stress during these years is related to the child's *separation* from home when he enters nursery school and kindergarten. The reactions of the child to these stresses are contingent on his security system. Insecure children express the fear of being abandoned or of being hurt when they are removed from the protective influences of the home, even temporarily. A child who has been made to feel that his own impulses are undependable and that the environment is fraught with dangers will, of course, be hesitant to reach out to others. Such a child is insecure about what he will do to others and what others will do to him.

Sibling rivalry can be pictured by the following illustration. Let us suppose that a husband comes home to his wife some evening and says: "Dear, I want you to know that I love you very much and that you mean as much to me as ever, but beginning next week I am bringing home another wife who will also live with us from now on. Please understand that this doesn't mean that I don't love you." The impact of such a statement on a wife would understandably be traumatic.

A child who has enjoyed all the attentions and privileges granted him by his doting parents will naturally resent the birth of a brother or sister who robs him of the key position in the household. The resulting jealousy is a direct outcome of the threat to his security, and he is bound to regard his newborn rival as one who threatens his place in the sun.

If, when the child is two or three, his mother has a baby and then lavishes her attention on the newcomer, a kind mother becomes a deserting, hateful mother, and the baby a threatening, hateful little brother or sister. Feelings of rage and hostility that result are powerful. Where, in the past, such feelings have compromised him with his parent, he will have to repress them in attempts to adjust himself to the existence of his rival. Doing this, he restores the mother again

91

to her place as the kindly, good mother, and he may extend an attitude of strained tolerance toward his younger sibling.

Intense jealousy is the result when the child sees his parents express their love and attention to a newcomer. This is especially the case where the child feels insecure in his relationship with his parents. Such a child may interpret the giving of love to the younger child as a sign of abandonment and an indication that there is something wrong with himself.

Sibling rivalry is also manifest in a young child in relationship to an older child, when he begins to develop attitudes of aggressiveness and strivings for mastery. Feelings of frustration developing from an inability to aspire to the status of the older sibling may be keenly felt.

Also, a younger child who is unable to attain to the performances of an older sibling, and who is whipped up into a frenzy of competitiveness by goading parents or relatives, is apt to develop strong devaluated feelings about himself.

Residual childish promptings from the failure to meet and master the crucial events of these years are: continued dependency on the mother, with or without repression of incestuous desires toward her; an inability on the part of a male to identify with the father, or of a female to relate to him; and rejection of or hostility toward the mother, with abandonment of sexual feelings of the male toward woman, or specifically toward those who resemble the mother.

Let us illustrate with some specific parent-child configurations. In the instance of a weak father and a domineering mother, the boy and girl may identify with the mother who is regarded as "the strong one," i.e., the male in the family. This is apt to produce sexual confusion. Where the mother is domineering and the boy fears being engulfed by her, he may seek to detach himself from her and build up defenses against women as a species who he believes overwhelm and mutilate men. This may lead to a choice of males as less frightening love objects, causing him to resort to homo-sexuality as an outlet for his interests. Where the mother is openly or covertly seductive toward the boy, this may stim-ulate him sexually, intensifying the oedipal situation, lead-ing to such solutions as detachment, abandonment of mas-culine identification, or the renunciation of sexual feelings themselves. This situation may survive childhood and cause the individual to enter adult life with a total blackout of sexual desire. Or he may selectively extend the lack of sexual feelings to persons who in some way symbolize his mother in appearance, temperament, social status, and so forth. Here he will be impotent toward certain types of women, yet potent with others.

In the case of a boy who feels overwhelmed by a seem-ingly powerful father, there may be a tendency to give up his assertiveness. Intense hostility may continue, inducing guilt, self-punishment, and submissiveness, with an abandon-ment of masculine strivings and a desire to relate passively to the father and to be loved by him. There is then an identification with the mother, which, in the mind of the child, is associated with being passive and with losing his masculinity.

Some girls emerge from the preschool years unable to accept their femininity because they are convinced that females are second-class, damaged, or unlovable persons. This gives rise to intense resentment against men on the basis that they victimize, dominate, and humiliate women. Such girls may need to compete aggressively with men, attempting to van-quish them at all costs, or they may assume masculine traits, gestures, clothing, and interests. Sometimes the girl may solve her conflict by a dependent kind of reaction to men, minimizing herself and her capacities, while concealing the powerful resentment that she feels inside.

The way in which the sexual impulse was managed in early childhood will obviously influence the manner of its expression in adult life, as well as the specific choice of a love object. Where the child is made to feel guilty for having sexual feelings, having been intimidated or humiliated for such feelings, guilt and fear of punishment will contaminate the prevailing sexual attitudes. Impotency, frigidity, and sexual perversions have their inception in the earliest attitudes that the child develops toward sexual feelings and genital organs.

On the other hand, where sex has been accepted as one of the joys of life, where relationships between persons are seen as opportunities rather than conflicts, a child emerges who is secure in his or her conviction about being male or female.

A Case Study

The case of Julie portrays the effects of a warm and stable infancy, a reasonable and supporting disciplinary stage, but a complicated oedipal involvement. Julie at age three and four was an outgoing, sunny child who bounced on her father's knee with immense enthusiasm and affection. During these years the relationship of father to daughter became intensified by a lack of rapport between the father and his wife. Further, the birth of a sibling at this time caused the mother to withdraw from involvement with both her husband and her daughter, with the consequence that father and daughter found more and more of their needs fulfilled through one another. The distance between the parents, the father's turning to his daughter, the normal sexual attraction of the four year old girl for her father, and the consequent jealousy and resentment experienced by the mother—all these factors together caused a situation of intense family conflict.

The mother began actively to deflate her daughter's confidence in herself, eventually causing Julie to have doubts about the reality of her own experiences, which had heretofore been generally positive. Her father obviously enjoyed her as a feminine creature, but Julie had difficulty identifying with her mother who increasingly became less feminine and more hypercritical of Julie's vitality. The relationship continued to be highly stimulating for both father and daughter, finally reaching a level that was so manifestly incestuous that the father in response to his own anxiety stopped almost all contact with his little five year old daughter. Julie felt bewildered and rejected, with residual self-doubts about her ability to be attractive. Her mother competitively found fault with Julie and predicted for her an impoverished and barren life. Her father, denying his true feelings for his daughter, insisted that she was not a "lovely charmer," and forced her to wear outmoded clothing and to observe prudish habits. Julie's coquettish character style continued nevertheless, but naïveté, denial, and repression were used to handle any sexual feelings that arose.

Her life through the school years was overtly successful, but her conflicts and the contagious influence of two repressive parents did not allow her to develop a self image that reflected the reality of her life outside her home. She continued to charm older men, but always felt that her successes were illusory and bound to be short-lived. She could not accept the role of a woman as harshly described to her by her mother, and she compulsively determined that she would have all the things denied her by her mother. Her femininity thus became an uneven function. While craving to be noticed as a woman, she doubted that this would be possible for her. She felt angry toward men for what she interpreted as rejection, and bitter toward any woman who exemplified the life style that had been predicted for her by her mother. She felt she had to settle for meager pleasures in life, but even while in conflict about it, she poured her energy into proving that her mother was wrong. In the case of Julie, many reparative experiences later in life enabled her to realize that she was not a damaged person, and her compulsive strivings eventually turned into more relaxed and solid achievements in the areas of both love and work.

Summary

The preschool years have a special importance because of the task of establishing a stable sexual identification. Being appreciative of the child gives to the child an appreciation of his own identity. Encouraging him works far more effectively than criticizing. With the importance during these years of sibling rivalry, competitive strivings, and ambivalent feelings, the need for cooperative teamwork among family members is paramount. Common tasks shared in a spirit of mutuality enable one to experience the combination of unity and diversity that develops an appreciation both for self and for others.

9

Challenges of the Early School Years

They had that wistful charm, almost sadness, peculiar to children who have learned early not to cry or laugh with abandon. . . . They lived on the even tenor found advisable in the experience of old families of the Western world, brought up rather than brought out.

F. SCOTT FITZGERALD

A child needs adventure. He needs to make mistakes and to profit by his mistakes. He needs challenges and demands and opportunities for stimulation. Some experimental trial and error is better for him than arbitrarily conforming to the dictates of others. He develops the use of his own mind and learns to pursue his convictions on the basis of his personal experience.

The Years Six Through Eleven

There are three features that distinguish a young person who is successfully negotiating his childhood years during

97

this period: the establishment of extra-familial contacts, the pursuit of intellectual growth through organized learning, and the expansion of physical skills, especially through organized team play.

These are the years when a youngster needs to have his latent potentialities challenged at school, at the same time that pressures and expectations are not so severe as to overwhelm him. If a child is placed among children who lag behind him, he will be deprived of the stimulation and competition essential to keeping his interest alive and his mind growing. If he is in a class where he cannot keep up, he will feel stupid scholastically, unappreciated and resentful, and may even respond with delinquent behavior. Reasonable success in school aids in the development of good interpersonal relations, cooperativeness, and capacity for friendship. There is an integration of social values and the acceptance of one's own social role. Belonging to a group or a club or a team or a gang serves the purposes of allowing a child to test both his physical and interpersonal prowess.

Let us examine the three basic concerns mentioned above in more detail.

As the child makes excursions into the outside world, he establishes group identifications; this presupposes a giving up of some of his individual rights and pleasures. It presupposes also the ability to feel liked and respected by others. Children who feel unlovable have difficulties in establishing themselves within a group. There may be several reasons for a child's inability to relate to a group, including: 1. Refusal to participate in group activities due to a need to maintain solitary pursuits. The child here has a tendency to detachment, since he fears being overwhelmed in a close relationship. The detachment may not be manifest, and on the surface the child appears to mingle with others. Yet beneath the facade of friendliness, the child feels isolated. 2. Manifestation of acts of aggression, with strivings for power and dominance. Here he exhibits a type of behavior characteristic of a bully. 3. Seeking out a stronger individual upon whom he can lean and to whom he subordinates himself in a dependent role. 4. Avoiding identification with a group due to a conflict between the need to perform perfectly and fears of inferiority. One of the ways of solving this problem is through an inhibition of function and avoidance of any situation where he does not perform well or where he does not appear in a superior or dominant role. The child may then refuse to play with other children his own age because he cannot dominate them. He may shrink from competition, avoiding all situations where there is apt to be a likelihood of failure. Fear of being compared with other children and of failing may produce a shyness and isolation that permeate all of the child's relationships, both in social groups and at school.

Inimical school conditions contribute their share to the difficulties the child may experience in the classroom. Where there are many pupils who manifest behavior disturbance or delinquency, where there is over-crowding, where inadequate school resources necessitate the employment of poorly trained teachers, where maladjusted teachers dominate the classroom utilizing the children as vehicles for their own neurotic drives, the outcome may be an inability on the part of the child to adjust to school conditions.

There are some handicaps that the child possesses that reinforce any emotional problems he may possess. Dull normal children, and those who are mentally defective, are unable to grasp the significance of the learning materials to which they are exposed. Certain physical conditions may also undermine the child's capacities for advancement. Acute or chronic illness, visual and hearing difficulties, malnutrition and undifferentiated handedness are among the most common of difficulties. The reverse is also common: as physical drawbacks may influence school adaptation, so also do emotional tensions. Anxiety and its derivatives may block a child's capacities for comprehension so markedly that the child can simulate a mentally retarded individual.

Home conditions, moreover, may interfere with the child's adjustment. Such things as parents' moving to different communities, for economic, social, or neurotic reasons, prevent the child from establishing a continuity in his relationships with others. There may be a clash between standards at home and those at school. The permissiveness of a progressive school may differ markedly from the rigidity and authoritarianism that prevail at home. Or the reverse may be true, where the child attends a conservative school and is reared in a progressive home atmosphere.

All these factors influence the child as he integrates social values with his developing personality structure. He tends to pattern himself along lines prescribed for him by the groups with which he identifies. Cooperation with others, helpfulness, and contributions to the group are conducive to his feelings of self-esteem, particularly where he is rewarded by others for these accomplishments. Great insecurity, lack of assertiveness, and an inability to exercise self-control will tend to interfere with proper relationships and will have obvious negative effects on his self-esteem.

Since the child simultaneously belongs to a number of groups, conflict between the respective values of each is inevitable. Thus a child may have to play the following roles: 1. As a male, he is expected to play, to dress, and to comport himself like the other boys. After school, school mates' tauntings of "chicken, scaredy cat, yellow!" are the worst words that a third grade boy can encounter. 2. As a family member he is expected to uphold certain customs and expectations of the family. How often quoted are the words from a Jewish mother to her son: "I just want you to marry a nice, Jewish girl." 3. As a school boy he must adhere to standards imposed on him by his teachers. The words written by an admired teacher, "Fine test, keep up the good work!" are immensely gratifying. 4. As a member of a gang he is subject to a code that he dare not violate under threat of expulsion. The secret code, the undiscovered hideout, the mysterious contents of pockets (or pocketbooks) speak of the child's need to be one with his schoolmates and to disengage himself from his parents.

The standards of his family may clash with those of his gang or of his school or of his sex. Thus his mother, responding to her own needs to dominate, may tend to infantilize and effeminize her son. The traits developed by the child to conform with his mother' demands will bring him into opposition with social expectations of how a boy must behave. They will definitely bring out scorn and aggression from his playmates. These residual conflicts may persist through life, causing the individual to be uncertain about who he is and what is expected of him in his relations with individuals and with groups.

Where the child has a social background different from that of the other children, where there are differences in race, religion, or economic status which are a focus of discrimination extended toward the child by the other pupils, a disastrous effect may be recorded.

The school situation often becomes the mirror where emotional problems are reflected. These take the form of reading disabilities, writing reversals, persistent school failures, school phobias, stuttering and other speech problems, habit disturbances, truancy, fire-setting, aggression, stubbornness, resistance to school routines and other conduct disturbances, shyness, timidity, examination panic, inability to perform in classroom, dawdling, clowning, showing off and exhibitionism, excessive meticulousness, tics, and psychosomatic problems. Such symptoms are often passing manifestations, but certainly not always so. In any event, they are evidences of the stresses attendant upon the tasks of childhood or of reverberations of earlier difficulties which have once again surfaced in response to new situations.

A Case Study

The case of Laura illustrates the residual effects of chronic illness and hospitalization during the years six through eleven, effects which deprived her of the opportunities to engage in the essential tasks of those years. When it was necessary for her at the age of six to undergo a long series of surgical operations, she was repeatedly separated from her family for months at a time. Hospital regulations precluded visits by her several siblings. The aesthetically unpleasant nature of her physical condition, particularly her shocking appearance and the accompanying unpleasant odors, further served to isolate her from fellow patients on the pediatric ward. She was hospitalized a total of some 40 months out six childhood years.

While Laura's situation is extreme, it illustrates what happens when social contacts, school experiences, and physical experimentation are not available to a youngster. As an adult, Laura is now at her best in the presence of ministering authority figures. She readily and comfortably complies in one-to-one relationships with older, helping figures. But relationships with peers are fraught with an uncertainty that nears panic. Laura is unduly suspicious that her peers know something that she does not, that they are engaged in activities from which she is shut out, and that behind her back they are being given advantages by authorities that surpass her own. She still does not know "what people are really like." Intimacies shared are infrequent occurrences for her. While her talents are adequate, she lacks inner certainty about how to evaluate them. While she is fully recovered physically, she is overly dependent on words from others about how attractive she is. Yet, she feels uncertain and has great repressed resentment for the persons on whom she relies.

Her situation is one in which the adult replacement for what she missed in childhood is virtually impossible. It will be necessary for her to accept the fact that her personality structure will lack, to a large extent, those elements that should have been acquired in her early school years.

Summary

Loyalty is the quality of human relationship which probably has the highest priority during the years six through eleven. Children crave the kind of loyal parents and friends who help them to overcome the fear of loneliness and isolation, the fear that one is somehow different and unacceptable. Parents must be loyal in their communication, loyal in the sex education that they impart, loyal in their backing and support of their child. They must loyally support a child's sense of loyalty—to his friends, to the tasks of his schoolwork, and to the world in which he lives.

10

The Explosive Epoch of Adolescence

The denunciation of the young is a necessary part of the hygiene of elderly people, and greatly assists in the circulation of their blood.
L. P. SMITH

In the book of Ecclesiastes are these familiar words: "For everything there is a season—and a time for every matter under heaven. A time to be born, and a time to die, a time to plant . . . a time to weep, and a time to laugh, a time to mourn, and a time to dance, a time to love, and a time to hate. . . ."

Adolescence is the time to grow up, and the word in fact derives from the Latin word "adolescere" which means "to grow up." Adolescence is that stage of growth that begins with the onset of puberty and terminates with the assumption of adulthood. It is a period of great strife for both parent and child. For the parent it is a state of perpetual frustration over what he considers the antics of his offspring, who, despite warnings and admonitions, continues to embark on ventures, many of which seem to end disastrously. It is a period in the child in which he feels himself to be exploited

104

and misunderstood, in which he balks at routines and rebels against parental authority, in which he is at the mercy of impulses which may tax his adaptive capacities, bringing forth neurotic and even psychotic-like manifestations.

The Years Twelve Through Twenty

During early adolescence, the child has tendencies toward irresponsibility, irritability, aggression; he resents any affectionate displays of his parents toward him; he has little penchant for cleanliness and many tendencies toward poor manners. As a general rule the child will choose one or two friends and no more. He has great sensitivity to criticism.

Characteristic of this period is a far-reaching personality alteration and a breakdown of functions that have managed to keep the individual in a state of equilibrium in the past. The psychic equilibrium of the adolescent is upset by upsurges of impulses that he seems unable to hold in check. These may be restored temporarily by certain traits and character patterns such as by intense idealism, perfectionism, recalcitrance, asceticism, and strong esoteric interests, none of which may have been apparent a year or two before.

The objectives that have to be resolved during adolescence are: 1. A dissipation of dependency ties to a point where the individual can enter into a more aggressive and independent attitude toward the world. 2. A learning of control of the sexual function so that a proper balance is maintained between restraint and expression. 3. A change from a subordinate attitude of the child to the more dominant attitude of the grownup, in order that the person may feel himself to be on equal terms with other adults. 4. The development of a cooperative attitude toward authority, without hostility or feelings of being victimized. 5. Development of assertiveness and creativity, with the ability to assume leadership on occasion.

The stresses of this period relate to a conflict between sexual desires and personal moral and social restrictions, between masturbatory impulses and fears of self-damage and social disapproval, between a love for and a defiance of the parents, between a desire to retain one's dependence and the need for independence and self-growth, between the need for and rejection of the parents, between impulses of passivity and those of activity.

In primitive cultures, the adolescent's struggle is less intense than in civilized societies, because there is much more continuity in the behavior patterns of child and adult. Primitive economies, being less complex, afford easier and earlier emancipation from parental support. Civilized living interferes more drastically with a ready solution of the adolescent conflict. There actually is little in the training of most children to prepare them for the adult role. They are expected to proceed from dependence to independence, from the assumption of a subordinate to a dominant status, and from sexual indifference to mating, with little real preparation. There is also the fact that frequently the parent seeks to hold onto the child and resents the final break of his dependency. While the adolescent is relatively mature biologically in our culture, he cannot become economically self-sufficient until well into adult life.

A great deal of conflict results from the biological impulse to break dependency ties and the need for material help and support. The child frequently experiences resentment and hostility as a result of this conflict. He then will feel an urge to lash out at his parents; yet he will realize that such action may result in retaliatory measures that threaten his security. In addition, he will be in conflict due to his ideal of maintaining respect for his elders. He will thus be at the mercy of many ambivalent and conflicting attitudes. On the one hand, he may desire to pursue his education and to accept a career in line with his projected ambitions and the wishes of his parents. On the other, he may have a desire to become self-supporting, even though this involves interrupting his education and taking a menial job. He will be torn between devotion to his parents and anger at them for hampering his freedom of action. There is constantly a need to defy, to minimize, and to challenge the standards and dictates of his parents. While he possesses a drive for emancipation, he fears such emancipation. He seeks independence, yet shies away from it. He flouts conformity and adherence to social mores, yet he tends to criticize those who fail to abide by his own mores. He is impulsive and unstable, and his reasoning is overwhelmed by momentary emotions rather than by sound judgment.

As a result of a profound glandular change associated with maturation in the sexual organs, sexual feelings become intensified, and the child will respond to these in accordance with the attitudes and patterns he harbors toward sexuality that are the product of earlier conditionings. These more or less reflect the mores of his social group. While he is prevented, by moral judgments and taboos, from expressing sexual curiosity and strivings, his sexual impulses motivate him strongly in the direction of other gratifying outlets. For instance, he may develop crushes on members of the opposite sex, with over-idealization of the love object to an unreasonable and even ridiculous degree. However, if the child's early sexual feelings have been subject to rigorous restraints and punitive measures, the appearance of the sex drive in adolescence will become for him a source of great insecurity and even anxiety, since the impulse is bound to be interpreted by him as something that will make him evil and unloved.

One way of coping with sexual tensions is through masturbation. Masturbatory indulgence is probably universal in adolescence as a tension relieving mechanism. Psychological complications depend upon the attitude of the child toward his own sexual organs and toward the practice of masturbation itself. Many children in our culture have been intimidated to such a point that they consider masturbation to be an act followed by dire consequences. Genital manipulation will accordingly be accompanied by a great deal of guilt and fear. Many children, reacting to their masturbatory practices with disquieting dread, will then develop neurotic methods of dissociating their sexual strivings from themselves. Where masturbation is an accepted outlet, it can lead to an easier tolerance of one's sexuality, and prepare one for the time when heterosexual intercourse will become an enjoyable reality.

Where heterosexual feelings and deeds are too anxiety provoking, substitutive homosexual attachments and even overt homosexual relations may be sought by the child. Toward peer members of the same sex there is rivalrous and competitive interaction with strong affectual attachments. Homosexual feelings may also be projected onto older members of the same sex, such as teachers. The rule in our culture is for a temporary homosexual phase at the beginning of adolescence, the boy mingling in gangs with other boys, believing any association with girls to be "sissyish," the girl developing intense loyalties to and crushes on female contemporaries. Such temporary homosexual attachments are not particularly harmful. However, where fears of the opposite sex are extremely strong, early homosexual impulses may persist as a permanent distorted outlet.

Heterosexuality may constitute a great threat to some girls, particularly to those who are unable to accept their femininity. Menstruation, childbirth, child rearing, and laborious house work constitute for them areas of great exploitation, suffering, and privation. The tendency may be, among girls in early adolescence, to deny the fact that they are feminine and to regard female functioning with terror and abhorence. The growing girl may view her enlarging breasts and menstrual periods with dread, and she may strive in her actions, her hair-do, her gait, and her dress to identify herself with males.

Abnormal solutions of adolescent problems take many forms. The adolescent's struggle for maturity is influenced adversely by unfortunate conditionings and experiences in earlier relationships of the child to the parents. Overprotected children, particularly those who have been dominated and overstimulated by neurotic mothers, are tremendously disturbed by adolescent impulses to be independent. A striving toward self-sufficiency conflicts with the need to cling to the protecting parent. The child here is plunged into catastrophic helplessness when his dependency drive is threatened. Often the parent resents the child's growth and seeks to infantilize the child and to exercise dominance over him. These attitudes impair the child's capacities for independent action. The mother, especially one with strong dominant urges, may resent the graduation of the child into the adult. Indeed, as far as she is concerned her child is still a baby. On the other hand, children with strong dependency needs, as a result of failure to develop normal assertive tendencies, may dread the termination of the period of their infantilism. There may be fear of breaking loose and expressing the hostilities associated with the break up of dependency ties. Compensations in the form of compulsive modesty and needs to make oneself inoffensive are consequent to this type of adjustment. On the other hand, the child may attempt to deal with excessive dependency urges by equally forceful aggression and hostility. Delinquency, violence, and behavior disorders of various sorts may constitute a means of mustering up sufficient hostile feelings to terminate the dependency situation.

Expressed forms of aggression during adolescence will depend on the freedom of the child to externalize his aggression. Verbal or physical assaults on the parents, runaway tendencies, and behavior problems result when overt aggression can be tolerated without too much anxiety. Where the child has been intimidated and cannot express his rage openly, or where he senses that his resentment will result in retaliatory abandonment and punishment, he may be unable to express his anger. Indeed anger may be so suppressed or repressed that it may not gain conscious recognition. It may, instead, be shunted off into other than motor channels, for instance the complex nerve system within the body (autonomic nervous system), resulting in such symptoms as depression and psychosomatic complaints. Guilt feelings are frequently coincident and may be appeased by self-punishing acts or religious preoccupations. In young persons with severely weak personality structures, the conflict may shatter adjustment capacities with the precipitation of psychoses, usually of a schizophrenic nature.

Some adolescents attempt to solve the dependency-independency struggle by inhibiting their aggressive impulses, taking refuge in even greater dependency on the parent. Desire for self-sufficiency, then, is either repressed or gains gratification solely in wish fulfilling phantasies, the daydreams involving such things as running away from home, achieving success and glory in a career, or engaging in various feats of assertiveness or aggression.

The need to cling to his dependency leanings may become extraordinarily important in an insecure or frightened adolescent who senses in the demands made on him the fact that he is obliged to grow up and stop being a child. Adulthood, he imagines, involves exposures to dangers in a menacing world where one is alone and helpless, bereft of the protection that comes from clinging to a supporting parent. Occasionally, the solution for the conflict is sought in a reaction of detachment. This is most commonly the case in the rejected child who has yielded his independence by submitting to the injunctions of demanding parents in order to win the few crumbs of love and understanding that are thrown his way so long as he complies. The emerging adolescent's desire for freedom may create such intense conflict that the child will detach himself from people while adopting an outward attitude of slavishness. In this way he maintains a gulf that protects him from others at the same time that he ingratiates himself with them.

In children whose personality structures are oriented around power impulses, the adolescent struggle may result in a further striving for mastery and in an attempt to overwhelm the parent with coercive rage. Adolescence may inject such vitality into the child's feeling of self-importance that he will strike out blindly at all forms of constitutive authority, pitting himself against forces of order and decorum at school and against restraints at home and in the community. He may come into difficulty with the law by engaging in delinquency, truancy, fire setting, and other antisocial acts. Or he may engage in sexual exploits and sadistic activities that require punishment and even necessitate his removal from the community. Some children seek out a subculture, such as a hippie group, with which to identify. While extracting economic support from parental representatives of the "establishment," they hold the latter in contempt and strive to pattern themselves in dress, hair style, political convictions, and values after their new-found friends, no matter how disturbed they may be. Indulgence in drugs and sexual acting-out are common practices.

Children express defiance and hostility through sexual practices when they realize that such practices arouse great anxiety and consternation in their parents. They may thus utilize their sexuality as a tool. Their behavior problems, all radiating into fields of interpersonal action, may become centered around sexual disorders as a cover for more fundamental fears.

How the child handles his sexual drives in general is contingent upon his past experiences. Children who have been frightened into conformity by strict or hostile parents may interpret the sexual feelings as a dangerous lure. One way of managing themselves is to adopt a technique of self-punishment to purge themselves of guilt whenever sexual thoughts or impulses enter their minds. This masochistic distortion of the genital impulse may later make suffering a condition essential to the enjoyment of sexuality. Indeed, a child so encumbered may seek out conditions under which he is punished, punishment taking on a gratifying sexual tinge. On the other hand children who have learned the technique of gaining liberation from authoritative suppression through acts of aggressions and violence may employ sadistic activities as conditions mandatory to the release of sexual feelings. There may be an indulgence in acts of cruelty or aggression, in torture of animals or smaller children, which become sources of exciting fulfillment.

Children whose personality structures force upon them the assumption of a passive role may interpret the sexual drive as a challenge to this attitude. Functioning aggressively in a sexual role may precipitate great anxiety. Sexuality then may have to be repressed, or the child may seek to relate himself in a passive way to a more active partner. In males, this may lead to homosexuality as the preferred sexual outlet.

Commonly during adolescence, the child may turn to religion for solace. In this he looks for something that will lend a meaning to things. When his aspirations are shared with a perceptive adult who understands the nature of his religious and idealistic strivings, the adolescent can often be guided into self-fulfilling activities that serve both society and his own needs. On the other hand, adults can often use the religious fervor of the adolescent in exploitative ways which serve the needs of the adult and later turn out to be a source of embarrassment to the young person. The adolescent's idealism in a way is a thing of beauty, and what the Apostle Paul wrote to young Timothy applies now as then: "Let no one despise your youth."

The most significant residual effects of an uncompleted adolescence are two: a fear of a lack of maleness in men and femaleness in women, and a continuing dependency.

A Case Study

The case of Tom, age 28, illustrates both features. These are his own words: "I have terrible anxiety around people. I don't know if I'm a homosexual, but I worry about it all the time. I'm an adolescent, really. I like to horse around. I go to movies a lot. I like passive entertainment. I'm not a good athlete. I feel like an inadequate male. I'm not good at serious conversation. I like parties where there is a lot of nonsense going on. I'm not close to people. I never share. I am drawn to mother images. I look happy-go-lucky, but I can't cope with the demands on me. I don't know what I want, ever. My strongest motivation is to have people like me. I never express hostility. With people that I respect and admire, I am the most worried about being homosexual. I can't live without people thinking well of me. But that means that I must not say or do anything except what will please them. And I never know for sure what will please everybody— except to be agreeable and friendly."

Tom's father was a construction foreman, a cheerful, hard-working man who loved to fish and hunt, go to football, basketball, and baseball games, and play poker with his cronies on Friday nights. He provided well for his family, was generous with his money, and took everything calmly. Tom's mother was more business-like and berated her husband for not being serious enough, for being too involved with sports outside the home. He responded to her nagging by avoiding her all the more. The mother felt Tom should be everything the father was not: studious, musical, and concerned about social advancement. She generally had the last word in an argument and would often complain privately to her son about the father's gauche habits.

While his father was obviously proud of Tom, he neglected to introduce his son to his own way of life, and left his upbringing in the mother's hands. Although Tom admired his father's style of life, he could not break into his father's round of activities. Strongly pressured by his mother, relatively neglected by his father, and unable to assert his own feelings with either parent, Tom developed a gracious and amiable personality, needing to please everyone, but uncertain about his own masculinity. He was not homosexual but feared that he was, particularly under stress. When called upon to perform a manly task, he felt inadequate; when in contact with a woman, he would rely on the passive pattern that he had used in order to please his mother.

Summary

Here is a summarizing group of quotations from a set of essays written by adolescents about parent-child relationships:

1. If parents today thought more about their social relationships with their teenagers, rather than the physical aspects (money talks) the family unit would be strengthened.

2. A youth walks in darkness . . . he must find a light which he will use as a reference point which will help him not to get lost.

3. Parents, don't ever close your ears and your mind to our thought waves.

4. We can think, we can create, we can be individuals, Help us to do so.

Clearly, the need is for intensified interaction between parent and adolescent.

11

Lingering Residues of the Growth Process

We are living in the period of the most rapid technological, social, and political change that the human race has probably experienced to date. The problems of adjusting to this rate of change are very great. They are primarily learning problems. It is literally true that anyone in middle life spent his youth in a world that has totally passed away. We learn about the world, however, in our youth and we seldom change our view of it. Most people therefore are living in a totally unreal world. This is the greatest potential threat to the continuance of change. KENNETH BOULDING

Personality structuring does not cease entirely at age 20. But the results of hereditary, mothering, and fathering determinants in personality development, described in Chapter Three, can have an inhibiting effect. More general interpersonal influences, cultural factors, and the values of society continue to dispose a person toward certain styles of satisfying his personal needs and drives.

Each age and stage confronts the individual with special tasks. With the passing of each stage, certain tasks are left behind unfinished. While each stage leaves the individual with specific unfulfilled residues, a summary of the entire process can be outlined under the following seven headings:

1. *Unpropitiated early needs constantly obtrude themselves on the individual, propelling him toward direct or symbolic actions to satisfy these needs.* A man deprived during infancy of adequate sucking pleasure may constantly be obsessed with a need for mouth stimulation, over-indulging himself with food and alcohol to the point of obesity and alcoholism. A woman, restricted as a child in physical activity and assertive behavior on the basis that she was a girl, may continue to envy men and their possession of the emblem of masculinity, the penis. Accordingly she will attempt to pattern her life along lines commonly pursued by males, masculinity being equated in her mind with freedom and assertiveness. With dogged persistence she will deny feminine interests, and she may even clothe herself in masculine-like attire, cropping her hair after the style of men.

2. *Defenses evolved in childhood may carry over into adult life with an astonishing persistence.* A boy, over-protected and sexually over-stimulated by a doting mother, may vigorously detach himself from her. When he grows up, he may continue to avoid contact with women; any attempts at sexual play may result in incestuous guilt to a point where he is unable to function. A child rigorously and prematurely toilet trained, may regard his bowel activities as disagreeable and filthy. Over-cleanliness, over-orderliness, over-meticulousness ensue which burden his adult adjustment. A younger sibling may carry over into adult life the conviction that he is small and ineffectual in relation to any person more or less unconsciously identified as his older sibling. This will promote withdrawal tendencies or provoke him to prove himself by fighting and pushing himself beyond his habitual capacities. An older sibling may continue to harbor hatred toward any competitor whom he equates with the preferred

and privileged younger child in his family who displaced him.

3. *Mechanisms developed in early childhood that have insured a gratification of needs will continue to be indulged to a greater or lesser degree in adult life.* Thus a child, intimidated by his parents to avoid masturbatory activities, responds with great hostility and, in a defiant manner, covertly continues his practice. Later on the mobilization of hostility seems to be a condition prerequisite for any kind of sexual expression, sexual sadism being the ultimate outcome. Another youngster may have been enjoined by over-scrupulous parents to perform meticulously on all occasions, on the threat of their condemnation or loss of love. Henceforth indulgence of the trait of perfectionism may become an essential factor in his experiencing any degree of positive self-esteem.

A pampered child whose temper tantrums compelled his parents and siblings to give into his whims, persists in self-oriented, selfish demands on the world to supply him with gratifications and satisfactions. Sensitive to the slightest rejection, he construes any casualness toward him as a designed personal injury. This mobilizes rage and releases coercive behavior to force people to yield to his demands.

4. *The individual will repetitively set up and attempt to live through early destructive situations which he has failed to master as a child.* A young woman repetitively involves herself in competitive relationships with older, more attractive, more gifted women in an attempt to subdue them. The feelings she experiences and the situations she creates parallel closely the rivalry experience with her older sister whom she could never vanquish. A child is severely rejected and physically maltreated by an alcoholic father. When she matures she is passionately attracted to detached, sadistic, and psychopathic men whose affection she desperately tries to win. A man in psychoanalysis develops paranoidal atti-

117

tudes and feelings toward the analyst imagining that the analyst wishes to humiliate and torture him. These are transference manifestations reflective of the same kinds of feelings he had toward his father during the oedipal period.

5. *The individual often unwittingly exhibits the same kind of destructive attitudes and behavior patterns that he bitterly protests were manifested toward him by his parents.* A woman reared by a petulant, argumentative mother may engage in the same kind of behavior with her own children, totally unaware of the compulsive nature of her pattern. A man victimized during his childhood by a hypochondriacal father may himself become obsessionally concerned with physical illness following marriage. Through insidious identification a son may become an alcoholic like his male parent, a daughter the victim of migraine like her mother, etc.

6. *The individual may fail to develop certain mature personality functions.* A child severely neglected and rejected during infancy comes into adult life with pathological feelings of impending doom, a conceptualization of himself as inhuman and insignificant, tendencies to depersonalization, and an inability to love or respect others. A boy whose father is passive and detached identifies with a strong, aggressive mother, emulating her manner and interests to the point of avoiding masculine attitudes and goals. Homosexual desires substitute for heterosexual impulses. A youngster who was discriminated against by his agemates because of his race may, from the beginning of his extra-familial contacts, develop a contempt for his kinfolk and a fear of groups. A girl victimized by "proper" and "gentle" parents who cannot stand scenes is shamed into abandoning any demonstration of anger. She continues to display a bland, forgiving manner in the face of exploitation and intimidation.

7. *The individual may tend to revive childhood symptoms in the face of stress.* Vomiting, colic, and diarrhea, which were manifestations of stress during one's early infancy, may

be mobilized by later episodes of tension to the embarrassment and dismay of the person. Fear of the dark and of animals, which terrorized the individual in early childhood, may overwhelm him in adult life when anxiety taxes his existent capacities.

Summary

In Chapters Five through Eleven we have explored two of the three major denominators of personality structure, namely, unresolved childhood promptings and nuclear conflicts. We have seen how the assets and the liabilities of a person's development combine to form his personality. In the next chapter we move on to the third major feature of personality structure—character drives.

12

Patterns People Pursue

One can acquire everything in solitude except character.
STENDHAL

The unity that underlies individual ways of behaving can best be understood if one discerns that there are operating in every person certain personal patterns made up of nuclear conflicts, unresolved childish promptings, and character drives. The former two have been discussed in previous chapters. This chapter deals with the characterologic dimension.

Character Drives

Among the most common character drives are exaggerated dependency reactions, submissive techniques, expiatory techniques; dominating techniques, techniques of aggression, techniques of withdrawal, and techniques aimed at the expansion of a devalued self-image. We shall examine each of these.

120

Exaggerated Dependency Reactions

A relationship is developed with a significant person patterned after an over-evaluation of the latter's strength and beneficence. Insatiable demands are then made on this individual for gratifications of almost every conceivable sort. When the parental figure falters in the least, security is cancelled and anxiety prevails. Hostility is commonly associated with this type of adaptation, issuing from two sources: first, dissatisfaction with the amount and quality of bounties derived from the authority, and, second, resentment at giving up one's independence and drives for self-growth. Because the expression of hostility is regarded as a threat to the dependency situation, rage is suppressed or repressed and may be converted into depression or psychosomatic symptoms. The resulting physical suffering may be utilized as a weapon of aggression against the authority, the individual coordinately experiencing masochistic gratification, and a compulsive craving for affection which may surface as the prevailing reaction. Some religious fanaticism is also at times a part of this type of adaptation. Here, the individual, in quest of yielding to a power greater than himself, exploits religion and worship with intense zeal. Agnostics may become devout, and those belonging to religious organizations of a non-authoritarian nature may obstinately change to one that demands greater homage to God or his priestly representatives.

Submissive Techniques

A common consequence of this type of relationship is submission to, and ingratiation with, authoritative persons. Compliance, passivity, obedience, humility, and the yielding of the self to injunctions believed imposed on one are common. Submission may take a sexual form, the individual relating in a passionate way to selected people. When members of the same sex have been elevated to positions of superiority or power, unscrupulous surrender may be the consequence. In males the dependent submissive role and strivings toward homosexuality usually mobilize fears of castration with bouts of violent anxiety, making the submissive technique a liability rather than an asset. Coordinate with the submissive technique is a great undermining of self-esteem, self-depreciation, fear of rejection, and an increasing sense of helplessness.

Expiatory Techniques

These techniques are based on a revival of the childish idea that criticism and punishment may be avoided by anticipation, such as by self-criticism and self-punishment. This enables one to get the punishment over with in order to regain the good will and love of the parental object. Often there is a confessional stage in which accusations are heaped on the self for actual or imagined misdeeds. Self-hate and remorse become magical means of "undoing" fantasied infractions against authority. An inhibition of pleasure impulses and a subjecting of oneself to suffering result in asceticism. Suffering may become a condition necessary to the experiencing of sexual pleasure, and the fusion of the two gives sexual excitement in torment (masochism). The individual may inflict injuries of various kinds on himself, for instance exposing himself to psychological or to physical self-mutilation. Certain painful physical disabilities, hypochondriacal preoccupations, and mild depressions may accompany this technique of adjustment.

Dominating Techniques

The motivating force behind the drive to dominate is to coerce people to yield to the individual's will. Manifestations of dominance range from mild temper tantrums to violent rage reactions. Domination may be exerted through physical illness in which the individual attempts to control the environment and persons on the basis of provoking their guilt. Domination may also be manifested through sexual control. Here sexuality is utilized as a means of overwhelming members of the the opposite or of the same sex. The consequence may be nymphomania, satyriasis, or active homosexuality.

Techniques of Aggression

Violence may be directed against outside individuals or against one's own conscience by crushing personal standards and moral values. This is usually achieved at the expense of personality integrity, the individual casting aside his habitual mores and adopting a way of life that seems foreign to his nature. Sexual licentiousness, perversions, fighting, and the shirking of responsibility may ensue.

The acting-out of destructive or hostile impulses may range from mild competition to sadistic displays which may proceed even to the extent of murder. Intense fear and distrust promote forceful and destructive attitudes. This is the core of the "paranoid personality" who, projecting his own hostile or murderous impulses, responds to others with suspiciousness and fear of violence.

Included here are reactions found in certain types of "psychopathic personality." This condition is characterized by a state of emotional infantilism. There is an inability to face responsibility, the sacrifice of prudence for immediate gratifications, and the failure to organize behavior in line with the pursuit of purposeful life goals. All are manifestations of an immature personality integration. The individual appears to be constantly at odds with the disciplines of society and with the prevailing moral code. His behavior is governed by his immediate emotional needs, and he shies away from shackling his current demands to reality restrictions. He will brook neither interference nor frustration and, like a child, reacts with aggression when his pleasure whims are denied. Intellectually the individual may be brilliant, but he is so easily sidetracked that his talents are fruitless. Boredom and lack of perseverance make success impossible; efforts become disorganized and unsustained; goals are fantastic and often beyond realistic achievement. Failure fills the individual with rage, and he attempts to compensate by the use of force, by pathological lying, or by the assumption of dramatic roles that symbolize his childish notions of great achievement. Because he is ruled by egocentric needs he is in perpetual conflict with the dictates of society. His personality lacks moral, ethical, and aesthetic qualities. Unable to handle frustration, tension, or anxiety, he takes recourse in such tension releasing mechanisms as alcohol, drugs, sexual overindulgence, and unmitigated pleasure strivings. Associated are such deviations as irritability, nomadism, thirst for adventure and excitement, perverse sexual attitudes, alcoholism, drug addiction, emotional instability and immaturity, poverty of sentiment, inability to profit by experience, lack of feeling for others, an incapacity to inhibit aggressive and sexual impulses, and a notorious failure to conform with social demands and the dictates of sober judgment.

Techniques of Withdrawal

Detachment may express itself by avoidance of competitiveness where there is fear of aggression or failure, by withdrawing from people where expectations of rejection or feelings of inferiority prevail, and by moving away from difficult challenges where frustration or failure are anticipated.

Detachment may consist of a retreat from specific situations and persons, or it may spread to a generalized withdrawal from the environment and people in the syndrome sometimes referred to as "schizoid personality." This condition encompasses a wide variety of reactions including a penchant for daydreaming, general inertia and lack of drive, impoverishment of affect with apathy, and veering away from close interpersonal relationships. There are tendencies toward disintegration and schizophrenic-like ego shattering in the face of stress.

Another type of personality reaction exhibiting detachment is what has been referred to as the "anal" personality. This disorder, characteristically found in our culture, consists of an exaggerated self-entrenched and withdrawn attitude motivated by a great distrust of people. There is a fear of being overwhelmed by others which produces intense suspiciousness and a need to preserve oneself by warding off all intrusions. The individual here seems to want to absorb things but to give up little. Associated are impulses of stinginess, orderliness, cleanliness, obstinacy, and sadism. The function of most of these traits is to preserve the wall that protects the person from others. Cleanliness becomes a means of warding off contacts with the outside world; orderliness is a technique that keeps things in place so that the individual may not be caught unaware; obstinacy is a technique of fighting off overwhelming power by negativism; sadism stems from a feeling of weakness within oneself and from the necessity to deal with others in kind through domination and force. One of the motivants of homosexuality which often appears in this type of personality is fear of people of the opposite sex who are not to be trusted because they are different from oneself and, hence, potentially evil. Intimacy with persons who are more familiar because they have the same sexual organs is less threatening. Homosexuality may be a cover for additional motives, for example making oneself passive and dependent, gaining power, and humiliating the love object. Love is conceived of as dangerous, indeed any outgoing feelings are dangerous.

Techniques Aimed at Expansion of the Self-Image

Narcissistic strivings. The individual's interest here is concentrated primarily in himself. Strong desires are present for constant admiration, for flattery, and for appreciation. These impulses may be extended toward certain people or toward everyone. They may merely be indulged in phantasy in the form of daydreams, for example, and identification of the self with great historical characters or outstanding current personalities who possess the qualities the individual seeks to possess. The individual may dovelop a penchant for perfectionism with a need to render himself unassailable in all fields of work and play. There may be an attempt to adorn and bolster the impoverished self by grandiose impulses. The person here may develop a fabulous bloated image of what he would like to be and live solely in the hope that some day this image will magically come into being. One of the unfortunate consequences of the grandiose striving is that the person may set up goals for himself that are superhuman in nature and that are impossible for any person to achieve. These goals are so high that failure is inevitable, and repeated failures light up the conviction of worthlessness, in turn exciting further grandiose strivings.

Power impulses. Here the individual is motivated by a need to make himself strong and invincible. There is a blind admiration for everything forceful. The person has contempt for softness and tenderness, and self-esteem appears dependent on the ability to be strong, even violent. The need to control and to achieve power may be sought in terms of the symbols of prestige or status contemporarily prevalent. Compulsive ambition is often a consequence of this impulse to render the self powerful and unassailable.

Summary

Character drives emerge as the child develops coping methods to gain security, to win parental approval, and to escape from the catastrophic helplessness of feeling unloved and unlovable. He is most apt to develop techniques in line with specific demands made on him by parents. Where parents are motivated by their own needs to exercise dominance to excess and to effect submission of the child, it is likely that the child, in order to adjust to these demands, will develop a subordinate, submissive, unobtrusive character organization. Where the parent is meticulous and insists on exacting and precise conformity as the price for his love, the child may develop strivings for perfectionism. Where the parent is motivated by an impulse to over-protect the child, the child may find it essential to suppress his own needs for independence. In this way he will perpetuate his dependency. An inhibition of impulses for independence and self-expression may result in a character structure of selflessness, with techniques of symbiotic fusion through parasitic dependency on a stronger person.

Where the child has found that he can gain security through aggression and compulsive assertiveness, his character structure may become organized around these drives, with the manifestation of defiance, recalcitrance, or detachment, traits of compulsive independence, and avoidance of any influence that threatens to encroach on his integrity.

Character drives are exploited chiefly to maintain emotional equilibrium as economically as possible. In propitious circumstances the person may manage to operate successfully. He may maintain an adaptive balance even though he is manifestly disturbed in his relationships. More likely the complications and contradictions inherent in the exercise of the character strivings, and the inevitable clash with his customary values and standards, make adjustment precarious. Difficulties will precipitate out at work and in his marital, interpersonal, and community relationships, creating additional foci of conflict and reinforcing the anxiety that he already finds hard to hold in check. However, where the character strivings are not unduly rigid and compulsive and where the stresses are not overpowering, a person may be able to meet his major needs, although somewhat crippled by stereotyped reactions.

Character distortions rarely occur in isolation. Usually interrelated, their admixture makes for a picture that is unique for each individual. Behavior is not the static product of solitary trends, but a composite intermingling of tendencies, the fusion making for a picture that is different from the mere sum of the component trends.

Despite damage to the personality in the formative periods of life, the individual may build up defenses against noxious experiences, and manage to make some kind of adaptation. This is particularly the case where his environment permits him to act out his deviant drives without compromising vital needs. Or, to protect himself the individual may circumscribe his activities within a narrow orbit, rigidly operating within its bounds, thus reducing frustration or hurt. He may also selectively choose the people with whom he relates, detaching himself from those who mobilize in him too much anxiety. He may yield a number of needs, the expression of which would engender anxiety, or he may disguise them in a manner that is acceptable to him.

Under these circumstances, an individual may be able to adapt himself even with a defective personality, proceeding toward goals of self-fulfillment and more or less satisfactory relationships with others. Indeed, most human beings are reared under conditions far from ideal, for there is probably no existing culture that does not contain destructive and neurotic values. We must thus assume that all persons sustain some damage in the process of their growth, harboring within themselves conflicts that hamper a completely harmonious integration. Yet the majority of people do manage to get along tolerably well, in spite of distortions in their character organization, fulfilling most of their basic needs, realizing many of their potentials, achieving ample self-realization and self-fulfillment.

But in many instances these happy contingencies do not occur. Feelings of insecurity may be so profound, the self-esteem so undermined, the ability to give and to receive love so depleted, that there is exposure to never-ending deprivation or threat. The individual will be diverted from objectives that are consonant with his best interests. Thus, instead of pursuing pleasure, he will be driven to seek safety. He will be constantly haunted by dangers that shadow his basic needs and demands. The very world in which he seeks gratification may be so menacing that he will exhaust his energies in building defenses against it. Additionally, unhealthy personality drives will contribute to the initiation of many inner conflicts. The individual will be unable to handle even average vicissitudes and will react to stress in an untoward manner. He will be riddled with tension which, when associated with helpless expectations of injury or destruction, will foster the reaction of anxiety. This physical and psychological upheaval brings into play all the defensive instrumentalities the ego has at its disposal to restore the balances that permit some kind of adaptation. The outcome may be a quieting of anxiety at the expense of the personality integrity, that is, the development of neurosis.

13

The Sense of Maleness and Femaleness: Identity and Sexual Role

We love women in proportion to their degree of strangeness to us.
CHARLES BAUDELAIRE

Personality develops into a structure that forms the adaptive machinery through which basic needs are gratified, external stresses are mediated, and conflicts are resolved. Personality in this context is not merely a repertoire of special abilities, attitudes, and beliefs. Rather, it is the implement that encases every facet of man's adjustment and the most elemental of his wants.

Identity

The issue of one's identity deserves its own special consideration in relation to the concept of personality structure.

Identity is described as the continuity experienced by a person as he deals with his inner world and with external reality. It is a subjective awareness of his uniqueness but also of his place in the world. Identity is an inner definition of self, more or less confirmed by the world. It has to do with the "identicalness" of oneself over a wide range of inner and outer circumstances. And ideally it quickens one to act on the basis of that unity of being and doing. As Paul Tillich has expressed it, identity issues in the courage to be (Tillich, 1952). In the emerging identity of a person, one's *sexual identification* is of central significance, but we will first consider the overall task of identification before we proceed to the specifics of sexual identification.

Identification involves the incorporation of the qualities of an outside person or object with one's self. The identification figures most easily available to a child are, of course, parents. There is a tendency to assimilate the characteristics of parents whom the child loves, admires, or even fears.

Several forms of identification are possible. In *narcissistic identification* the individual identifies with the aspects of another person that are similar to one's own qualities. Where narcissism is strong, the choice of a loved person or object is a reflection of the idealized image of the self as seen in another person. In *goal-oriented identification* one identifies with the person who has something desirable. He vicariously satisfies his own wishes in this way. For example, a boy envies his father's strength and wants to be like him for that reason. In *object-loss identification* there is an effort to recover or obtain a valued person or object by being like that person. Thus the child patterns himself after the demands of a parent in order to gain and not lose that parent's good will. In *identification with the aggressor* there is a desire to avoid punishment from an authority by identifying with his prohibitions. Such an example, ruefully learned by many a serviceman, is the story of the army private who suffered much abuse at the hands of his drill sergeant. When the private himself became a sergeant, he passed on the same kind of behavior to which he had been subjected.

The total of these four kinds of identification makes for a variety of personality traits that are unique for every individual.

Sexual Identification

Identification proceeds at every age and stage. However, there are two particularly crucial periods in the development of one's *sexual identification:* the years three through five, and the early years of adolescence.

Sexual identification is a learned relation between the abstraction of male and female on the one hand, and certain attitudes and behaviors on the other. A boy acquires the conviction that if he feels a certain way and does a certain thing—in our culture the name of the game is called "being masculine"—he will become a man. It is a game that has enormously high stakes in terms of emotional well-being, vocational options, and personal affiliations. Sexual identification summarizes what our society endorses as being male or female. It is the task of the preschooler to learn something about what constitutes male and female. Usually his notions about this matter are well-established by the time he is in the first grade. He has learned that people are of two basic kinds, and he has discerned this through the contagious influences of voice quality, physical characteristics, how people act at the toilet, the basement or kitchen, or when buying tickets at the movie. Some cues are easily discriminable, others are more subtle or even ambiguous: hair style, clothing, boots, the style of behavior toward children, the person who washes the dishes, who leaves for work in the morning—these secondary signs are increasingly subject to variation.

During these years a child comes to sense that he is masculine or feminine. Several interpersonal phenomena are known to be of essential significance: the identification task is facilitated by a person of the same sex who can give a child the kind of generous attention and acceptance that makes the child feel a sense of communion with the other person. The model with whom to identify should also be seen as somehow idealized, even heroic. The chronically unemployed father in Appalachia may be able to give his young son plenty of time and affection, but if the son senses that his father is far from being heroic, the son will not be drawn to emulate him as a masculine model. On the other hand, one's model cannot be totally beyond reach. How would it feel to have been the child of a Thomas Jefferson or a Winston Churchill? A child must be able to feel that he shares some characteristics in common with the person he is drawn to model himself after.

There are several crucial psychophysical characteristics that are perceived by a child as having broad sexual significance. The first would be the physical qualities of the male and female. There is even here some difficulty in identifying with one's own sex, although more psychological factors probably bias the perception of one's physique. The obvious dissimilarity of a young girl's body with that of her mother can occasion a child to wonder if having a vagina is enough to be considered female. And a young boy, intimidated by seeing the size of his father's penis, may question if he can ever measure up to that masculine standard!

A second sign concerning what is male and female in this world involves the way people—men and women, boys and girls—tend to act. Boys are active; girls are quieter. Boys go out and do things on their own; girls are more compliant. Men seek conquests of all sorts out in the big world, whereas women show a greater interest in domestic skills. Men have more interest in things mechanical. Women appear to take care of people in a more direct, physical way. In summary, a child gets a general picture that boys and men are to be more assertive, especially toward the wider world; and girls and women are more dependent and conserving.

It can readily be seen that these signs of maleness and femaleness are often uncertain. What applies in one family may not apply in another. Yet, it is the reading of these signs that confirms or clouds a child's impression of his own sexuality.

Beyond these behavioral signs, there are attitudinal marks of sex differences. Here again these are at times ambiguous and debatable. The female attitudes involve being sexually attractive and sought after by a man, being emotionally affectionate to husband and child. The male formula can perhaps be answered by the reader as he responds to this question: "What is brought to your mind when you think of the word 'manly'?" The answer in our culture usually involves being rather strongly aggressive, independent, not unduly emotional, and virile in the sense of being able to win and hold a woman.

No one emerges from the vicissitudes of childhood with a perfectly invincible certainty that he is masculine, or that she is feminine. But the more nearly one approximates that kind of certainty, the greater will be a person's self-regard. Our culture has placed enormously high status value on being male or female. Sometimes the stereotypes are impossible standards to reach, with consequent feelings of hopelessness or despair about one's ability ever to measure up. James Bond for the men, or the current sex symbol for the women, are unrealistic models. Their very ridiculousness may be one factor in causing the pendulum to swing, among some groups, to the point where physical appearance, clothing, and child-rearing activities on the part of male and female are contrived consciously to be as indistinguishable as possible. Those who tune out and turn off say, "If you can't win, why try?" Or if the effort spent is not worth the victory to be achieved, who needs the struggle?

Making a child sexually secure must take into account several perceptions about himself and the perceptions of others concerning him. He needs to be told that he is masculine; the validation by others that he is indeed very much a fine young man, that he is "all boy" will help confirm in him that he has those qualities. He becomes what he was appraised as being. This leads our young man to see himself as he sees his father. The external appraisal forms a unit with his inner conviction that he is a chip off the old block. He senses the similarity of his characteristics with those of other males.

A child also needs to do the things that other members of his sex are seen to do. If the boys are gathering for a baseball game, he needs to be there. When one of his peers finds a package of cigarettes, he needs to be a part of the experimenting. If someone's big brother is offering motorcycle rides around the block, he needs, despite his fears, to have a turn at it.

When a child is told he is masculine, when he sees his own congruence with his father, and when he does what the boys are all doing, the young child is securely on his way toward a positive sexual identity. This identity then issues in an integrity of behavior in widely diverse areas of a person's life. The joyful use of one's (masculine) skills acquired in childhood continues throughout life, broadening in scope and effectiveness. Certain activities that are not regarded as masculine in our culture will continue to be shunned, unfortunately often at the expense of what might otherwise be richly valued. The nimble athlete will thus often not consider ballet, and the brilliant girl may eschew the research laboratory.

Once firmly established, the easy acceptance of one's sexuality leads also to expect success in heterosexual relationships. One needs be neither Don Juan nor Casper Milquetoast, when one has had a comfortable success doing all the other things that males do, previous to the time when dating is initiated!

On the other hand, if one has felt lacking in the factors that constitute and confirm one's masculinity or femininity, almost by default homosexual fears arise. There is often a vast difference between fearing that one is homosexual and actually being homosexual. Lacking the cultural marks of maleness, the young man may say "what else is there but homosexuality?"—and that thought may compound his fears and even stimulate his proclivity for embarking on such behavior. If he has not had masculine interests, has had no particular interest in girls, and if his doubts have been reinforced by testing or criticism of his maleness, he becomes plagued with fears about his identity.

Doubts about one's competence and a shaky self-confidence are the soil in which grow the feelings that one is not masculine. This then prompts the following chain of ideas: Lacking faith in his own masculinity, he then becomes frightened of being beaten up, hurt, attacked, and even sexually assaulted by strong men. He begins to feel he is more feminine than masculine. Next he assumes that he is homosexual—and his fright knows no bounds.

The process of sexual identification during the adolescent years is closely linked with a number of social factors that correlate with the strengthening of one's sexuality. During adolescence, relationships with members of the same sex become particularly important as a setting for establishing sexual identity. Since assertive independence and a show of mastery are masculine qualities, boys tend to band together to foster their autonomy in a common stand against the parents. And since social relationships are especially signifi-

136

cant for girls, they use their peers in order to develop intimate affiliations. The familiar neighborhood scene of the early adolescent boys exploring the territory together on their bikes, and the girls huddled furtively together discussing who is in love with whom, illustrates the different ways in which the two sexes express their pivotal psychosexual tasks. This central difference in what constitutes the sexual identification of each continues to show itself in schoolwork, vocational choice, and parental relationships, as well as specifically in the relationship to members of the opposite sex.

A boy will look upon high school as a setting in which to demonstrate his sense of mastery. Boys who drop out of school have simply been unable to demonstrate the mastery in a school situation that their emerging sense of identity demands. They generally have not done well academically nor achieved success in extra-curricular affairs (Sofokidis and Sullivan, 1964). School represents failure to them, and young persons generally do not voluntarily persist at activities which are continuingly painful. The boy who fails in school will look for another setting that will meet his needs for a sense of masculinity, sometimes behind the wheel of his "hot-rod." Achieving triumphs with the girls can be accomplished after school hours, while continuing in school as a failure does nothing to enhance one's status.

The central quest of a teenage girl is more consonant with staying in school, even if her grades are not extraordinary. While the boy seeks assertive mastery, the girl will evidence a relatively greater concern with whether she is making the grade socially as a desirable female. She needs a social setting for the pursuit of her feminine goals. She wants to become poised, graceful, and sought after. If it is a choice between an "A" or being liked, she generally would choose the latter. (Fortunately, however, such forced choices need not be made.) Vocational plans for a girl usually serve the same ends: to be where the interpersonal action is, to find the right kind of friends, and eventually a husband.

Recognition of the differing (and certainly legitimate) needs of adolescent boys and girls, and, in fact, men and women, is a part of human wisdom as dictated by the culture. There is some truth in the cliche that a man's face is toward the world, and a woman's toward the home.

Sexual identification is at the core of the adolescent's identity (Kagan and Moss, 1962). High masculinity feelings in boys are indicative of good mental health (Mussen, 1961). Douvan and Adelson's study of adolescents (1966) indicated that girls with low feminine orientation were less poised socially in relationships with adults, and were less purposeful and socially energetic. Again, it was found that personal *achievement* was central in the self-concept of boys, while interpersonal *attractiveness* and popularity were crucial with girls. Girls have their glorious daydreams too, but they are not so much about becoming famous or successful, but rather about attracting and holding someone to love them.

While it has been our purpose to present positively the factors that make for healthy sexual identification, it must be remembered that sexuality is influenced, as are all the other drives, by the character strivings inherent in one's personality structure. Character distortions will reflect themselves in disturbances of sexual functioning. Because exercise of this function involves the presence of a partner, it is understandable that the manner in which sexuality is expressed will be colored by attitudes toward the partner. The sexual relationship, constituting perhaps the most intense form of interpersonal experience, may become a means, to the person, of seeking out security, of expressing dependency, of asking for reassurance, of exercising hostility, of enhancing or of devaluating the self.

Where the individual's security is gained by self-subjugation, the sexual relationship may be contaminated by this impulse, and sexuality may mean to the individual a form of annihilating himself or of permitting himself to be victimized by another. Or if power strivings are the means to security, the sexual drive may become an avenue of establishing dominancy over others. In a person who has impulses of detaching himself from people, in order to gain freedom from hurt, the sexual impulse that drives him toward cohabitation may conflict with this tendency. Where security is maintained through hostile and aggressive attitudes toward people, sexuality may become a means through which the individual humiliates or punishes other individuals. If self-humiliation and self-punishment are important to the general adjustment of the person, sexuality may become fused with pain and suffering in a masochistic way.

Without attempting to exhaust all the possibilities, we shall supplement the story of sexual identifications by indicating several significant factors that make for homosexuality as the preferred mode of activity. First, fear of being mutilated (castration anxiety) is present. A definite danger is or has been experienced in relation to having and using one's masculine powers, e.g., one's penis. The dread of this loss has led to the renunciation of one's use of masculine sexuality. Second, strong identification with his mother may have led the individual, during boyhood, to feel that the preferred way to be is feminine. There is a variation on this theme in which the male, in identifying with his mother, wishes to receive love from a male in the same manner that his mother received attention from his father. Third, a homosexual may derive his satisfaction through sexual contact with strong men, feeling in this way that he absorbs strength and masculinity from them.

Conversely, the lesbian either experiences anxiety in relation to seeing male genitals, associating this in some way with the possibility of castration, or she deadens her reaction by detachment from intimate relationships with males or by frigidity. In her homosexual behavior she derives not only a recapitulation of her earliest pleasures, but also of past deprivations and fears at the hands of a female. In a way, making love to a female is a form of self love (narcissism) as well as a reversal of the usual oedipal roles of identification with the same-sexed parent, together with sexual attraction for the opposite parent.

Homosexuality is not merely the simple selection of a partner of one's own sex. It is rather a complex behavioral manifestation, symptomatic of a variety of nuclear conflicts, residual childish promptings, and character distortions. Nonetheless, the most crucial contributory element is the lack of positive identification with an esteemed and nurturing person of the same sex.

Summary

Sexual identification involves the incorporation of an outside person of the same sex with one's self. The task of sexual identification is facilitated when one's model is admirable, approachable, and accepting. A child needs to identify with both the physical and psychological qualities of his own sex. As a boy, for example, is complimented on his maleness, is compared favorably with his father, and is companionable with other boys, he is achieving a healthy sexual identity.

14

Breakdowns in Adaptation: Conflict, Stress, and Anxiety

Anxiety seems to be the dominant fact—and is threatening to become the dominant cliche—of modern life. It shouts in the headlines, laughs nervously at cocktail parties, nags from advertisements, speaks suavely in the board room, whines from the stage, clatters from the wall street ticker, jokes with fake youthfulness on the golf course and whispers in privacy each day before the shaving mirror and the dressing table.

TIME *March 3, 1961*

Neurosis is man's greatest saboteur. It undermines his health. It destroys his working efficiency. It ruins his marital happiness. It complicates his relations with his children. It engenders deep, destructive hostilities toward his fellow man. It fosters intercommunity, interracial, and international tensions.

Every reader is familiar with examples of how neurosis makes its inroads on each of these areas of living: Linda is about to go away to a resort for a holiday weekend, but on Friday afternoon she learns that her mother is not feeling well, and perhaps ought not be left alone for the next three days. As she has done so many times in the past because of the exploitative way in which her mother "used" her illnesses, Linda stays home that weekend.

Steven is in despair at having failed his major subject. A term paper was due on May 15, and Steve had known about it for the whole semester. He had many good ideas, but couldn't seem to get them down on paper. He would start and stop, go for a coke, have a smoke, talk to his roommate, pace the floor. And the deadline came and went.

Two young people are having sexual difficulties. Enthusiastic about sexual relations before they were married, their excitement and pleasurable feelings had zoomed simply at the touch of one another. Marriage brought mutual responsibilities—washing clothes and sharing the paycheck—and bedtime wasn't any big deal with a partner who was all too human, and with whom the mystery seemed to be fast disappearing.

A new baby is born, and the mothering process takes endless hours, until both parents feel deprived themselves. Never having been sufficiently gratified as children, they had developed a marriage style of leaning on one another. Both parents saw the baby as a rival for the attention which they demanded from each other, and they expressed resentment to the child who had upset the neurotic balance of their marriage.

New neighbors move into the block who do not seem to have the same values as "the rest of us." Some neighbors are able to welcome the new cultural patterns the newcomers exhibit. But other oldtimers who derive a certain neurotic security from warding off contacts with the outside world, because of their own feelings of inner weakness, exhibit prejudicial attitudes and create community antagonisms.

At every level, emotional problems intrude on optimum living. The environmental situations that tax adjustment range from average burdens of living—variegated work, interpersonal, and social difficulties—to extraordinary stresses such as accidents, severe illnesses, physical disasters, economic calamities, and the catastrophies of war. The basic needs that may be vitiated are diverse. They include such *physical needs* as food, shelter, warmth, activity, rest, relaxation, sexual gratification, and freedom from dangerous stimuli. There are *ego needs*—the giving and receiving of affection, the exercise of assertive aggressiveness, the experiencing of positive self-esteem, the achievement of creative self-fulfillment, and the living up to personal standards, potentialities and ideals. Finally, there are *social needs* which include belonging to a group, identifying with other group members, and fulfilling important group standards and ideals. The conflicts that victimize mankind are even more myriad. These operate on different levels of consciousness. There are those conflicts, known to the person, which he may attempt partly to resolve. There are others, for reasons we shall consider later, which are shunted from awareness so that the individual is unable to come to grips with them.

Emotional illness represents a collapse in the individual's capacities for adaptation. This collapse is sponsored by environmental stress, by unpropitiated inner needs, or by a medley of conflicts that violently upset the equanimity of the person.

The capacities to mediate stress, to gratify important needs, to endure deprivation, and to deal with conflict in a constructive manner are ensured by a harmonious blending of the various aspects of personality. For it is through the operation of his personality structure that man manages his

143

functioning in society. A balanced personality makes for an adequate adjustment. An unbalanced personality engenders deep disturbances in adjustment. Categorically, then, we may say that personality integrity is the mainspring of good mental health.

As a result of blocks in the evolution of a mature personality, the individual evolves attitudes, values, and patterns of behavior that are the product of a defective security system, incomplete conception of reality, imperfect social control over bodily functions, lowered sense of assertiveness, stunted independence, devalued self-esteem, inadequate tolerance of frustration, improper mastery of sexual and hostile impulses, deficient group identification, faulty integration of prevailing social values, and impaired acceptance of his social role. Pressure of early unsatisfied needs, anticipation of the same kinds of turmoil or the actual setting up of conditions that prevailed in childhood, and survival of early, outmoded defenses, symptoms and their symbolic extensions are incorporated into the personality structure of the individual. The damage wrought by the resulting distortions is great. Compulsive in nature, they permeate every phase of thought, feeling and action; they govern the random and purposeful activities of the individual, forcing him to conform in a merciless way.

What are the common denominators that underly neurotic symptoms? What constitutes personality pathology? In this chapter we shall examine some half dozen elements that are involved in pathology. Basic elements are *conflict, stress,* and *anxiety*. Conflict, stress, and anxiety are not in themselves pathological. Nor are the coping attempts of adaptation and defense. Each of them may be utilized constructively. Analogously, a rock in one's path may be the occasion for one's stumbling, or it can become a building block in some fine structure. We shall look at the elements of pathology, both as stumbling blocks and building blocks.

Conflict

Conflict is inherent in the process of personality development and apparently is inevitable to human existence. Growing up entails an inevitable clash between inner needs and reality demands, between innate drives and the restrictions and demands of acculturation. The end product of this clash is a host of conditioned coping mechanisms and defenses. Unresolved residues of needs, and actions against them of incorporated social disciplines, continue to operate within the individual the remainder of his life, leading to a variety of reactions ranging from the search for direct forms of need satisfaction, to their repudiation by reinforcement of restrictive controls. Compromises are inevitable through attenuated gratification of needs via socially condoned and institutionally available practices, and by various modes of managing the conflict through such mental mechanisms as sublimation, displacement, transformation, renunciation, and repression. These compromises may suffice to keep the individual in an adaptive equilibrium. On the other hand, environmental restrictions and periodic uncontrollable needs may break down the adaptive reserve with an eventuating stress reaction.

The Motivational Model of Conflict

Conflict may perhaps best be understood by means of a motivational model which is conceptualized in the following chart.

145

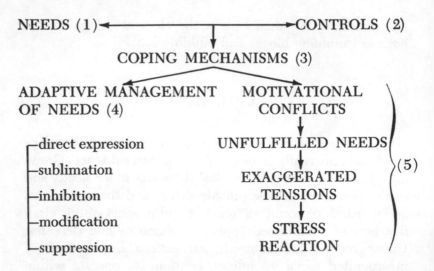

NEEDS (1) ◄────────────────► CONTROLS (2)

COPING MECHANISMS (3)

ADAPTIVE MANAGEMENT   MOTIVATIONAL
OF NEEDS (4)   CONFLICTS

 —direct expression UNFULFILLED NEEDS

 —sublimation   EXAGGERATED

 —inhibition   TENSIONS

 —modification   STRESS

 —suppression   REACTION

(5)

1. *Needs.* All living things are inexorably driven to a discharge of vital needs. These needs increase in complexity as we ascend the phylogenetic scale. Simple needs for nutrition, equitable temperature, and freedom from noxious stimuli are complemented in the human being by a host of complex needs essential for functioning in a complex environment. Some of these are an inherent part of the biological organismic matrix; others are social needs, environmentally conditioned and so intricately fused with biological drives that it is impossible to differentiate them. A unique biological-social compound precipitates out with characteristics distinctive from the basic elements that enter into its formation. Some of the needs operate outside the zone of awareness. Other needs are partially or completely conscious.

In the main, six groupings of needs may be differentiated: (a) physiological drives, such as for food, elimination, sex, etc.; (b) residues of early maturational promptings, unsatisfied during the developmental process, which press implacably for gratification. Thus needs for sensory stimulation, oral satisfaction, "mothering," aggressive exploration, restrictive discipline, sexual curiosity and other ingredients of the growing-up process may preoccupy the individual directly or in symbolic form—incorporative, eliminative, incestuous tendencies—giving rise to a host of strivings and contingent conflicts; (c) expressions of nuclear conflicts which are the inevitable precipitations of essential deprivations and disciplines extended toward the crude impulses and rebellious promptings of infancy and childhood such as, separation anxiety, ambivalency, castration anxiety, penis envy, or their symbolic extensions; (d) manifestations of unresolved experiences of strife and improper discipline with parents and siblings during the developmental process in the form of the setting up, the acting out, and the attempting to master the early discordant situation, such as abandonment, rejection, over-protection, sibling rivalry, oedipal jealousies, etc. (this phenomenon was referred to by Freud as the *repetition-compulsion*); (e) characterologic drives, reaction formations, and defenses; (f) expressions of assertive, social, and creative drives ("self-actualization," "self-realization," "group identity," "creativity"). Needs express themselves through tensions which unsettle homeostasis and promote motives for its restoration.

2. *Controls.* Needs, irrespective of origin, complexity, or propriety are always subject to restrictive *controls* which reflect the incorporated values and restraints evolved through experiences with parental agencies and other identification models. Needs undergo diminution, enhancement, or transformation in this conflux. The area of psychic control (often referred to in Freudian terminology as the *superego)* imparts a special coloration to needs as they press for fulfillment. What emerges in this metamorphosis is a compromise which embodies both elements of needs and controls.

3. *Coping mechanisms.* Needs, modulated in various degrees by inner controls, gain expression through *coping*

mechanisms. These, developed through painstaking conditionings in childhood, embody reward-punishment ordeals and form the basis for problem-solving propensities brought into operation by need tensions.

4. *Adaptive management of needs.* Through the instrumentality of coping mechanisms (*adaptation*) and favorable environmental circumstances, a direct discharge of need tensions will occur with restoration of homeostasis. If on the other hand the needs are of a regressive quality, this may complicate adjustment. In the individual with adequate coping mechanisms and adequate self-understanding, the drive to act out nuclear conflicts or to indulge early patterns compulsively will promote tendencies to sublimate, inhibit, modify, or suppress such immature promptings in the interests of adjustment.

5. *Tensions.* Where motivational conflicts are created by an exaggerated clash of needs and controls, by the interposition of oppositional drives liberated by the expression of a need, or by coping mechanisms which are incompatible with reality or bring the individual into rifts with others, *tensions* will become intensified and even brew to the point where they will initiate a "stress reaction."

Tension excitations reach the central nervous system at various levels of integration: visceral, somatic, and psychic. Under average conditions, excitations arising from disturbed homeostasis are psychically perceived. The conscious appreciation of the state of unrest fosters an integration of adaptive behavior patterns and their effective application toward gratification of needs in line with past successful patterns of response. Restored homeostatic equilibrium dissipates the tension state.

In many neurotic persons, on the other hand, there is faulty passage of excitations to cortical levels,with incorrect information processing and, therefore, failure in what should be the consequent marshaling of resources and defenses toward restoring equilibrium. This is usually due to an extraordinarily severe repressive mechanism. Inimical experiences in the individual's relationship with past authoritative figures often result in a hypertrophied conscience that initiates anxiety and guilt feelings whenever basic impulses and needs even in mimimal form are expressed. The child may, as a result, come to regard self-assertiveness, sexual curiosity, and the display of aggression as prohibitive strivings. He will then feel that he has no right to gratify personal needs and demands. Their very penetration into his awareness serves to stimulate anxiety. Where the ego is thus menaced by natural needs, the individual may attempt to organize his life so as to avoid their expression. His indigenous impulses will, nevertheless, continue to strive for release, stirring up tension. Repression, however, blocks the very awareness of unpropitiated inner needs. The result is the virtual obliteration of the psychic apparatus as an adaptive tool.

In addition to the danger that invests the expression and even appreciation of basic impulses, the neurotic person suffers from a distorted sense of values that make the normal pursuits of living vapid and meaningless. The past relationships of the person with his models were so disturbed that he had to elaborate character patterns (such as inordinate dependencies, power strivings, masochistic impulses, submissiveness, detachment, and compulsive perfectionism) to gain for him a vicarious fulfillment. Life becomes an arena in which there is ceaseless quest for spurious goals. Interpersonal relationships lose their normal meaning, and primary goals are subordinated to those that fulfill neurotic character strivings. The neurotic individual, consequently, will feel himself threatened by his natural needs, and he will respond to expressions of these with anxiety.

The average individual is capable of substituting compensatory gratifications for those needs which circumstances make it impossible for him to fulfill. The neurotic person, on the other hand, may look upon frustration of his drives as a sign that he is being victimized by the world. Hostility is the usual consequence. As a complicating factor, hostility is often regarded as dangerous and is consequently repressed. While the psychic apparatus is shielded from hostility by repressions, there is no such barrier to the deeper neuro-vegetative connections. Drainage of hostility through autonomic channels may produce such syndromes as cardiovascular abnormalities, migraine, epileptiform seizures, peptic ulcers, and a host of other ailments.

Thus the neurotic individual has a psychic and physical apparatus which is constantly in uproar. He feels himself unable to satisfy security needs, self-esteem, and strivings for love and companionship. He is confronted with feelings of helplessness, with convictions of worthlessness and even contemptibility. He is at the mercy of excessive tension, anxiety, and hostility. As a result his vegetative nervous system is subjected to incessant bombardment. A perpetual state of psychologic emergency is maintained to support his crumbling defenses. The slightest adverse environmental circumstance may unbalance him. A harsh word, a cold glance, a head cold, or a trifling inconvenience may suffice to upset his delicate equilibrium tumbling him into the depths of distress.

On the other hand, the healthy person is able to perceive his needs for love and assertiveness directly; he can adapt his life to achieve those needs without resorting to repression and denial which lead to the stirring up of more tension and the development of further neurotic symptoms.

The Freudian Model of Conflict

Having looked at a comprehensive motivational model of conflict, we will now examine in some detail the Freudian model of conflict which has served as the progenitor from which later dynamic models have sprung and which is at least of historical interest. It will be seen that the Freudian conception is the base from which elaborations, refinements, and revisions have been made in the light of modern sociological observations and the results of empirical research.

While personality organization is much more complex than originally described by Freud in his monumental contributions, his three-fold differentiation of the psychic apparatus as a source of conflict is still conceptually useful, though requiring supplementation. Freud divided groupings of psychological functions into systems of *id, ego,* and *superego.* The *id* was that aspect of mental functioning that dealt with primitive drives and impulses. It was unconscious and dominated by "primary process" operations such as fluidity, timelessness, inconsistency, illogic, and absence of negatives. It fostered immediate impulse gratification through direct expression or through indirect means such as displacement and fusion with other unrelated impulses. The *ego* was a differentiated part of the id emerging out of contacts with reality. As symbolization proceeded, the ego elaborated adaptive and defensive maneuvers which permitted discharge of impulses in line with "secondary process" operations, i.e., those that were reality determined and logical. Perceptual, cognitive, motor, physiological, and interpersonal functions were pressed into the service of adaptation. The defensive functions of the ego were unconscious, serving to mediate internal needs and external demands, to keep id activities in check and to balance the pressures from the third system, the *superego.* The latter, derived from contact with authority, contained the incorporated values, prohibitions, and approbations impinging on the child in the course of his development. It acted as if it sat in judgment on the individual's activities, approving or punishing them with a tenacious relentlessness. Unconscious to a large extent, it operated in an arbitrary and irrational way, with the bludgeon of guilt mobilization and threats of retaliatory abandonment and punishment. This primitive core was the nucleus around which later moral and ethical behavior crystallized. A harmonious integration of id, ego, and superego was essential for proper personality functioning. Discordant interactions made for serious malfunctioning.

A most important Freudian contribution to an understanding of conflict was the concept of a dynamic unconscious, embracing "nonreporting" activities—needs, impulses, attitudes, defenses, controls—that motivated the individual outside of his awareness. Operations of the id and superego and defensive maneuvers of ego fell within the unconscious embrace and were only minimally available to consciousness through aspects lying in a borderline zone, the "preconscious." For the most part unconscious mental activities revealed themselves indirectly through phantasies, dreams, slips of speech, behavioral distortions, and neurotic symptoms. Their manifestations were available to a trained observer in techniques of free association, dream interpretation, and observance of transference phenomena which formed the methodologic base of psychoanalytic therapy.

Under the lash of the superego and with the help of defensive operations of the ego, unacceptable needs and impulses underwent a symbolic transformation to fashion them to demands of reality. This metamorphosis was entirely unconscious and hence was subject to denial. A fear of biting dogs thus might reflect an impulse to destroy, fuse with and be incorporated by a maternal object. A phobia of snakes could be a mask behind which a desire for and fear of a father figure was concealed.

Symptom formation was consequently a complex operation embracing id, ego, and superego components, and the quality of symptoms reflected the maturity of defense. Projective and introjective mechanisms were most primitive and reflected profound instabilities of personality as well as highly un-resolved and traumatic experiences in infancy to which the individual could regress with symptoms of a neurotic or psychotic-like nature. Repressive defenses indicated later dif-ficulties and somewhat more mature capacities. The ease and depth of regression were related to the fragility of the id-ego-superego mosaic. The stronger the ego defenses, the less inclined the individual would be to resort to primitive mental operations.

Basically the Freudian model was a method of explaining how a person handles the inevitable conflicts of human exist-ence; the clash between instinctual drives and the demands of one's environment.

Learning Theory Models of Conflict

A bewildering variety of motivations operate within the individual, some conscious, others unconscious. These are shaped by biological and cultural factors.

Some of the most serious conflicts occur when the same activity is related to simultaneous approach and avoidance motives. There is abundant experimental evidence, both animal and human, to confirm the hypothesis that a need associated with pain or punishment results in a disorganiza-tion of the problem solving capacities of the individual and is apt to bring into play regressive, maladaptive defensive mechanisms.

The induction of experimental conflicts in animals suggests some of the mechanisms of conflict formation in man (Mas-serman, 1961). An animal motivated to satisfy an organic need (hunger, thirst, sexual tension, physical discomfort) pursues patterns in line with past successful need-satisfying responses (coping mechanisms). Faced with obstacles, the animal will exploit various other techniques contingent on learned successful auxiliary responses. With further frustration more elaborate problem-solving pursuits will be indulged contingent on the repertoire of instinctual or learned facilities at the animal's disposal. When in the quest of need satisfaction the animal encounters a stimulus fostering a need avoidance response, such as an electric shock upon approaching food, it will be faced with two mutually exclusive motivations: satisfaction of hunger and avoidance of pain. An impasse will be reached. Tension will mount and aberrant responses, such as aversion reactions, will develop. A generalization of the aversion reaction may then occur, such as a phobia related to any or all aspects of the feeding situation. Stereotyped withdrawal and rage reactions and a variety of somatic responses, even convulsions, may eventuate. Regression to earlier modes of behavior may follow. Many of the responses to conflict suggest symptoms seen in humans. The child who wants to play football (a need satisfaction), but who is threatened with his mother's disapproval if he does so (withdrawal of love equals pain) may reach an impasse, respond with tension, and regress childishly.

The application of learning theory, and specifically *social* learning theory to personality development has resulted in many concrete hypotheses that can be tested. Experimental situations can be devised which produce dependent or aggressive reactions in rats, monkeys, or even nursery school children. And conversely, the reduction of such behavior can be attained through strategies consonant with the same theory. Strategies of psychotherapy have been devised to extinguish unwanted behavior and promote the desired behavior.

For example, immature attention getting behavior such as clowning and noise-making, has been found to be eliminated most quickly when it is ignored; the learning theory hypothesis states that paying attention to such behavior is precisely what the subject is looking for, and even negative attention (i.e., punishment) is seen as something of a reward, and rewarded behavior will tend to be repeated. The intuitive reaction of many parents to provocative behavior is usually to make a fuss about it and then be mystified that the immature behavior persists, despite their every effort to condemn it.

The example just cited indicates something of the complexity in applying learning theory to all of human behavior. In a laboratory animal, punishment is more easily defined. In humans, the reward may be so subtle as to defy description. When a masochistic trend motivates a person, a person's behavior may seem to contradict common sense. A higher order of learning theory is then called for, with particular reference to the historical development of the person.

While it is dangerous to draw conclusions from animal experiments, the parallels in conflict formation and solution in animals and humans are convincing enough to merit further exploration. The simplicity and clarity of the conflict presented to the animal and its obvious response encourages the human to look for the similar common denominators in the more complex relationships between parent and child or between husband and wife.

In humans the outline of the conflict is most usually in terms of inner needs versus environmental demands. It may eventually be possible to provide the kind of society that allows for the optimum balance between these inevitable claims and counter-claims. And with conflict at more manageable levels we can expect less anxiety, fewer personality distortions, and the more effective achievement of man's aim of self-fulfillment.

In summary, there are inevitable clashes between needs, controls, coping mechanisms and the environment. Discordant interaction promotes emotional disturbance.

Biological as well as social needs make legitimate demands on the individual and on society as a whole. Through proper, conscious acceptance of a young person's needs, he comes to feel that somehow he can manage himself in a world in which he does not feel strange. On the other hand, the environment can make a person feel like a dangerous intruder because of the unaccepted and therefore seemingly dark impulses that he harbors within himself. With the necessity for the massive use of repression, his inner life indeed becomes a place of unknown terrors.

Where there is the recognized and approved opportunity for the reasonably direct discharge of one's needs, tensions are reduced and harmony achieved, and the human organism is fulfilled in regard to both his desires and his duties.

Stress

One can measure environmental stress only from the gauge of its special meaning for the individual. What may for one person constitute an insurmountable difficulty, may for another be a boon to adjustment. During World War II, for instance, the London bombings for some citizens were shattering assaults on emotional well-being; for others they brought forth latent promptings of cooperation, brotherliness, and self-sacrifice that lent a new and more constructive meaning to the individuals' existence. Indeed, for some persons wartime with its threat to life marshaled an interest in survival and subdued neurotic maladjustment, which returned in peacetime to plague the individual.

Misperceptions of the environment are universal, and one's attitudes toward reality are tainted with childish misinterpretations, with prejudices gleaned from erroneous education and from unfortunate experiences. Role expectations dominate notions of what is right or wrong in human relationships. The way men, women, wives, husbands, children, parents, grandparents, college graduates, laborers, negroes, Puerto Ricans, Mexicans, Jews, Russians, Germans are *supposed* to be and to behave determines one's feelings irrespective of the actual behavior of individuals. Stereotypes are accepted without peering into their essential falsity. The person may perceive stress where there is no stress.

Man's concepts of the world and of himself are colored by his prejudices. Of all the prejudicial taints, the magical world of his childhood is the strongest. Persisting are residues that force wishes, deeds, and angry feelings to be confused with expectations of hurt from others. Parental separation or death may be regarded as a mark of willful abandonment for which the child may hold himself responsible.

These are only some of the aspects of unresolved infantile and childish needs that cause one to perceive the world as a stressful place. An individual who felt unloved and unstimulated in his childhood—for example, the product of a sterile environment ruled by cold, undemonstrative, or rejecting parents—may attempt to engulf the world in unrealistic expectations and may make unreasonable demands on others for affection, attention, and recognition. At the same time he may feel conflicted about this demandingness and for the hostility that he harbors in himself as a result of his continuing sense of disappointment toward his world.

The understanding of stress necessitates acknowledging that there is no objective measure of it. One cannot say that such and such an environment is, for the average adult, 70 percent stressful and 30 percent nurturant. No matter how benevolent or stressful the environment, the individual will impart to it a special meaning as it is filtered through his conceptual network. This shades his world with a significance that is largely subjective. Conceptual distortions particularly twist feelings toward other human beings and especially toward the self. A self-image that is hateful or inadequate plagues the individual the remainder of his life and causes him to interpret most happenings in relation to his feeling that he does not have much value. Most of what happens to him in life will be viewed as confirming his own conviction that he isn't much good and that nothing that he does will amount to anything. Such a pervasive belief, of course, makes nearly any occurrence productive of considerable stress.

With this as an introduction we may go on to state that there *is* such a thing as realistic environmental stress.

1. *The environment may expose the individual to grave threats* in the form of genuine dangers to life and to security. Exemplary are exposure to disasters such as war, floods, storms, and accidents as well as severe deprivations to fundamental needs for food, shelter, love, recognition, and other biological and social urges engendered by a cruel or barren environment.

2. *The environment may be partially inimical*, the individual not having the resources to rectify it. A book on wilderness camping cites an example of a hunter who froze to death. When his body was found, there was evidence that the camper had used all his matches in a vain attempt to start a fire with the wrong kind of kindling wood. A few feet away from the frozen hunter, cites the guidebook, was a hollow tree trunk, the inside of which would have produced a crackling fire with only one match. In this instance, the temperature was indeed freezing, but the environment was beneficent enough, had the individual only had those early formative experiences "that would have enabled him to use the resources that were potentially available."

In this case, where does the blame lie? The ghetto child, deprived of educational and vocational skills, may persist in ineffectual attempts to wrest from his environment the satisfaction of his needs. The outsider, with a different array of skills available as a result of a different upbringing and training, may chafe at the futility of what he sees his impoverished neighbor trying to attempt. The solution lies in helping each person develop the resources necessary for coping with his own particular environment—and, when necessary, to escape from it, or to change it.

3. *The environment may contain all elements essential for a good adjustment,* yet the individual may, as has been cited above, be unable to take advantage of it because of a personality structure which makes him experience essential needs as provocative of danger. Such defects may cause him to project out into the environment his inner dissatisfactions, and he may actually create circumstances that bring upon himself the very hazards from which he seeks escape.

Some persons invariably regard their environment as one in which their assertiveness brings punishment. Such a person may be able to play an excellent game of ping pong until the score reaches 18-17. Somehow in trying to gain the final three points he will sabotage himself, being largly unconscious of the fact that he would find victory more stressful than defeat. He loses in order not to be punished by his opponents, who are actually within himself. He also may buy second-rate clothing, choose a second-class wife, engage in a second-class career far below his potential—all the while complaining that the world is full of stresses that deprive him of fulfillment.

4. *Character distortions engendered by defects in development,* such as extreme dependency, detachment, aggression, masochism, perfectionism, or compulsive ambitiousness, may engender problems in interpersonal relations. They make for the creation of abnormal goals and values that may seriously interfere with adjustment.

The compulsive pursuit of a neurotic style is not the same as the achievement of meaningful personal relations and a fulfilling, productive vocation. One's life can be consumed in the quest for safety, so that the joys of growth, expansion, and development are almost unknown. The quest for safety, if exclusively indulged, would deprive a child of learning how to ride a bicycle or how to swim. It would make dating out of the question, since no adolescent ever felt entirely secure on his first date. No woman would attempt that first turkey dinner for her family, since surely the possibility of failure is present in such a venture.

We agree with Kierkegaard "To venture is to cause anxiety, but not to venture is to lose all." Life, vapid and meaningless, as a result of the pursuit of spurious goals, brings with it a kind of stress that is eventually more debilitating than the stress that is a part of meeting and mastering the ongoing confrontations and challenges of an expanding life.

So long as a person is capable of coping with the current life situation, so long as he can gratify his most important needs and dispose of others he is unable to satisfy, so long as he can sustain a sense of security and self-esteem, and so long as he is able to mediate troubles that vex him, he will not experience stress beyond the point of adaptive balance. When, however, this is not possible, the threat is registered as a state of tension, with altered homeostasis affecting the viscera, the skeletal muscles, and the psychic apparatus. The person mobilizes himself to cope with the stress and, if he is successful, homeostasis is restored.

The manner in which a person responds to stress is described by Selye (1950), first, as a temporary "shock phase" or alarm reaction in which there is hypotension and a lowering of muscular tone. In the second phase, there is a "counter-shock and resistance," characterized by heightened hypothalamic and autonomic stimulation. At this point are developed the sensations of apprehension, tension, and anxiety, which in themselves become additional sources of stress.

Among the chief reactions invoked during this second stage are an increase in muscle tonus, enhanced locomotor activity, elevation of blood pressure, tachycardia, increased sensitivity to sensory stimuli, and other signs of an alerted psychic state. A breakdown of cellular substances occurs to supply the increased energy demands. Eventually, the cycle is balanced by a recuperative and protective reaction to restore the body to homeostasis. The para-sympathetic nervous system is involved here. Stimulation of this system results in a decrease in muscle tonus, lowered locomotor activity, reduced blood pressure, bradycardia, decreased sensitivity to sensory stimuli, drowsiness, and sleep. These reactions encourage a restoration of the cells to their previous integrity.

For the understanding of what stress does to one's psychological and physical status, it should be noted that the stress reaction is a nonspecific one: it can be provoked by any source which disturbs the homeostatic balance. Being caught in a burning building, learning that one has had a heart attack, or imagining that one's boss is going to be angry on Monday morning—all stimulate the same physiological stress reaction.

The following chart, "Adaptation Syndrome." (Wolberg, 1966), extends the previous chart relating to conflict. When conflict eventuates in a stress reaction, the following elements are mobilized.

The outcome of the person's adaptive measures to cope with stress hopefully produces a return to homeostatic balance. When this does not occur, the same stress keeps producing the same internal uproar, which results in even further anxiety. When attempts at adaptation keep failing, the continuing presence of anxiety in turn sabotages the development of more effective coping patterns. Thus a person who is introduced to someone may tend to forget the latter's name if he is anxious when he is being introduced; this in turn makes him more anxious because he must carry on a conversation with a person whose name he cannot remember, and his conversational facility is further hampered by this fact. His compound anxiety makes it all the more unlikely that he will be able to remember the name of his new acquaintance when his wife walks over and waits to be introduced.

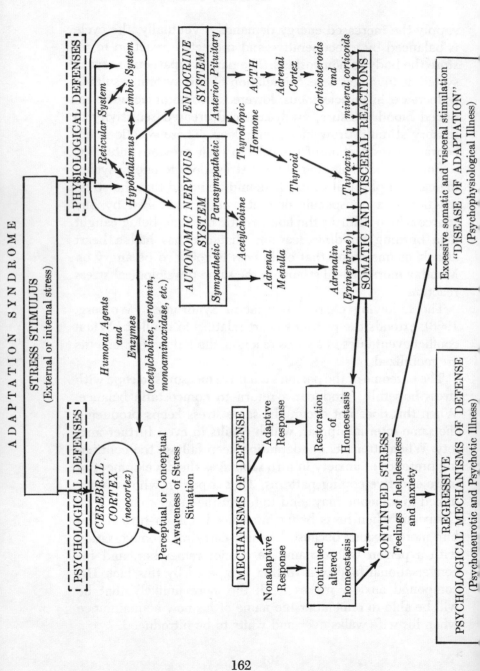

ADAPTATION SYNDROME

STRESS STIMULUS
(External or internal stress)

PSYCHOLOGICAL DEFENSES

PHYSIOLOGICAL DEFENSES

CEREBRAL CORTEX
(neocortex)

Reticular System — Limbic System

Hypothalamus

Humoral Agents and Enzymes
(acetylcholine, serotonin, monoaminoxidase, etc.)

ENDOCRINE SYSTEM
Anterior Pituitary

ACTH → Adrenal Cortex → Corticosteroids and mineral corticoids

AUTONOMIC NERVOUS SYSTEM
Sympathetic | Parasympathetic

Thyrotropic Hormone → Thyroid → Thyroxin

Acetylcholine

Adrenal Medulla → Adrenalin (Epinephrine)

SOMATIC AND VISCERAL REACTIONS

Perceptual or Conceptual Awareness of Stress Situation

MECHANISMS OF DEFENSE

Adaptive Response

Nonadaptive Response

Restoration of Homeostasis

Continued altered homeostasis

CONTINUED STRESS
Feelings of helplessness and anxiety

Excessive somatic and visceral stimulation
"DISEASE OF ADAPTATION"
(Psychophysiological Illness)

REGRESSIVE
PSYCHOLOGICAL MECHANISMS OF DEFENSE
(Psychoneurotic and Psychotic Illness)

162

Visceral symptoms are the product of a massive autonomic situation brought about by anxiety. Changes occur in the smooth musculature and in glands throughout the body. Furthermore, a lowered threshold to sensory stimuli creates a generalized increase of reflex activity. Spasm of the cardiac and pyloric portions of the stomach, hyperchlorhydria, intestinal spasms, constipation, or diarrhea are common phenomena. Changes in the tonus of vessels affect the blood distribution throughout the body. Cardiac responses include palpitations, tachycardia, and extrasystoles. Spasm of the respiratory apparatus commonly develops. There may occur an alteration of secretions of the various organs, urinary frequency or retention, dysmenorrhea and other menstrual disorders.

The general irritability and oversensitivity to stimuli may be registered as paresthesias, hyperesthesias, and defects of the higher sensory organs involving such functions as vision and hearing. There is an increased tonus of the striated musculature. This potentially facilitates adaptive motor reactions, but in prolonged states of stimulation, muscle spasms, and tics interfere with proper functioning. Electrical measurement of skeletal muscles and peripheral nerves may show action potentials as very high, even in a resting state. Excitations penetrating the higher brain centers produce constellations of ideas, memories, phantasies associated with a state of unrest. A wide variety of symbolic material may be mobilized in this representation, depending upon individual experiences and upon the degree of repression that exists in relation to the specific needs or problems that produce stress.

Overstimulation resulting from *continued* stress is bound to register its effect on the bodily integrity ("exhaustion reaction"). Bombardment of the viscera with stimuli will tend after a while organically to disturb the functions of the various organs and systems. To such ensuing disturbances Selye (1950) has given the name "diseases of adaptation."

Where the sources of stress are known to the person, he will best be in a position to deal with them constructively through adaptive mechanisms of defense. Where the sources are unknown, as in unconscious conflicts, the higher psychic apparatus is virtually obliterated as an adaptive tool. The person will then be handicapped in coping with anxiety, which, acting as a constant stress stimulus, will sabotage his adjustment on all levels of integration.

The Anxiety Attack

"What does it feel like? Like the jaws of death closing in; fear where is no threat, agony when there is nothing that should hurt. You breathe, but you can't get air. You feel like you are drowning; you reach for someone to pull you out, but there's nobody around. You want to get out, but you don't know how, or where to find the escape hatch." These are the words of a person describing a typical anxiety experience.

Anxiety is a universal phenomenon, and its management constitutes one of the major preoccupations of the human race. It has been described as the experience of "becoming nothing"—a happening so intolerable that "two broken arms and two broken legs would be a preferable fate."

Anxiety is a generic term that covers a vast amount of human psychopathology. It is characterized by a violent biochemical and neurophysiological reaction that disrupts the physical, intellectual, emotional, and behavioral functions of the individual. It is indicative of a collapse of a person's habitual security structure and his successful means of adaptation. It is nurtured generally by *unconscious conflict*, of which the person is unaware, and thus with which he feels helpless to deal. So catastrophic are its effects that the individual attempts to escape from it through various maneuvers. These are usually self-defeating because those very maneuvers are often regressive in nature, that is they revive outmoded childish ways of dealing with discomfort. They only further interfere with assertive and productive adaptations.

Where anxiety is uncontrolled, an actual return to infantile helplessness with complete loss of mastery may threaten. Reality testing may totally disintegrate, ending in confusion, depersonalization, an inability to locate the limbs in space, incoordination, and loss of capacity to differentiate the "me" from the "not-me." This threat to integrity may initiate "parent-invoking" tactics ranging from screaming, tantrums, bewildered cries for help, and fainting. Such complete relapse to infancy is rare, occurring only in individuals with fragile personality structures.

All people experience minor grades of anxiety that are usually quickly resolved. For instance who has not had that strange feeling, just as he is about to introduce someone, and he realizes that he cannot remember the person's name. At that moment he feels embarrassed and dismayed; he feels like nothing: his identity was to be that of an "introducer," and suddenly, at least for that moment, he lost that ability which gave him identity, meaning, and purpose. He stood there tongue-tied and was as "nothing."

Magnify that example into some loss which seemingly constitutes the *total* meaning and identity of a person, and we have described a full blown anxiety attack. Unlike the healthy individual, who experiences minor grades of anxiety when external provocations are present, the neurotic individual feels so insecure, and his self-esteem is so vulnerable that he is a victim of anxious attacks even when there are no external causes to account for them. Minor cues disregarded by the average person suffice to precipitate anxiety. The defensive and adaptive modes of the personality are brought into play to avoid the experience of "becoming nothing." The threat of nonbeing, i.e., of anxiety, strikes at the heart of whatever it is with which a person identifies himself. This may be anything from his ability to love and work, to the status value of his new car.

Anxiety is the experience of threat to values which one equates with his meaningful existence as a person. A person *has* a fear, but he *is* anxious—which illustrates the centrality of what is attacked in the phenomenon of anxiety. In our tendency to identify certain objects, possessions, or symbols with our security as human beings, we can see how our value systems, our conventions, our modes of child-rearing serve to nurture anxiety reactions.

Let us use our automobiles as one such example. It is obvious in our culture that a good number of us have made our automobile a personal extension of ourselves. When our automobile is threatened, we become threatened. When our automobile is not new and shiny, then we personally feel as if we were less. Following an automobile accident, some persons have been known to examine the damage to their *cars* before they even noticed if their own bodies had been injured—not to mention their wives, or children.

Anxiety does not always have to be harmful. As a matter of fact, some anxiety is an adaptive necessity; its release acts as a signal to alert the individual and to prepare him for emergency action. Small amounts of anxiety sponsor somatic and visceral reactions that lead to attack or flight. Anxiety even facilitates information processing in the forebrain. The physiological and biochemical patterns of anxiety are innate in the organism. Its psychological ingredients are unique to the experiences and conditioning of the individual. These, constituting the security apparatus, are organized to reduce and to remove threats to the integrity and safety of the individual.

The signal of anxiety, therefore, activates an adaptive mechanism stimulating somatic and psychological mechanisms to prepare for an emergency. The individual learns to react to minimal cues of anxiety with a constructive reaction which dispels the anxiety and perhaps eliminates its source. But where the defenses fail to operate, anxiety can reach a pitch where it cannot be dispelled. Somatic reactions of a diffuse, undifferentiated, and destructive nature then flood the body. Psychological reactions become disorganized. Regressed, childish kinds of behavior, which cannot be effective in handling an adult anxiety situation, may then take over.

What generally shatters the defenses of the person so that he responds with global anxiety? The provocative agent may be any external danger or internal conflict, recognized or unrecognized, that disorganizes the individual's reality sense, crushes his security and self-esteem beyond mediation of his available resources, and fills him with a catastrophic sense of helplessness to a point where he cannot realize himself in existence. It is the *meaning* to the individual of an experience or a conflict that is the fundamental criterion for whether he feels he is ceasing to be, i.e., responding with uncontrollable anxiety.

Let us proceed with examination of the physiological and psychological manifestations of the individual suffering from extreme anxiety.

First, there is a vast undifferentiated, explosive discharge of tension which disorganizes the physiological rhythm of every organ and tissue in the body, including muscular, glandular, cardiovascular, gastrointestinal, genitourinary, and special senses. Long continued excitations may produce psychosomatic disorders and ultimately even irreversible organic changes.

Second, there is a precipitation of catastrophic feelings of helplessness, insecurity, and devaluated self-esteem. The victim often voices fears of physical illness or disease as interpretations of the peculiar somatic sensations or symptoms that are being released by the physical concomitants of anxiety. Fear of cancer or heart disease are especially

167

common. There is an interference with spontaneous psychological reparative forces which normally tend to bring the individual back to homeostasis.

Third, there is a wearing down of repressions to the point where they become paper thin in certain areas. Consequently, a breakthrough of repudiated thoughts, feelings, and impulses, ordinarily controllable, now may occur at random. These outbursts further undermine security and produce a fear of being out of control, of not knowing what to expect.

Fourth, various defenses are mobilized, their variety and adaptiveness depending upon the flexibility and maturity of the individual. If these strategies fail to control or dissipate the sense of terror, then a further set of maneuvers is initiated which we shall illustrate in later sections when we consider the various levels of adaptation to anxiety, stress, and conflict.

Having described anxiety and illustrated its effects, we will now turn to the sources of anxiety. These sources are unique for the individual, since the threat to existence correlates with whatever in one's upbringing originally gave meaning to existence. If a child most clearly experienced himself as having an identity when he followed his mother's injunctions to "be a good boy," then the later years will make him vulnerable to anxiety especially at the point where he is not seeing himself as a good boy.

Freud distinguished by their source *three types of anxiety: objective* anxiety, in which the danger element is in the external world; *neurotic* anxiety, rooted in an instinctual impulse or object choice, and *moral* anxiety, originating in the superego and reflected in the dread of punishment.

The helplessness of an infant exposes him to many hurtful experiences, and this is the prototype of objective anxiety.

Neurotic anxiety, according to Freud, is caused by fear of danger from the instincts; essentially it is fear of being overwhelmed by instinctual energy should ego controls fail. Three types are discernible: (a) free-floating anxiety with readiness to fasten itself to any available environmental situation; (b) attachment of anxiety to a specific object that in itself was innocuous but which symbolized something dread-inspiring. The feared object represented a virtuous transgression: for example, a woman walking in the street may in her fantasy equate herself with being a street-walker. She then transfers her fear to the street; (c) acting-out behavior which evoked threats from the environment. Here impulses break through when controls relax. The sources of neurotic anxiety are within oneself, there being an association of an instinctual demand with an external danger.

Moral anxiety is the guilt or shame aroused by fear of the conscience. Here the internalized parental agency threatens to punish the person for thoughts, phantasies, impulses, or acts that transgress the aims of the ego-ideal. Originally the fear was in relation to outside parental agencies, but with superego formation, the conflict became an intra-psychic one. Many authorities today believe that Freud's classification and description of anxiety are oversimplified, but this does not lessen the value of the fundamental contribution Freud made toward the understanding of this phenomenon.

It is significant that it is the *meaning* of any event that shades it with the quality of menace. Thus David, after sleeping with Bathsheba and putting Uriah to death, exhibited all the classic signs of anxiety which he expressed in the Thirty-second Psalm: " . . . my body wasted away through my groaning all day long. For day and night thy hand was heavy upon me; my strength was dried up as by the heat of summer."

David's plight appears to indicate that in his time, as in our culture, the most commonly punished and hence repudiated strivings are related to aggression, sexuality, and self-assertiveness. In his upbringing the child learns that successful control of these drives preserves parental approval, and later self-approval. Ultimately they may be automatically repressed. However, at certain epochs these strivings may become overwhelmingly powerful and break through the repressive forces, initiating anxiety. For instance, during puberty sexual impulses may obtrude themselves annoyingly on the young person.

Anxiety is also conditioned by a failure of defenses which, for one reason or another, are no longer functionally active. Thus, a person with excessive dependency needs may experience anxiety upon death of a parent or parental substitute. An individual whose vitiated self-image is covered by compulsive ambitiousness may collapse in the event of a demotion or cut in salary. One whose defenses are centered in perfectionism may show anxiety when he perceives his mediocrity in any line of endeavor, or when he finds it impossible to perform without flaws in any new task or enterprise. Threats of interpersonal closeness in a detached person, of being put into a dominant position in the case of a submissive soul, of being obliged to serve a subordinate role in one with domineering tendencies, may detonate anxiety.

A consistently powerful source of anxiety is any situation interpreted as damaging to one's self-image and which cannot be counteracted by a compensatory reaction. An attack of anxiety may then follow. For example, the mother of an infant may become terrified if she suddenly realizes that she is so angry that she would like to do away with her child. The actual circumstance that shatters the individual's confidence in himself will, of course, depend on his symbols of self-worth. Circumstances that cause him to feel evil, contemptible, destructive, and incapable of loving and of being loved are most disastrous.

Fortunately, most people are capable of coping with anxiety in ways not too interfering with their adaptive potential. The healthy personality structure, harmoniously balanced, and with sufficient plasticity to permit the expression of one's needs and the meeting of environmental demands, will be able to mediate the daily experiences of life without the threat of psychological annihilation, i.e., global anxiety.

Summary

Einstein is quoted as having remarked that he made many mistakes in his life, "but never in principle." What he was saying was that he had the necessary equilibrium in his basic stance, so that he would not "come undone" by the ordinary mistakes of living.

Harry Golden showed the same admirable perspective when he wrote that he never complained in a restaurant when, in ordering green beans, he was brought lima beans instead by the waiter. His explanation for not complaining had something to do with the fact that our sun is 93 million miles away, that there are several trillion other stars in our universe, and they all move in perfect order through the heights and depths of space. In the face of all this, said Harry Golden, his getting lima beans seemed rather inconsequential.

The best defense against undue anxiety is a self-confident awareness that one's place in the world allows for the meeting of one's needs, rich relationships with one's fellow man, and the sense that one's full capacities can and are being fulfilled. In short, the marks of the healthy personality, described in Chapter Two, form the basis of a varied repertoire. This allows one to have a meaningful part to play and liberates the courage to be.

15

Coping with Anxiety: Levels of Defense

*What other liberty is there worth having, if we have not
the freedom and peace in our minds—if our inmost and most
private man is but a sour and turbid pool?*

HENRY DAVID THOREAU

A rabbit, bounding through the woods, is frightened by a
hunter. The rabbit freezes in his tracks, his coloration blending imperceptibly with the foliage to a point where he is not
observed by his enemy, and he is safe. This is the rabbit's
habitual defensive maneuver, a hereditary technique evolved
over countless generations.

Now we take this same rabbit, bounding not through the
woods, but across the Pennsylvania Turnpike. As a speeding
automobile approaches, the rabbit may adopt the same maneuver that he utilized so well in the woods, i.e., he may
freeze directly in the path of the automobile. This defensive
technique will result in his own destruction.

The mode of adaptation to threat is at least as significant
in a person's life as the nature of the threat itself. As in the
case of our rabbit, a rigid adaptive repertoire is unable to

172

adjust to unfamiliar situations, and causes the person to function under great handicap. A more plastic personality structure possesses an almost infinite flexibility and resourcefulness in marshaling defenses to meet with new and unexpected contingencies.

The Adaptative Process—An Overview

In this chapter we shall begin with an overview of what prompts the adaptive process, and how it functions. Then we shall delineate four specific levels of the adaptive process, indicating how each level is successively called forth when the previous level has failed to cope with the anxiety experience.

As we have seen, adaptation and defense arise out of the necessity to cope with anxiety. Since anxiety is the strongest motivant of all human behavior, its avoidance becomes the most powerful of all drives. A person will tend to eliminate any impulses, attitudes, memories, or strivings which produce anxiety. Since the earliest anxiety experience is the fear of the loss of love—a nurturing experience which produces in the child a sense of well-being—a child will readily make every effort to reduce his chances of being cut off from the sources of being loved. As we have said before, in our culture the sexual, hostile, and self-assertive drives are most frequently subjected to disapproval or punishment, and hence have the greatest anxiety-provoking value.

The formula in its simplest form is as follows: Sex, anger, and assertion may be disapproved of; such disapproval is tantamount to the loss of love; without love the conceptual equivalent is "I am as nothing; to be as nothing is that intolerable experience of anxiety that I must avoid; ergo, I had better somehow deal with sex, anger, and assertiveness in a way that still enables me to feel safe, i.e., loved." Such an adaptation may mean that one will circumscribe his needs, narrow his interpersonal and social orbits, limit some of his activities, and, if he thus operates within the bounds of his restricted environment and his limited demands, he may be able to function in a relatively normal way.

Anxiety represents a collapse in adaptation. Most persons, as indicated previously, during their life are confronted with minor and temporary attacks of anxiety, especially at times when they are overwhelmed by external difficulties. These attacks, however, are usually short-lived and disappear upon the resolution of the disturbing environmental crisis. Flurries of periodic anxiety are indicative of the inadequacy of the person's defenses against it and signal the fact that the adaptive resources of the person have collapsed to a point where he is overwhelmed by catastrophic helplessness.

Solutions for anxiety will depend on the source of the anxiety as well as the specific personality configurations of the individual.

The human organism is constantly evolving defenses to external stress and inner tensions which if successful restore the functional equilibrium. An individual may, for example, buttress his failing repressions and, by sealing off noxious conflicts, restore to himself his shattered sense of mastery. He may coordinately bolster his depleted defenses and even evolve more constructive modes of dealing with his current difficulties. The means by which this is accomplished will vary with the circumstances which plague him and with the opportunities at his disposal. Thus a passive man whose dependency needs are threatened by the obtrusion of hostile and murderous impulses toward his host, may extricate himself from his immediate involvement with the latter and develop a new relationship with a person who is, in his opinion, more powerful, more bountiful, more omniscient, more loving. The repression of his hostility and the restoration of dependency (oral) gratifications will, for the time being, neutralize his anxiety and permit him to function at his optimal level.

A woman, whose self-esteem has habitually been bolstered by success in competitive enterprises, may, because of marriage and the birth of children, be relegated to what she considers an unrewarding and humiliating role as housewife. She may respond with feelings of mutilation which are symbolically reflected in physical disturbances. She may then spontaneously escape from her conflict by involving herself in voluntary organizational activities in which she indulges her competitive needs and emerges supreme in her contest with other women.

A wide assortment of means may be indulged by different persons to restore the status quo which range from extricating oneself from situational difficulties that cannot be controlled, to altering values that nurture distress, to imbibing new attitudes in a different philosophical or religious frame that give existence a different meaning. Or there may be the learning of new and better responses to situations which habitually have provoked maladaptive reactions. The repertoire of available modes is in the average person quite extensive. Not only may these restore the old neurotic balance of power; sometimes surprisingly they may, without design, promote enduring personality growth.

The specific types of defense are chosen by the individual for reasons that are not, at our present state of knowledge, fully known. The following factors are probable: (a) The individual's unique experiences and conditionings focus emphasis on certain periods in his life. For instance, as a child the individual's dependency needs may not have been satisfactorily resolved, causing him to measure his self-esteem chiefly in terms of how well loved he was by his parents. This will have

175

caused him to yield any drives or impulses he believes would compromise him with his mother, father, and other significant persons. He will then tend to conform and to give up the expression of such impulses as independence, assertiveness, sexuality, and hostility, if these are in any way condemned by the parental agency. Later on, he will tend to run away from facing up to situations that display such impulses. Because his lack of compliance and his defiant attitudes and behavior threaten his standing with his parents (and later their internalized images in his conscience), he will be insecure when confronted with circumstances where he must take an aggressive stand. The defenses he may employ are projection, undoing, and isolation, giving rise to such syndromes as obsessional neurosis, compulsion neurosis, and paranoidal manifestations. Or he may utilize repression to excess as a technique in order to avoid anxiety. He may demonstrate inhibitions of function, resulting in hysterical, phobic, and depressive manifestations. On the other hand, the child who has challenged the parents' right to control him, and who has, against the threat of punishment or abandonment, managed to indulge his assertiveness, hostility, and sexuality, will not employ these defenses as rigidly. (b) Certain defenses appear in childhood which net the child a special gain. Such defenses, if successful, establish a pattern of behavior which may be pursued later on. For example, where violent and aggressive displays intimidate parents into yielding to the child's demands, he may tend to have outbursts of anger and to intimidate others as a preferred way of dealing with opposition. (c) Unresolved childish fears, needs, and striving, with persistence of archaic concepts of reality, will influence the patterns adopted in the face of stress. Fears of the dark or of being alone may return whenever stress is excessive, where these were excessive in childhood. (d) Defensive reactions are often conditioned by parental neurotic attitudes and illnesses which the individual may take over in the process of imitation. A mother's terror of lightning storms or recourse to headaches when difficulties come up may be adopted by her child.

The neurotic individual thus utilizes archaic techniques of adaptation to which he was exposed, or which originally helped solve the difficulties in his childhood. But when these techniques have long outlived their usefulness, they create many more problems than they solve. Nevertheless, the individual is apt to employ them in a reflex manner, almost as if they were the most natural of devices to utilize under the circumstances.

One would assume, on the basis of the laws of learning, that when the original conditions which inspired anxiety (e.g., the fear of punishment) no longer prevailed, then the person, particularly as he became older and more mature, would no longer experience the same anxiety. This actually is not the case. Freud demonstrated that the individual continued to respond to the world even after the parents have died, as if the world continued to be a representative of the parents. He noted the incorporation of parental prohibition into the psyche of the person. His responses to these prohibitions were as if the threatening parents actually still existed within himself. Violation of those directives, originally prohibited by the parents, then would serve to inspire anxiety of a character and intensity similar to the early experiences which initially inspired the reaction.

Anxiety is thus apt to occur whenever there is any reappearance of the original anxiety-provoking situation, or it may precipitate with partial cues or with symbols that represent the traumatic circumstance. With each reaction of anxiety, the response to the specific situation or to symbolic cues associated with it becomes reinforced. This continual relearning of when and how to become anxious is repeated hundreds and thousands of times. The anxious response to certain provoking situations is then triggered habitually and without conscious awareness, and the defenses to counter the anxiety become equally automatic and unconscious.

Many defensive responses to anxiety which are directed toward the reduction of anxiety may lead to a crippling of a person's flexibility and adaptiveness. The defensive technique of the phobia illustrates the destructive influence that a mechanism of defense may yield. The inhibition of function characteristic of phobic states is calculated to isolate the individual from certain sources of danger onto which he has projected his inner anxieties. For instance, a woman fearful of yielding to unrestrained sexual impulses may develop strong anxieties while walking outdoors. She may shield herself from such anxiety attacks through the symptom of agoraphobia, i.e., by avoiding leaving her home, except perhaps in the presence of her mother. The phobia ultimately results in her incapacitation, interferes with her livelihood and her capacity to establish normal relationships with people. She may, as a result, undergo a shattering of self-esteem, and her feelings of inferiority may stimulate a further attempt to isolate herself from others. Her hostility, which is usually directed at her parent on whom she is so helplessly dependent, may become extreme, and she may have difficulty in expressing or even acknowledging her hateful feelings, because they threaten her standing with her mother. Thus, while she has employed a defense to shield her from anxiety, she has suffered from gross difficulties in her functional relationships with life and people. The defense against the original anxiety plunged her into difficulties as great or greater than the stress that initially inspired her reaction.

Levels of Defense

The various maneuvers of an individual in response to anxiety can be labelled "the adaptation syndrome." In general, four levels of defense are employed: 1. conscious efforts at maintaining control, by manipulation of the environment; 2. characterologic defenses, aimed at manipulating interpersonal relations; 3. repressive defenses, which manipulate the intrapsychic forces; and 4. regressive defenses which regulate physiological mechanisms. The individual may stabilize at any level, while retaining symptoms and techniques characteristic of previous levels. At different times, as stress is alleviated or exaggerated, or as ego strengthening or weakening occurs, there may be shifts in the lines of defense, either up or down. The manner in which these four levels of defense are employed in adaptation is as follows:

The First Level of Defense: Control Mechanisms

When tensions and anxiety are experienced, the first maneuver on the part of an individual is to fashion his environment to his needs, to escape from it, or to change his mode of thinking about it. Thus he may avoid certain activities or places or people. He will try to manage in some different way whatever he feels to be the source of stress. He may change his job, his wife, his haircut, his nose shape, or his domicile. Or he may attempt to change existing attitudes, attempting to think things through and to arrive at some new intellectual formulations about what his life is all about. In this regard, he may try to suppress certain thoughts, to keep his mind on more positive channels, to exercise self-control, or to read self-help books that stimulate him to think through a new philosophy of life. He may develop different leisure time activities, attempting to find satisfaction in a new hobby, a new social activity, or different friends. He may try to "get outside himself," or just the opposite, he may become more absorbed in bodily satisfactions such as eating, drinking, tranquilizers, drugs, and medicines. He may deaden his feelings with sedatives, with stimulants, and with alcohol. Daydreaming of a wish-fulfilling nature may help him to escape the painful realities of his daily troubles.

His emotional equilibrium may also shift, so that he permits himself emotional outbursts, fits of crying or laughing, and impulsive outbreaks designed to release tension.

All these, and other maneuvers like them, are the first attempts to be made when a person feels the uncomfortable tension that indicates a breakdown in homeostasis. Every person alive at various times employs some of these environment-manipulating devices. Sleeping late, taking a day off, buying a new hat, having an extra ice cream sundae, may all be such attempts—and they may often be enough to restore a sense of well-being. The judicious use of certain preventive measures, even some deliberate self-indulgence, may accomplish the purpose of staving off further stress and tension.

Pathological reliance on the first line of defense can cause habitual and addictive disorders such as alcoholism and drug addiction. The first line defenses, when employed with conscious insight regarding the basic nature of one's conflict and anxiety, may fortuitously provide more or less lasting relief. On the other hand, their hit or miss exploitation, without awareness of the nature of one's difficulties may lead to habits and patterns that prove eventually unsuccessful, necessitating the use of the next line of defense.

The Second Level of Defense: Characterologic Defenses

In Chapter Twelve we have examined the character strivings of dependency, submissiveness, expiation, domination, aggression, withdrawal, and self-image restoration. In situations of increasing threat, it is typical for a person to exploit an exaggerated form of his normal characterologic drives. What a person ordinarily subsists on will become even more predominant when problems beset him. Analogously, in time of a threatened civil riot, the police commissioner will tend to see a great need for more policemen, the educator will call for better education, the welfare worker will find the solution in greater public assistance allowances, and the clergyman's answer will be in the direction of greater depth of religious sentiment. In other words, the characteristic solution of each individual will be intensified when stress and conflict are at hand.

Idiosyncratic adaptations to stress are developed early in life, primarily in coping with the parental figures who are the first source of a child's security. Certain character styles were promoted by the parents, and the child learned that there was a certain manner of relating to people and events which had the best chance of keeping him free of anxiety. Later in life, when anxiety is experienced there is an unwitting return to the mode of life that worked most effectively in the past.

If the first line of defense may be called manipulating one's environment, then the second line of defense may be termed "manipulating one's interpersonal relationships." If dependency is characteristic for a person, then in time of stress he may become abjectly dependent. If detachment is the way in which a person handles untoward experiences, then a serious tragedy will cause him pathologically to isolate and withdraw himself for long periods. It is the exaggeration of the usual mode that is the key to understanding this second level of defense.

For instance, a university president is confronted by a band of rebellious students who demand more confrontation between students and administration. Depending on the

181

character strivings of the university president, he will respond in various ways. If he is essentially a detached person, he will attempt to withdraw to his office, busy himself with other "important" matters, and try to ignore the intrusion of the rebelling students upon his inner world. Perhaps he will be critical of the students because they did not go through the channels of the dean's office, etc., and the entire matter is thought not to be of the type for the president to become involved with at all. At every stage of his thought and action, the pattern of detachment is the guiding influence behind his administrative approach to his students.

If the university president is the dependent type, he will rush to his advisors, hoping to gain the help from others that will provide release from his conflict. If he is of the aggressive, dominating type, he will attempt to put down the students with force. And the more force that the students demonstrate, the more anxious the president will probably become, and the more insistent he will be that the countering coercion of the administration be sufficient to suppress the student momentum.

It is typical of the exaggerated maneuvers of the second defense line that they get the individual into interpersonal difficulties. If a high school principal is accused by his teachers of being too controlling, the principal may become threatened. When threatened, he fears that he is losing control over his teachers, perhaps asking that they submit to him more complete lesson plans and that they sign out of the building when leaving for lunch. It is this very control that the teachers objected to in the first place, and the interpersonal conflict becomes exaggerated.

Examples of pathologically exaggerated character drives include may kinds of interpersonal, vocational, and educational difficulties. The following are typical: Educational and work disorders may be symptomatic of such excessive dependency that one is unable to pursue any independent, assertive line of thought or action. The writing of a term paper or the making of a business call may represent the exercise of personal responsibility; a person with a devalued self-image may not be able to pursue such an activity on his own. Marital problems, so ubiquitous in our society, and parental mishandling of their children may represent the exaggeration of any or several character strivings.

Delinquency and criminality are syndromes representing the excess of hostile aggression. Sexual disorders often portray the nature of the interpersonal disorder. Hypochondriacal preoccupations may depict the fear of injury; psychopaths demonstrate the extravagant caricature of many interpersonal needs; immature, obsessive, schizoid persons have all, under the threat of anxiety, pressed their life styles to extreme lengths. Usually, second line defenses do not work effectively. Rather they plunge persons into such interpersonal difficulties that conflict and stress are heightened, rather than reduced. The chronic employment of dependency reactions, for example, is eventually resented by others on whom one leans, serving to alienate the person from his sources of support. Rather than have his needs gratified, he drives others away and is more alone. The emotionally poor get poorer if there is a blind repetition of the same pattern. Because of the ultimate ineffectiveness of the second line of defense, the person usually goes on to the next level.

The Third Level of Defense: Repressive Maneuvers

The third level of defense consists of the manipulation of one's *intrapsychic* structure. It is an attempt to gain peace by pushing troubles out of one's mind.

In *repression* a barrier is set up to the motor discharge of needs, impulses, memories, ideas, or attitudes, awareness of which will set off anxiety. To avoid anxiety, selected ideational segments are sealed off along with any associational memories or links, the activation of which may challenge the repression. In this process there may be a blocking in the perception, processing, storage, and retrieval of experiences; an inhibition or distortion in the functions of intelligence, such as attention, learning, discrimination, judgment, reasoning, and imagination; the operations and expression of emotions; and in behavior. The necessity of maintaining repression can absorb the energy resources of the individual. Constantly threatened are breakdowns in the repressive barriers, a filtering of the sealed-off components into consciousness, and a mobilization of anxiety. The individual may consequently be victimized by a ceaseless stress reaction, his physical system being in a perpetual uproar. Vulnerable organ systems may become disorganized with outbreaks of organic illness. At the same time a symbolic discharge (*displacement* of affect) may occur in attenuated or distorted forms, which will provide some gratification for the repudiated drives. At phases when repressed needs become particularly urgent, or for some reason or other are activated physiologically, such as a previously quiescent sexual drive stirring during adolescence, or experientially, as when an insult excites slumbering rage and aggression, a direct expression may occur followed by retributive defenses which will appease guilt feelings and serve to restore repressions.

The understanding of the repressive line of defense can best be seen in the two groupings: those efforts directed to reinforcing repression, and the direct or symbolic release of repressed material.

First, *reaction formations* (such as chastity or heightened morality as a cover for perverse sexual or antisocial desires) may become pathologically exuberant in the urgent need to deny the existence of forbidden impulses. It has been reported, for example, that a 19th century Prime Minister of England, widely known for high moral standards, would go out alone for a walk each evening at 11:00 p.m. for the purpose of finding a prostitute walking the streets of London, and upon finding her, would proceed to try to reform her by pointing out and persuading her of her errors and then taking her to a home where she could begin a new life. In this instance, it would appear that there was a very fine line between the sexual impulse of the Prime Minister and his reaction formation to that impulse. Otherwise why would so politically important a person focus on prostitutes?

Second, there is an inhibition of function, disturbed apperception, attention, concentration, and thinking occurring as one selectively inattends to certain disturbing aspects of his inner or outer world. Disturbed consciousness may take the form of fainting, stupor, or excessive needs for sleep. Disturbed memory to the point of amnesia may develop. Emotional dulling can be seen in a person who exhibits indifference or apathy as a defense against being involved in a potentially threatening situation. Sensory defects, motor paralysis, and even visceral inhibitions may be conversion reactions which serve to block out the direct awareness of an anxiety-provoking thought or deed. Thus one may literally not be able to feel a frightening object, see a threatening event, or experience a sexually arousing stimulus—if such awareness would provoke undue anxiety.

Another effort at reinforcing repression is the development of a phobia. In *phobia formation* there is a displacement from a fearsome inner drive to an external object which symbolically comes to represent this drive. Thus a fear of snakes in a woman may conceal an exaggerated but repressed interest in the male sexual organ. A fear of heights may be a cover of a murderous impulse for which one may anticipate retributory punishment.

185

Further attempts to gain peace through repression are through *undoing* and *isolation*. By these maneuvers the individual, almost magically, robs a forbidden impulse of any vitality. When he thinks an angry thought, he quickly follows it with a thought that "un-does" the first thought. Or he does not "feel" the thought, and so he believes his sexual or hostile impulses have no real significance for him.

The release of repressed material through direct or symbolic means is the second form by which repressive maneuvers attempt to maintain a psychic equilibrium. As we have just noted, the first form of repressive maneuver reinforces the repression itself. This second form allows for an intermittent direct or symbolic discharge of the repressed material.

One such type of release is simply an impulsive breakthrough of some forbidden word or deed. Occasionally, an excited episode of acting out of some impulse can be noted in a person who otherwise relies heavily on repression as his typical form of defense. The fighting drunk may actually be a sober Casper Milquetoast whose repressions are temporarily deadened by alcohol permitting a hostile release.

Obsession, that is the repetitive use of "unwanted thoughts," together with the immoderate use of reveries and day-dreams, is a second means that serves to drain away the repressed material. While one might not openly castigate his neighbor for having, let us say, a terrible looking lawn that detracted from the uniform appearance of the neighborhood, one might find himself having phantasies of his own elegant lawn surrounded by high walls, beyond which was a pauper's hovel set amidst much debris. A symbolization of forbidden inner impulses through obsessional thinking, drains off energy but promotes anxiety in their release. The individual may murder, rape, or torture special people in his phantasies, or explode the world with atom bombs, to his own dismay and anxious discomfort. He may then neutralize his released impulses by engaging in compulsive rituals, which on the surface make no sense, but which symbolically appease his guilt or divert his mind from his preoccupation. Thus "evil" thoughts may inspire repeated hand washing as a cleansing ritual.

A third measure for liberating repressed material is through *dissociative states,* such as somnambulism, fugues, and multiple personality. Acted out are the repressed impulses, too threatening to be integrated into one's conscious activities, but not remembered when the usual consciousness is restored.

Psychosomatic disorders may be a fourth evidence of the release of tensions that have not made their way into conscious awareness. Sensory, somatic, and visceral changes may reflect the inner conflicts of an individual. Tics, spasms, and convulsions are often symbolic revelations of inner psychic processes that cannot find direct expression.

The fifth means are the *sexual perversions,* such as homosexuality, fetishism, exhibitionism, etc., which discharge erotic tensions when these become uncontrollable.

The *use of the self as an object for aggression* is a sixth method by which unacceptable impulses gain some measure of expression. Angry impulses originally directed at others are repressed and then directed against the self. The resultant condition may be neurotic depression, a feeling that one is a miserable creature. The continuing self-recriminations in which the depressed person indulges serve to discharge his hostility—albeit in the wrong direction. There may also be dangerous abuses of the self, with accident proneness, mutilation tendencies, and even suicide.

Finally, a defense mechanism that allows for releasing repressed material is *projection.* Projection is a means of repudiating inner drives that are painful and anxiety provoking by attributing them to outside agencies and influences. Thus inner feelings of hate, too dangerous to accept and manage, are externalized in the conviction of being hated or victimized by an oppressor. Avarice may be concealed by a belief one is being exploited. Homosexual drives may be credited to persons toward whom the individual is pervertedly attracted. The projective mechanism serves the purpose of objectifying a forbidden and repressed danger which will justify certain measures, such as the expression of aggression without guilt. In this way, punishment and self-blame are avoided. By projecting impulses and desires onto the outside world one may insidiously gain acceptance for his own forbidden drives. For example, insisting upon the fact that the world is sexually preoccupied, and finding prurient examples for this point of view, a sexually fearful individual may try to lessen the severity of his own conscience that punishes him for his sexual needs.

Projection was operating when a little boy, standing at the lion's cage at the zoo, said "the lion is afraid of me." Unacknowledged hostile and sexual impulses often are projected onto other racial groups. Certain politicians, in fact, appear even to have a conspiratorial view of history, that is, it is the other country that has all the bad motives.

The Fourth Level of Defense: Regressive Defenses

When all other measures are failing to restore emotional equilibrium, psychotic states are the last instrumentality with which to escape the painful demands of reality. There may be a return to helpless dependency, a repudiation of and withdrawal from reality, excited acting-out impulses without reference to reality demands, and depression that has reached delusional and suicidal proportions. In this fourth level of defense the individual shows evidence of psychotic functioning. There may be dereistic thinking; disorders of perception (illusions, hallucinations); disorders of mental content (ideas of reference, delusions); disorders of apperception and comprehension; disorders of stream of mental activity (increased or diminished speech productivity, irrelevance, incoherence, scattering, neologisms); defects in memory, personal identification, orientation, retention, recall, thinking capacity, attention, insight, and judgment. There is evidence that special syndromes, such as manic-depressive psychosis and schizophrenia have genetic components that bring out their peculiar characteristics in the face of fourth level defenses.

These four levels of defense must not be regarded as arbitrary, static states. Each level never occurs in isolation. Each level is always mixed with manifestations of other defensive levels.

Summary

The understanding of a person's emotional condition relates to everything that has been said about personality development, personality structure, personality pathology, and personality adaptation.

Adjustment necessitates the achievement of a harmonious balance of personal needs and group standards, integrating defenses and drives toward a blending of what is most fulfilling for the individual. This necessitates a balanced, productive interplay of component ingredients of the personality, an ideal state which is never completely achieved or achievable. Conflict is inherent in all human adjustment. Successful adaptation presupposes not the absence of conflict, but its reasonable solution in line with what is best for the individual at the time of its mediation.

Modulation of repudiated strivings from the unconscious, of immediate conscious ego needs, of idealistic, ethical, and moral values, and of environmental standards, is the essence of a good adjustment. It goes without saying that this modulation must be anchored in reality.

To achieve these adjustment aims necessitates a flexibility of defenses, an ability to shift from one set of maneuvers to the next, conditioning these to the existing needs and to the prevailing exigencies of one's own life and the lives of others.

PART TWO

Introduction

The progressive changes in Beethoven's nine symphonies reflect both his own struggles to be free, as well as the increasing freedom of the western world in which he lived and wrote his glorious music. Beginning in the more formal style of Mozart, he moved from that classical mode into a pattern that perhaps made him the first of the romantics. The years of Beethoven's life (1770-1827) span the American and French revolutions—political changes which might well be characterized as movements from a classical to a romantic mode. Politics, music, and life were undergoing complementary and momentous changes.

Personality and life are inextricably bound. Man's inner struggles are lived out on the broad arenas of history. And history in turn becomes a determiner of personality through its myriad of social, economic, political, and religious influences on human development. Beginning with a troubled world within oneself, it may be assumed that there will be a troubled world without—and vice versa. Whether it be the irrational fury of a Hitler, or a John Doe's passive acceptance of his humble lot in life—internal psychological factors led each of them to choose their careers. But it was not *only* Hitler's sadistic father and his masochistic mother who drove him to avenge his damaged self-esteem on an international scale; it was also the fact of Versailles, which blended with Hitler's intrapsychic needs to form a conflict of truly monstrous proportions.

In Part Two, we attempt to indicate how the dramas everywhere before us on the stages of history can be understood as having been shaped in significant measure by those factors which mold personality.

In the first fifteen chapters we have examined the structure of personality. This machinery for adapting to one's inner and outer worlds has been studied in its physiological and interpersonal manifestations. Chronologically, we have observed the individual grow from the amorphous infant to maturity.

In the last six chapters we shall be more global in our observations, deducing from the dynamics of personal adaptation some of the salient problems and opportunities that now confront us as a nation and a civilization. Translating theory into practice is, to put it mildly, an imprecise science. But to bridge theory and practice is an obligation incumbent upon us if we are to know the powers that rule man from within, and also to gain control of the forces that manipulate him from without.

Chapter Sixteen begins with a summary of a typical life style that should be familiar to many Americans. The pressures of the western ethic, in combination with a neurotic family interaction, produced the case of Roger Thorne, which illustrates the axioms of personality development in upper middle class America.

Moving from the individual pattern of Roger, we describe several cultural patterns in the following three chapters. These social patterns of main street—violence, the generation gap, and the sexual revolution—are traced from their roots in personality formation and structure. Why these patterns are such problems today will be studied in terms of both society's values and the current interpersonal practices which mold personality.

The two final chapters contain exercises in maturity and guide lines for parents. Based on the principles developed earlier in the book, suggestions for an ongoing program of personality growth are proposed that will serve as a guide for the stages and exigencies of life. Optimistically proposed, these suggestions are intended as instruments for the betterment of man's life, through the daily application of what we know about personality development, personality pathology, and personality adaptation.

The six chapters which form Part Two of this book are macrocosmic in nature, contrasting with the more microcosmic principles set forth in Part One. We boldly make this transition, trusting that the study of personality development is also the study of mankind.

16

The Neurosis of Main Street U.S.A.

This is the age of the half-read page,
the quick hash and the mad dash,
the bright night and the nerves tight,
the plane hop and the brief stop,
the lamp tan and a short span,
the big shot in a good spot,
the brain strain and the heart pain,
and the cat nap till the springs snap
and the fun's done.

ANONYMOUS

What about our normal Jeff Parker whom we looked at in Chapter Two? What actually happens to *him* when, as he put it, he gets a bad case of nerves? What is the neurosis of Main Street U.S.A., and how does it specifically show itself in the average person in this present generation?

Let us chart the personality maneuvers of the average American fellow, who, like so many others, is too busy, involved in too many activities, perhaps is spending too much money, is wondering if it is worth it all, and feels pressured just about wherever he turns.

The Five Motors of Mr. American

If our harried picture of Mr. American is at all accurate, then we may be sure that his *dependency needs* are quite insistent. The ideal relation between a healthy degree of dependency and a healthy degree of independence does not exist. It is out of balance. Most likely the average person's childhood needs for nurture and care and affection were not optimally met, leaving him with a residue of unmet needs which tend to express themselves intensely when the pressures of life mount. And people are apt to blame their troubles on the world: The revolt of youth. Governmental corruption. Inflation. Communism. Or the atom bomb. But they will somehow muddle through, working out their troubles in one degree or another. It is only where their dependency needs are too intense that solutions will not be found.

People with powerful dependency needs will often cast about for individuals who demonstrate stronger qualities than they themselves possess. When a swimmer tires, he looks about for something or someone on whom to lean or with which to grapple. A dependent person can be likened to a tired swimmer, and he wants to find someone or something who can do for him what he feels he cannot do for himself. What he generally looks for is a *perfect* parent, an ideal that exists only in his own fancy. Actually there are no perfect parental figures who are able or willing to mother or father another adult. So our dependent person is continually being frustrated, because his hopes and expectations are not met by someone else. A man who weds, expecting an all-giving mother figure for a wife, is bound to be disappointed. And further, if he does find a person who fits in with his design and who treats him like a helpless individual, he will begin to feel that he is being swallowed up, that he is losing his individuality, that he is trapped. Consequently he will want to run from the relationship. Also, as he senses his dependency, he will feel that he is being passive like a child. And this is frightening because he knows that he is not being manly; he may actually have homosexual doubts and fears.

We will call his *first* maneuver his *dependency motor*, which begins to operate especially at times when he is under pressure. As he searches for the element missing in his psychological diet, namely a parental figure, he will most assuredly be disillusioned.

Mr. Main Street has a *second* motor that inevitably accompanies the first, namely the *resentment motor*. Resentment invariably fires off because either he cannot find a perfect parent who will take care of him, or he feels trapped when someone does take care of him, and he senses his own passivity and helplessness. Resentment breeds guilt, because people just are not supposed to be hateful where Mr. Main Street lives. But even guilt does not always keep the hostility hidden. Sometimes when our man has had too much to drink, or when he is very frustrated about something, his hate feelings leak or pour out. That in itself can be terribly upsetting, because he may fear he is getting out of control; or the mere awareness of his inner angry condition can make him despise himself. Self-hate complicates his existence because it sponsors tension and depression. Hatred directed outward and then turned in results in masochism, in the form of major and minor self-punishments. These may range from fouling up a business deal to spilling soup on one's new tie.

Now he has two motors going most of the time when under pressure: the dependency motor and the resentment motor, with its accompanying kickbacks of guilt and masochism. But the picture is not complete without a *third motor, low independence*, which is an invariable counterpart of high dependence. Low independence is a feeling that one cannot gain, by his own reason or strength, the desirable prizes of our culture, whether they be love and justice, or wine, women, and song. A spin-off of low independence is a feeling of inferiority, a lack of proficiency in achieving desirable goals. Part and parcel of inferiority feelings is the uncertainty about being manly and masculine. Self-doubts about one's sexual integrity are torturous; the usual sequel is to try to compensate by being the quintessence of everything masculine: overly-aggressive, overly-competitive, and overly-dominating. Our man may have phantasies and images in his mind of strong men and may be particularly attracted to them because of their strength. But his awareness of how *much* he thinks about men may cause him to wonder if he is homosexual and to fear the very things he admires. He may actually on occasion be sexually attracted to idealized male figures. Interestingly, low independence feelings in women lead to the same self-doubt and compensations as in men. Mrs. Main Street will try to repair the fancied damage to herself by acquiring and acting as if she has the symbols of masculinity which in our culture is equated with independence. She will compete with and try to vanquish and even figuratively castrate males. In its exaggerated form she will act toward other females as if she is a male, dominating and homosexually seducing them.

By now we have a fully operating *fourth motor, a devalued self-image*. With the constant reverberating of his first three motors, our man is now feeling spiteful toward himself. He feels he is miserably incompetent, undersirable, and unworthy. Everywhere he sees evidence of his insignificance: he is not tall enough, he has developed a paunch, women do not seem to pay attention to him, his hair is thinning, his job is not outstanding, his car, his house, his wife—nothing is perfect. He may even think his penis is of inadequate proportions. He feels like a damaged person. These feelings torment him, and he vows to prove that he is not as devalued as he feels. He commits himself to the task of being all-powerful, ambitious, perfect, to repair his devalued self-image. Then he imagines he can surely respect himself. If he can live without a single misstep all will be well. He tries to boost himself on his own to the point where others will have to approve him. He may only day-dream all this, or he may, if events are fortuitous, accomplish many of his over-compensatory goals But if he climbs high, he will most likely resent those below who now lean on him and make demands on him. To those who exhibit weakness he will show his anger. While he may be able to be giving on his own terms, an unexpected appeal from someone else will be regarded as a vulgar imposition. He actually wants for himself someone on whom to lean and be dependent. However, giving in to such a desire speeds up all his motors and makes him feel even worse. He pursues just the reverse course from his original dependency drive; he competes with any strong figure on whom he might want to lean. He shows the pseudo-independence reminiscent of the adolescent who disagrees on principle with whatever his parents say. And he may compensate for his devalued self-image by exploiting all the cultural symbols of being a worthy person, such as being perfectionistic, compulsively ambitious, and power driven. These compensatory drives may preoccupy him mercilessly and he may organize his life around them. One failure means more to him than twenty successes, since it is an affirmation of his lowly status.

These difficulties are compounded by the way they interact with our man's sexual needs. When one's dependency needs are being gratified, there is often a pervasive feeling of well-being that floods one's whole body. Upon awakening following surgery, for example, the confident, smiling face of a nurse can suffuse a man with grateful, loving feelings, at least part of which may be sexual. The sexual feeling is not that of adult male to adult female, but rather that of a helpless child toward a warm mother. Such a feeling is tantamount to an incestuous surge and brings with it great conflict and guilt. Should this dependency be the nature of a husband's continuing relationship to his wife, he may be unable to function sexually with her, since he is virtually involved in a mother-son relationship. On the other hand, if the nurturing figure is a man, homosexual fears and feelings may arise. And for Mrs. Main Street, the dependency situation does just the reverse. A nurturing mother figure calls up in her fears and feelings of homosexuality which may or may not be acted out. Moreover, low feelings of independence may inspire ideas of defective masculinity in males with impulses to identify with muscle men. Phantasies of homosexuality, or the direct acting-out of homosexual impulses, may follow. In women, feelings of defective independence may inspire a rejection of the feminine role.

The reverberating of all these machines calls for strenuous efforts on the part of our subject. It all began with the dependency motor, which then activated the resentment motor (together with its components of aggression, guilt and masochism). This threw into gear the third motor of low independence, which in turn gave power to the fourth motor of self-devaluation with its over-compensations and sexualizations.

Where can a man turn next to gain some sense of composure? He often turns to the *fifth motor, detachment.* Detachment is an attempt at escaping from life's messy problems. Our man by now is fed up with the rat-race and wants to get out. He says no more committees, no more parties, no more responsibilities, no more extras of any kind, no more involvement with people. He wants an island fortress, or at least a castle with a moat around it, and he would pull up the drawbridge and say "no" to everything and everyone. He is sure that this is the solution; he decides not to become rich and famous.

But it doesn't work. People need people. Life is not satisfying alone. Our man finds loneliness to be a worse state than what he was enduring before. He realizes that people constitute one of life's richest gratifications. So, he plunges in again; by now his first motor of dependency is really driving him. And if he is desperate enough, he may attach himself all over again to a figure who holds out some promise of being the perfect parent. And the neurotic cycle is on its way again. The fifth motor of detachment has again revived the first, second, third, and fourth motors.

These drives, these five motors, are never entirely quiescent. In the average person there is invariably some fuel to keep them going. There is no one whose dependency needs were perfectly met early in life. This hunger lives on, and with this hunger, the mechanism of dependency is continually operative. And in our culture, in this generation, the unmet dependency need sets in motion the successive motors just described. So long as fuel is available and the speed of the motors can be controlled, the individual may manage to keep going, switching on one or the other motors and turning them off if they threaten to carry him away.

Dependency inevitably breeds resentment in our culture. If outlets for the resentment are not available, and if compensations for a devalued self-image cannot be pursued—in other words, if the individual cannot readily switch from one engine to another—then the conflict and stress reach proportions where one feels catastrophically overwhelmed. When the tension mounts excessively, and there seems to be no way of escape, anxiety strikes—which is the feeling that one is overwhelmed and lost. Operations to defend against the anxiety will be instituted, but, as we have seen, the defense is often ineffective or more burdensome than the condition it was designated to combat.

The Case of Roger Thorne

The case of a man from Main Street, America, illustrates all that has been said.

Roger Thorne is the younger of two brothers. He was reared by a domineering mother who was resentful of her role as housewife which had halted a successful career as a fashion designer. Unhappy in her love life with her husband, she transferred her affection to her younger son, ministering to his every whim and smothering him with cloying adulation. Roger's brother, George, bitterly contested this situation, but getting nowhere, subjected his sibling to cruel reprisal. Roger's father, recoiling from the not too well concealed hostility of his wife, removed himself from family life as much as he could manage and had very little contact with his sons.

The dynamics in Roger's case became apparent during therapy. Basic to his problem was a disturbed relationship with his parents, particularly his mother. The yielding of her unmarried professional status to assume the role of housewife apparently had created in the mother resentment toward her husband and rejection of her children. This inspired a "reaction formation" in the form of over-protection, particularly toward her younger child, Roger. Frustrated and unfulfilled, she used Roger as a target for her own needs and ambitions with the following effects: a) encouragement of over-dependence and passivity, b) strangling of gestures toward assertiveness and independence, c) stimulation of excessive sexual feelings toward the mother, and d) hostility displayed directly by his brother as aggression, and indirectly by his father in the form of detachment.

Over-protected by his maternal parent, neglected by his father, and abused by his brother, Roger took refuge in the relationship offered him by his mother. His dependency on

202

her nurtured submissiveness and passivity, with alternative strivings of rebelliousness and fierce resentment which he repressed because they threatened the security he managed to derive through compliant behavior. Roger both cherished and loathed the crushing attentiveness of his mother. Toward his father and brother he felt a smothering fear which he masked under a cloak of admiration and compliance.

The withdrawal of his father made it difficult for Roger to achieve the identification with a masculine object necessary for a virile conception of himself. Roger turned to his mother for protection. He revolted, however, against dependency on her, fearing that excessive closeness would rob him of assertiveness, and that aroused sexual feelings would bring on him disapproval from his mother as well as punishment from his father and brother. Repudiating competitiveness with the other male members of the family, he attempted to win their approval by a submissive, ingratiating attitude.

These contradictions in attitudes and feelings had an impact on Roger as a boy. He was a sickly child, ever complaining, and his mother made routine rounds of the local practitioners and specialists. A facial tic and a slight stammer which persisted for months were especially distressing.

That tension was being generated within Roger was apparent from his functional physical ailments which failed to yield to the medicaments and other prescriptions offered him by the many medical practitioners his mother consulted.

During adolescence Roger emerged as a quiet, detached lad, never permitting himself to be drawn into very intimate relationships. He was an excellent and conscientious student, and he was well-liked for his fairness and amiability. At college, he was retiring, but he had a number of friends who sought his companionship because he was so easy to get along with. His romantic attachments were superficial, and the young women he squired to parties admitted that he was attractive but complained that it was difficult to get to know him.

Adopting detachment as a defense against a dependent involvement and compliance as a means of avoiding physical hurt, Roger evolved a character structure that enabled him to function at home and at school, although at the expense of completely gratifying relationships with people.

Upon leaving college, he entered a business firm, arrangements for this having been made by his father. He resisted for two years the exhortations of his mother to marry the daughter of one of her best friends; but finally he succumbed, and he seemed satisfied and happy in his choice. The young couple lived in harmony, and he was considered by his group to be an ideal example of an attentive husband, and after his son was born, of a devoted father. His steadfast application to his work soon elevated his position, until he became a junior member of the firm. His best friend and confidant was one of the senior members, toward whom Roger bore the greatest respect and admiration.

His work and marital life, which were more or less arranged for him by his parents, turned out to be successful since he was able to employ in them his compliance and detachment mechanisms. Towards his best friend and other senior firm members, Roger related passively as he had related previously toward his father and brother. Toward his wife he expressed conventional devotion, keeping himself sufficiently distant to avoid the trap of a tempting dependent relationship which would threaten the independent assertive role he was struggling to maintain.

The only distressing element in Roger's life was his failing health. Constantly fatigued, he evidenced a pallor and listlessness that inspired many solicitous inquiries. Dyspeptic attacks and severe migrainous headaches incapacitated him from time to time. As annoying as his physical symptoms was a pervasive tension which could be relieved by recreational and social distractions.

Inner conflict between dependency, submissiveness, compliance, detachment, and aggression, however, constantly compromised Roger's adjustment, producing a disruption of homeostasis with tension and psychosomatic symptoms. His failing health, fatigue, pallor, listlessness, dyspeptic attacks, and migrainous headaches were evidences of adaptive imbalance. What inspired this imbalance was an invasion of his capacity to detach, produced by the demands made on him by his wife and associates. In addition, his submissive and compliant behavior, while protecting him from imagined hurt, engendered in him overpowering hostility which drained itself off through his autonomic nervous system.

Not long after his tenth wedding anniversary, at age 33, Roger was promoted to a senior member of the firm. His elation at this was short-lived as he became conscious of a sodden depressed feeling that progressively deepened. Inertia, boredom, and withdrawal from his ordinary sources of pleasure followed. Even his work, to which he had felt himself devoted, became a chore. Always eager to cooperate, he experienced, during work hours, a vague dread of something about to happen which he could not define.

So long as he was able to satisfy to a reasonable degree his needs for security, assertion, companionship, love, sexuality, satisfaction in work and play, and creative self-fulfillment, Roger was able to make a tolerable adjustment even with his psychosomatic symptoms. The precipitating factor that had brought about the undermining of Roger's capacities for adaptation was his promotion to senior membership in the firm. While Roger had ardently desired this promotion, for reasons of both status and economics, actually being put in a position of parity with his friend violated his defense of passivity, compliance, and subordination, and threatened him with the very hurt he had anticipated as a child in relation-

ship to his father and brother. To accept the promotion meant that he would be challenging of and perhaps triumphant over father and brother figures. This might expose himself to injury and destruction at the hands of a powerful and punitive force he could neither control nor vanquish. Yet Roger's desire for advancement, inspired by realistic concerns, made it impossible for him to give up that which he considered his due. Since he was aware neither of how fearfully he regarded authority nor of how he was operating with childish attitudes, he was nonplussed by his reactions.

While discussing seemingly casual matters with his best friend and partner during a lunch hour, he was overwhelmed with a feeling of panic, with violent heart palpitations and choking sensations, which forced him to excuse himself on the basis of a sudden indisposition. Back at work, he recovered partly, but a sensation of danger enveloped him—a confounding agonizing sensation, the source of which eluded all attempts at analysis. Upon returning home, he poured himself two extra jiggers of bourbon. His fear slowly vanished so that at dinner time he had almost completely recovered his composure. The next morning, however, he approached his work with a sense of foreboding, a feeling that became stronger and stronger as the days and weeks passed.

Had Roger at this point refused to accept senior membership in the firm, or had he left his position for a minor one in another firm, he might have escaped the catastrophe that finally struck him. His legitimate desires for advancement, however, enjoined him to accept. His conflict became more and more accentuated until finally in the presence of the provocative stress symbol, his friend, he no longer was able to marshal further defenses. Collapse in adaptation with helplessness and expectations of injury announced themselves in an anxiety attack.

The most upsetting thing to Roger was the discovery that his tension and anxiety became most violent while at work.

He found himself constantly obsessed at the office with ways of returning home to his wife. Week ends brought temporary surcease; but even anticipating returning to his desk on Monday was enough to fill him with foreboding. He was unable to avoid coming late mornings, and, more and more often, he excused himself from appearing at work on the basis of a current physical illness. Because he realized fully how his work was deteriorating, he was not surprised when his friend took him to task for his deficiency. Forcing himself to go to work became easier after Roger had consumed several drinks, but he found that he required more and more alcohol during the day to subdue his tension. At night he needed barbiturate sedation to insure even minimal sleep.

Roger attempted to gain surcease from anxiety by implementing mechanisms of control (first line defenses) such as attempting to avoid the stress situations of work and deadening his feelings with alcohol and sedatives. These gestures were not too successful since he was obliged to remain in the conflictual situation no matter how much he wanted to avoid it.

Wild, unprovoked feelings of panic were, however, not confined to his work. Even at home, his habitual haven of comfort and safety, he experienced bouts of anxiety which burst forth at irregular intervals. His sleep, too, was interrupted by nightmarish fears, which forced him to seek refuge in his wife's bed. A pervasive sense of helplessness soon complicated Roger's life. Fear of being alone and regressive fear of the dark became exaggerated. Other fears developed, such as fear of heights, of open windows, of crowds, and of subways and buses. In the presence of his wife, however, these fears subsided or disappeared. Roger consequently arranged matters so that his wife was available at all times. For a while she relished this new closeness, for she had resented Roger's habitual detachment from her. Nevertheless, she realized from his irritability and explosiveness, that something was seriously wrong with her husband.

Unable to restore an adaptive balance with first line defenses, second line characterologic defenses were next elaborated. Chief among these was exaggerated dependency. Roger sought safety through a dependent relationship with his wife that paralleled that of a small child with a mother. Various fears such as of the dark and of being alone were indicative of his child-like helplessness. By turning to his wife for protection, Roger attempted to ward off panic. In so doing, however, he was forced to yield his detachment which had served as a means of buttressing his sense of self. He placed himself then in the very position he had managed to elude as a boy, namely that of being reduced to a vassal of his mother who had resented his growing up. By becoming dependent on his wife, he re-experienced the same threats to his assertiveness he had had as a child. His dependency defense, therefore, not only failed to protect him, but imposed more anxiety on his crumbling ego.

When Roger confided to his wife that he was greatly upset by recurring phantasies of bloody accidents and mutilations, she enjoined him to consult a doctor. He rejected this advice contending that he was merely overworked, and he promised to take a winter vacation which he was sure would restore his mental calm. Fearful thoughts continued to plague Roger. He became frightened whenever he heard stories of violence, and he avoided reading news accounts of suicides or murders. Soon he was obsessed with thoughts of pointed objects. Knives terrified him so that he insisted that his wife conceal them from him.

The return to a childish dependent position mobilized fears that in too close association with a mother figure he would be subjected to mutilation and destruction by overwhelmingly powerful brother and father figures. Sexual feelings toward his wife became forbidding incestuous feelings

*for which the penalty was bloody mutilation. Fantasies of ac-
cidents and bloodshed were reflections of Roger's castration
fears. The repetition of the oedipal drama followed a shattering of Roger's repressive system. Attempting to reinforce
repression by the third line repressive defenses, Roger employed phobia formation striving to remove himself from
symbols of mutilation such as knives and other cutting instruments.*

Other annoying symptoms developed. In the presence of
forceful or strong men, Roger experienced a peculiar fear
which he tried to conceal by affable and compliant behavior.
Sometimes he was aware of a desire to throw his arms around
men and to kiss them in a filial way. This impulse disturbed
Roger greatly, as did phantasies of nude men with huge
genital organs. Roger's sexual life was seriously affected by
his illness. While he had never been an ardent lover, he had
prided himself on his potency. His sexual powers now seemed
to be waning; when he approached his wife, he was impotent
or had premature ejaculations. This upset Roger and created
fears that he never again would function well. To disprove
this he forced himself compulsively to attempt intercourse,
only to be rewarded by further failures. Anticipatory anxiety
soon made sexual relations a source of pain, and, when his
wife suggested that they abstain, he agreed, but he was
frightened that she would leave him for another man.

*The fear Roger manifested of strong males, the desire to act
in an affectionate way with them, the terror of homosexual
assaults by nude men with huge genital organs, were products of his fear of attack by father figures irate at his appro-
priation of the maternal object. A disintegration of Roger's
sexual life was inevitable due to the fact that he was relating
to his wife not as a husband but as a child. Abandonment of
a male role with his wife was therefore necessary to avoid
anxiety. While serving as a spurious protective device, his
sexual inhibition further undermined his self-esteem.*

209

Roger's symptoms became progressively exaggerated, until his incapacitation finally convinced him that he needed professional help.

Diagnostic considerations. It may be opportune to discuss at this point the contemporary dilemma of diagnosis. For example, when we consider the diagnosis in Roger's case, we are confronted with the usual problems of classification. All emotional difficulties spread themselves over a wide pathological area, involving every aspect of the person's functioning—intellectual, emotional, physical, and behavioral. Systems of nosology, based as they are on presenting complaints and symptoms often lose sight of the fact that the entire human being is embraced in any emotional upheaval. The particular classification into which a patient fits then may depend merely upon the relative emphasis the diagnostic agent or patient puts upon selected symptoms.

This may be illustrated in the case of Roger. His complaints were those of tension, irritability, explosiveness, anxiety, depression, psychosomatic symptoms, phobias, and obsessive thoughts. In addition, he exhibited a character disturbance in such manifestations as excessive submissiveness and dependency. Were Roger chiefly concerned with his physical ailments—his headaches, dyspepsia, listlessness, fatigue, failing health, or impotence—we would be inclined to regard him as a person suffering from a "psychophysiological reaction." Should his anxiety attacks have caused him greatest concern, and were he to have focused his attention on his anxiety, we might classify him as "anxiety reaction." In the event his depression was of prime interest, a diagnosis of "psychoneurotic depression" might be entertained. If emphasis had been put on his obsessive concern with bloody amputations, death, and pointed objects, he might be called an "obsessive reaction." His fear of heights, subways, buses, crowds, of solitude and the dark, are those often found in "phobic reactions." Finally, had his submissiveness, passivity, and other character defects been considered his most significant problem, he might be labeled as a "personality disorder." The matter of diagnosis, then, would be essentially a matter of immediate focus. Actually we might say that Roger suffered from a mixed psychoneurotic disorder with anxiety, depressive, psychophysiologic, obsessive, phobic, and personality elements. This diagnostic potpourri is not surprising when we consider that every individual whose homeostasis has broken down exploits dynamism characteristics of all four levels of defense in addition to displaying manifestations, psychological and physiological, of homeostatic imbalance and adaptational collapse.

This much has been his life history and his diagnosis. The question now is, what kind of treatment might be accorded Roger? First, he might have been handled on a symptomatic level, in which an effort was made to treat his symptoms through medicaments, sedatives or tranquilizers for his anxiety, energizers for his depression. He might have been enjoined to slow down in his activities and to detach himself as much as possible. He might have been requested to take a vacation, engage in hobbies and recreations in order to divert his mind and his difficulties. Referral to a physician might have accomplished this for Roger.

Another way of handling the problem might have been possible if a counselor were able to realize the source of the problem of Roger's work situation and to get to the difficulty before Roger's habitual defenses had disintegrated—before he had developed the dependency technique and had stopped being detached from his wife. Were it possible to have gotten to Roger early enough, then one might have been able to enjoin him to accept a subordinate status at work, or to give up his position and take another position elsewhere that did not bring him into the same kind of conflict.

Even if Roger were approached at a later stage in the development of his neurosis, when he had begun to give up his detachment, it might have been possible, by changing his position, to help him restore his defensive detachment, to become more independent and productive, and slowly to begin functioning again on the basis of the customary distances that he erected between himself and others. Active guidance and reassurance may have made it possible for Roger to return to his own bedroom and to begin to assume the reserve with his wife that made it possible for him to function without anxiety.

Approaches such as these understandably would not modify the basic character problem that lay at the heart of his distress. Yet they might have made it possible for Roger to get along, perhaps as well as he had ever done, prior to the outbreak of his neurosis.

In the event that the actual modification of character structure was attempted, or should the problem have progressed to a point where a return to the old status quo was impossible, Roger himself refusing to employ his old way of life, the therapeutic goal would be the modification of the rigid patterns of living that circumscribed Roger's creativity and capacities for happiness. Reconstructive psychotherapy would be the essential intervention, with a warm relationship with a therapist, one in which Roger would work through his hostilities and defenses which prevented him from achieving a fulfilling life. Roger would be brought to an awareness of how he functioned with people, the reasons for his functioning, its genetic origins, how he was projecting into his present day situation attitudes and impulses that were rooted in past conditioning and experiences. He would be encouraged and helped to modify his interpersonal relationships in line with reality and to divorce his present relationships from attitudes rooted in past misinterpretations and faulty conditionings.

Actually, reconstructive therapy was instituted when Roger finally presented himself for treatment. A brief fragment of one psychotherapy session will illustrate some of our patient's maneuvers that became operative and apparent in therapy.

PATIENT: I had a dream last night that upset me. I am in bed with this big woman, big wonderful breasts. She's my wife, but she changes into a negress. She strokes and touches me all over and I feel completely loved and accepted. I awoke from the dream with a strong homosexual feeling that upset me. (Here Roger symbolizes in dream structure his dependency impulses, his repulsion against his dependency, his incestuous desire, and the resultant homosexual residue.)

DOCTOR: Yes, what do you make of this?

PATIENT: I don't know. The woman was comforting and seductive. I always like big-breasted women. Exciting. But my wife isn't as stacked as I'd like her, or as she was in the dream. (Pause)

DOCTOR: How about the negress?

PATIENT: I never liked the idea of sleeping with a colored woman. Makes me feel creepy. Colored people make me feel creepy. I know I shouldn't feel that way. Last time I was here I noticed you had a tan like you had been in the sun. I said 'maybe he's got negro blood.' I know I shouldn't care if you did or not, but the idea scared me for some reason.

DOCTOR: Sounds like the woman in your dream was partly me. (This interpretation was proffered in the hope of stirring up some tension to facilitate associations.)

PATIENT: (Pause) The idea scares me. Why should I want you to make love to me? (Pause) By God, maybe I want you to mother me, be giving, kind.

DOCTOR: How *do* you feel about me?

PATIENT: I want you to be perfect, like a God; to be accepting and loving; to be wise and strong. I realize I'm dependent (*motor one*). I resent my need to be dependent on you (*motor two*). When you show any weakness I am furious.

213

I feel guilty and upset about my feelings. I feel like killing anybody who controls me. I know I must face responsibility, but I feel too weak and unmasculine (*motor three*). I feel like a shit (*motor four*) and hate myself. I am a nothing and I'd like to be a somebody, but I can't.

DOCTOR: Apparently it scares you to be a somebody. When you were promoted, you started getting upset.

PATIENT: Why should I? I suppose I feel like I'm stepping out of my depth. Like I'm not man enough. The whole thing puzzles and frightens me.

DOCTOR: So what do you do?

PATIENT: I am constantly running away (*motor five*). I get so angry at people. I don't want to see anybody. I'm so upset about myself. I try not to feel. But I can't seem to make it on my own. (*The re-instituting of motor one*.)

The patient in the session was manifestly groping with his passive-dependent strivings (*motor one*), his rage (*motor two*), his feelings of low independence (*motor three*), his devalued self-image (*motor four*), his detachment (*motor five*), together with concomitant unresolved incestuous drives and homosexual impulses. All aspects of Roger's personality problem were being projected onto his therapist.

These patterns are delineated in the accompanying chart. Interpretation of the patient's reactions to the therapist in terms of his habitual personality responses, connecting them with his experiences in growing up, and relating them to the incidents leading to the collapse in his homeostasis enabled Roger to approach a different relationship with his therapist, which acted as a nucleus for different feelings toward himself. Not only was homeostasis restored with cessation of his symptoms, but he was able to accept his post as a senior member of the firm with subjective and objective strengthening of his ego.

PERSONALITY MECHANISMS

THE FIVE MOTORS

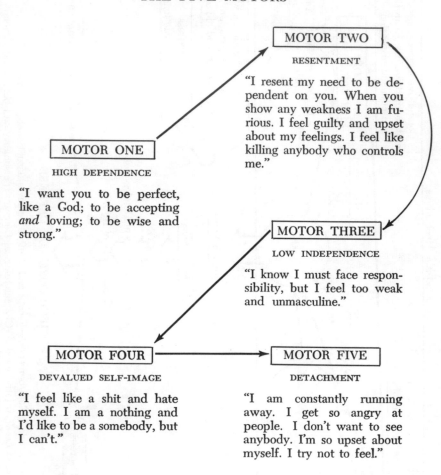

MOTOR TWO

RESENTMENT

"I resent my need to be dependent on you. When you show any weakness I am furious. I feel guilty and upset about my feelings. I feel like killing anybody who controls me."

MOTOR ONE

HIGH DEPENDENCE

"I want you to be perfect, like a God; to be accepting *and* loving; to be wise and strong."

MOTOR THREE

LOW INDEPENDENCE

"I know I must face responsibility, but I feel too weak and unmasculine."

MOTOR FOUR

DEVALUED SELF-IMAGE

"I feel like a shit and hate myself. I am a nothing and I'd like to be a somebody, but I can't."

MOTOR FIVE

DETACHMENT

"I am constantly running away. I get so angry at people. I don't want to see anybody. I'm so upset about myself. I try not to feel."

In addition to the five primary motors, there are offshoots from the resentment motor that include aggression, perhaps to the point of sadism, and also guilt, resulting from the hateful feelings, even eventuating in masochism.

215

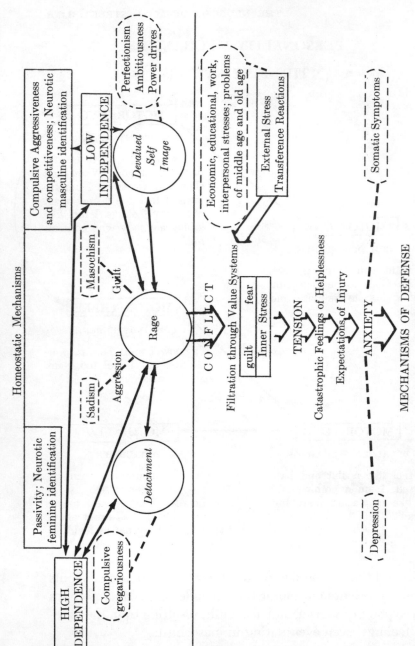

PERSONALITY STRUCTURE

Homeostatic Mechanisms

Passivity; Neurotic feminine identification

Compulsive Aggressiveness and competitiveness; Neurotic masculine identification

HIGH DEPENDENCE

Compulsive gregariousness

Detachment

Sadism

Aggression

Rage

Guilt

Masochism

LOW INDEPENDENCE

Devalued Self Image

Perfectionism Ambitiousness Power drives

Economic, educational, work, interpersonal stresses; problems of middle age and old age

External Stress Transference Reactions

CONFLICT

Filtration through Value Systems

guilt   fear
Inner Stress

TENSION

Catastrophic Feelings of Helplessness
Expectations of Injury

ANXIETY

Somatic Symptoms

Depression

MECHANISMS OF DEFENSE

First Level: Environmental—Escape and Control Defenses (situational problems)
Second Level: Interpersonal —Characterological Defenses (personality and behavior disorders)
Third Level: Intrapsychic —Regressive Defenses (psychoneurotic disorders)

216

The low independence motor prompts the overcompensatory strivings of compulsive aggressiveness and competitiveness, making for a neurotic masculine identification.

The devalued self-image motor also leads to compensatory measures such as perfectionism, ambitiousness, and power drives.

And the detachment motor often provokes one to abandon his isolation and plunge into compulsive gregariousness.

And as we have seen, any and all of these drives may become sexualized, so that one's sexual impulses become linked to feelings of incestuous passivity, or competitive domination with consequent fears of retaliation, or with masochistic or sadistic impulses.

The more general personality structure chart, which appears on page 216, indicates the corollaries to the five motors. When the five motors fail to maintain homeostasis and conflict is unresolved, then anxiety results and the four levels of defense mechanisms operate to cope with the anxiety.

Summary

A typical middle class neurosis has been described in this chapter and exemplified in the case history of Roger T. Emotional equilibrium was achieved when the "motors" of his personality functioned in balance. These motors of the personality were the motors of dependence, resentment, independence, devalued self-image, and detachment. The erratic firing of these motors kept Roger in a state of stress and anxiety. When he gained a balance between dependence and independence and a consequent healthy self-regard, he was able to regain his ability to love and to work.

17

The Social Problems of Main Street U.S.A.: Our Heritage of Violence

In times when the passions are beginning to take charge of the conduct of human affairs, one should pay less attention to what men of experience and common sense are thinking than to what is preoccupying the imagination of dreamers.

ALEXIS DE TOCQUEVILLE

Every age has its style accented by legends about its leaders. Thus Henry the Eighth had his women and his feasts. Alexander the Great sorrowed because there were no more worlds to conquer. Machiavelli explored means of achieving mephistophelian ends. On the other hand, Socrates chose death. Gandhi bespoke nonviolence. St. Thomas Aquinas described an infinite orderliness in the universe. Queen Victoria wielded a hegemony that nearly put half the world to sleep. Jesus said: "Whoever would be great among you, let him be your servant."

These individuals each evidenced a charisma that reflected, or established, a cultural style, sometimes lasting a generation, sometimes even a century or more.

Cultural Life Styles

As there are styles in art, music, religion, literature, and politics, there are also styles in emotional problems that reflect the era. Consider, for example, the difference between the popular expression of emotional disorder in the Victorian age in contrast with our own. Victorian living has come to be synonymous with repressed, Puritan prudery. The vigorous display of one's impulses was forbidden. Women concealed even their ankles; to faint in response to some earthy confrontation was expected. With this kind of life style, it was natural that the typical neurosis was hysteria, characterized by the tortured, taut, constricted, self-punitive, turned-inward person who was his own worst enemy and who hurt himself far more than he hurt his environment. Except for occasional breakthroughs of the repressed impulses, shut-up-ness was his typical condition. The virility of the period of the French and American revolutions, followed by the romantic era characterized by Lord Byron and Wagner, had by 1885 largely petrified into the *form* of emotion, but not its *vitality*—plenty of frosting, but no cake. The gingerbread of a Victorian house exemplifed the excessive frills of the era, frills which were essentially divorced from solid structure. The saccharine, even naive, quality of a Browning or Tennyson examplifed the age. It was in this atmosphere that Freud, all his life a very proper Victorian, but also a genius, began to comment on mankind.

Contrast today's behavior with the repressed tendencies of Victorianism. Pathology is much more likely now to be

219

acted out, rather than held in. A student protest that once would have involved merely a series of dormitory gripe sessions, now takes the form of lying down in the president's office. Religious services once lasted two hours, and the preacher preached for at least one of those hours. Now congregations rarely sit through a sermon of more than 12 minutes. This is the era of the march, and the letter to the congressman is altogether too tame to be meaningful. This is a generation of deed more than word, of doing more than thinking. It is more behavioral than verbal.

The last 25 years have seen the lessening of the impact of words. Franklin Roosevelt's fireside chats and Churchill's oratory probably would not have the same effect today as in the 1940's. The proliferation of words has made them cheap, and they have relatively less effect on people today. (Could it be that we do not have the proper pied piper whose tune the present generation can "dig"? When Senator McCarthy began attacking the Establishment, many isolated hippies did listen, and even scrubbed their necks.) The students of today may not learn to appreciate the thought of Hegel and Schleiermacher as well as they did 50 years ago, but this student generation will learn how to talk to a ghetto child, and organize a community action program.

We are witnessing a change in cultural life style in our generation. The change is in the direction of greater freedom of thoughts and words, but especially deeds. The world has seen such changes before. The violent, free-swinging style of Martin Luther in 1530 evolved 100 years later into a pedantic intellectual and theological obscurantism that would have dumbfounded Martin himself. The preciseness of the early Mozart gave way in the course of a generation to a glorious freedom in the later symphonies of Beethoven. The entire culture of their time followed the same patterns.

The change of life style in our era can be noted in all the art forms. If one of the functions of an art form is to tell us what we are like, it is well to note the almost monolithic message that we are being given. The message of art is that man is alone, nearly solipsistic, and that as he acts out his lonely sufferings, there is no one who can offer him relief. It is the cry of unmet dependence of our motor number one from Chapter Sixteen.

Witness the popular songs. The lyrics consist of laments over lost loves. The distances are too great, the barriers too insurmountable, the other person too fickle. And the singer cries that he is hurting and alone.

What other musical forms are the specific product of our era? There is the atonality of Stravinsky and Schönberg, music that is constructed almost mathematically, rather than by the flow of intuitive musical feeling. Our generation has seen the advent of electronic music, again bearing witness to the relative absence of the human factor.

What is new in art? Abstracts, op, and pop. The frenzy of Jackson Pollock gave way to the mathematical precision of op art. And pop art is the grotesque expression of sick humor—but the sickness lies not in the art, but in the supposed idols of our culture: superman, the gas station, and the soup can.

Literature again reflects the acting out quality of our time. The new literary form that Truman Capote initiated, in *In Cold Blood*, is a portrayal of the perversion of mutuality, as are so many recent novels. On Broadway, those things that people laugh at actually would grieve the sensitive person if he stopped to consider what he was laughing at. The trend in movies is to indicate "for mature audiences only" which is another way of saying that some aberration of human intimacy will be acted out. And what of the poets? Odes to life are not being written, but portrayals of tragedy and emptiness mark current poetry.

Dancing is characterized by two persons accompanying each other to the floor, and then each performing what amounts to a solo routine. People do not have to talk to each other when they dance now, in fact conversation would be nearly impossible. But even more than that, the deafening intensity of the music serves another purpose: An adult chaperone once asked a teen ager at a dance how she survived the incredible volume of the music. "It's great," she replied. "You don't have to think."

What, then, is being said through the artistic media? The message is reflected in all the new art forms of our era: There is a vast emptiness amongst people, and the times are lonely; the emptiness prompts on the one hand a restless acting out, a hyperactive, impulsive search for satisfactions, alternating with a despondent disdain for any possible meaning in life—a tuning out and a turning off.

The historian of the psychological signs of our times sees empty disillusionment in the new music, art, literature, and dance. The emptiness is coupled with intermittent acting out, the angry attack to wrest from the world the commodities that satisfy elemental human needs. In our schema of the previous chapter, our culture is witnessing a violent see-saw between the detachment motor and the dependency motor.

While one can see other psychological signs of the times, if one focuses on what is *new*, what is distinctively characteristic of our own era, then the emptiness and the acting out are the most unmistakable marks of current culture. But even at this writing there seem to be some faint early signs that something even newer is being introduced. Could it be that we are entering an era of hope? Perhaps the pendulum is beginning to swing away from the declaration of life's meaninglessness toward a measure of conviction in the ability of an individual to make a difference. Or as the Peace Corps advertisement used to say, "You know you don't expect to change the world, but that doesn't mean that you have to leave it exactly the way you found it." If there is a change in life style on the horizon, it will be the result of complex changes in family patterns, environmental influences, and the values already operating in our society. We hazard the conjecture that there *is* a new hopefulness extant, which may begin to counteract the nihilism that followed two world wars and other assorted conflicts. Hope is the expectation of fulfillment, confidence concerning one's prospects for satisfaction. Such a trend in our society could change the feelings and the behavior of the next generation. Perhaps that is what lies ahead.

But this moment in history is characterized by intermittent acting out and turning off. It is in this context that we purpose to examine three acute problems of our time: 1. violence, 2. disaffection of the young with our society, and 3. sexual behavior. In the remainder of this chapter we shall deal with violence, and in the following two chapters with the other key problems.

Violence

Three of the most illustrious men in America were shot and killed in five years. In the first three months of 1968, reported serious crime rose 17 percent over that of a year earlier, which in turn had been up 20 percent from the year before that. Are we a sick society and a sick people?

Violence is a concept that includes homicides, insurrections, riots and strikes, political terrorism, and civil war. Measured on that scale, the United States ranked 42nd in overall violence when compared with 114 nations during the years 1961 through 1965 (Gurr, 1968). Our country is considerably less violent than Mexico, Colombia, Burma, and Indonesia. But it is more violent than England, Australia, and Japan. On one of the measures, the homicide rate, our incidence is four times that of Canada, Australia, and Japan, and it is eight times that of England. But our homicide rate is only about one fifth that of Colombia and Mexico.

In terms of all the people injured and killed in the United States by violent means, our country is less violent than in previous times. In July of 1863, there was a riot in New York City that makes all the recent "racial" riots seem like minor squabbles. By the end of just five days, 1,200 persons were killed and some 6,000 were injured. The angry resentful people of the ghettos then were not the negroes, but the immigrant Irish who had the miserable jobs, the despicable living conditions, and who were then about to be subjected to a draft lottery for an unpopular war. They were the angry underdogs, and they poured into the streets in mobs that required ten regiments of the U.S. Army to stop them (McCague, 1968). They destroyed property, set fire to buildings. Even women with crowbars eagerly tore up streetcar tracks.

In 1871, a Congressional investigation revealed that in that year alone there had been thousands of lynchings, shootings, whippings, and mutilations of negroes in the south. An army general in Texas said, "Murders of negroes are so common as to render it impossible to keep accurate accounts of them."

It is the individual act of violence that has caused great concern in the United States more recently. Kennedy, McKinley, Garfield, and Lincoln were assassinated, and attempts were made on the lives of Truman, both Roosevelts, and Jackson. Such occurrences are not confined to the United States. Since the end of World War II, 11 heads of state have been assassinated, and there are records of 66 other attempts in 28 different countries.

What the United States does not witness within its borders are the more general kinds of overt violence: Stalinist purges, Algerian terrorism, mob action in Pakistan and India, enforced Biafran starving, 200,000 deaths in Colombia, and the massacre of 400,000 persons in Indonesia. Since World War II there have been more coups d'etat, guerrilla wars, and revolutions in the world than national elections. Between 1961 and 1967, civil strife occurred in 114 of 121 nations surveyed in the Gurr study (1968). In the last 2,400 years each country in Europe has had a ratio of significant political violence that is frightening.

Whatever the precise figures in the United States may be, it is acknowledged that there is too much violence. The causes are not fully known, but recent attention has been increasingly focused on the interrelationship of brain pathology and frustrating life experience. It has long been understood that violence begets violence, and that intense frustration leads to rage and aggression. But it also appears that there are different levels of ability to tolerate that frustration. In many known cases of violence-prone persons, it has been possible to detect brain damage, which apparently interferes with the normal electro-chemical circuitry of the brain. These malfunctioning circuits discharge in an irregular manner, leaving the individual prone to respond erratically and violently to minor provocations. Thus excessively hot weather or a minor insult may enrage some persons to the point of physical force, while others might feel simply annoyed.

No one can categorically attribute violence to brain damage, but much needs to be learned about the effects of tumors, certain types of epilepsy, virus infections that affect the brain, blows on the head, and even congenital, chromosomal abnormalities. Any or all of these factors may have a bearing on a person's tolerance level and on his consequent tendency to react violently under certain conditions of provocation.

Freud (1946) provided an instinctual model for explaining man's violence. Freud alleged that while many instincts were operative in the human being, two large groupings could be differentiated: those that served life and those that served death. Survival and propagation were reflected in the life instincts among which the sex instinct was particularly prominent, expressing itself in the energy force, *libido*. The death

225

instinct, *thanatos,* was the expression of the universal tendency on the part of organic matter to return (regress) to the original inorganic substances from which they were derived. Aggression and destructiveness were among the human derivatives of the death instinct. The life and death instincts, and their derivatives, manifested themselves in many forms independently and in fusion. A characteristic of instincts was that they persistently expressed themselves (*repetition compulsion*). The *source* of all instinctual drives were body needs (hunger, sex, elimination, etc.) which activated the instincts, generating energy, and tension. This promoted goal directed strivings in the ego toward motor actions (feeding, sexual behavior, eliminative functioning, etc.) to gratify the needs, thus discharging tension and bringing about a state of relaxation. The *aim* of the instinct was to eliminate the need source and to bring about a state of physiological quietude. The *object* of the instinct was the instrumentality through which the aim was satisfied. The object or its image (psychic representations) became invested with energy from the id leading to a discharge of energy onto the object. The impetus of the instinct was the force that propelled it in terms of the energy that was mobilized. No instinct acted in isolation; rather there was a fusion of instincts accomplished by the synthesizing action of the ego. All activity consisted of a compromise of drive energy and the resisting forces. *Displacements* occurred as a result of this compromise. Where the displacement failed to discharge sufficient tension, the involved instinct was *aim-inhibited* with a resulting accumulation of energy. Adjustment required the constructive distribution of energy, with proper harmonization of the operation of the id, ego, and superego.

Where the ego broke down in supplying a means of discharge of energy, or where it blocked the discharge too strenuously, the id threatened to break through the resistance and discharge energy in a disorganized and regressive way.

A potent source of anxiety was danger from the instincts. The ego evolved defense mechanisms to cope with this danger. Among these was a change of object choice. For instance, the death instinct was diverted from the self and projected in the form of aggression, dominance, destruction, competition, and exploitation. Since the instinctual aim was inhibited by this diversion, tension continued to foster attenuated forms of discharge. Substitute object choices served to safeguard the ego from anxiety. When the substitutive symbolisms failed in their disguise, the ego responded with anxiety.

It may be seen that Freud postulated a biological base for man's destructiveness. On the other hand, he allowed that given a healthy ego, i.e., a healthy captain of one's personality strivings, there is the possibility of adaptive living without the disorganized breakthrough of destructive instincts.

The more recent works of Lorenz (1966), Ardrey (1967), and Storr (1968) have been contentions that aggression is instinctual. Storr, for example, as an advocate of this school of thinking, has written " . . . the infant is potentially aggressive from the moment of birth, and . . . infants inevitably entertain destructive fantasies of terrifying intensity. These fantasies . . . arise partly from innate aggressiveness" (p. 2). " . . . it is probable that when no outside stimulus for aggression exists, men actually seek such stimuli out in much the same way as they do when sexually deprived . . . there is so far no convincing evidence that the aggressive response is, at a physiological level, any less instinctive than the sexual response . . . " (pp. 18, 19).

Even more specifically, Lorenz reports that the aggressive instinct is so powerful in cichlid fish that if they are deprived of other fish to prey upon, they will greatly increase the time that they spend biting the bottom of a fish tank. The implication is that animals need hostile territorial neighbors on whom they can vent their aggression.

Admittedly, part of the problem is in understanding what is meant by aggression and violence. But we would stress here that it is the *machinery* for aggression (and for mating) that is an innate heritage of man. What is inborn is the capacity to respond to stimuli. Early in childhood, complex patterns for the expression of aggression are laid down through social conditionings. The circumstances of life determine how and when the "aggression machinery" will be turned on and off. "Releasers" will be developed based on an individual's needs and the prevailing social sanctions. Thus, an elderly woman on crutches who bumps us may not provoke any retaliation, while a 13 year old smart aleck who elbows us on a crowded bus may provoke an outraged complaint. The black man in this country will understandably be more angry than his white counterpart, as a result of the accumulated irritations that he experiences in his daily living. Or if any infant is seriously deprived of mothering during his earliest weeks and months, a pattern of distrust and anger may be developed that indelibly colors his interactions with all people throughout his life.

We affirm with Scott (1958) "that there is no physiological evidence of any spontaneous stimulation for fighting arising within the body . . . there is no need for fighting, either aggressive or defensive, apart from what happens in the external environment." When lives and rights and values are at stake it can be understood that men will fight. When physical and psychological life are not threatened, the capacity to respond aggressively can remain quiescent.

What are the provocations in our way of life that cause too many acts of violence to be committed? In the United States two kinds of violence should be delineated: the violence that leads to assassination, and the violence that is a more general physical aggression, ranging all the way from teasing to murder. Assassinations for seemingly ideological reasons have often been the acts of persons suffering from severe mental disorder. A climate of intense political strain may be a pro-voking factor, but there are those who feel that even at such times, only a schizophrenic person has attempted, or com-pleted, an act of assassination (Hastings, 1965). All such per-sons, it is alleged, had long histories of emotional disorder, often with delusions or hallucinations, and had shown marked instability in interpersonal relationships and vocational re-sponsibilities, particularly with the most extreme hostility and resentment toward authority figures. This does not rule out the fact that under the press of personal conviction an individual may not be induced to eliminate by murder an-other human being he is convinced has injured or humiliated him, or who is a symbol of a hated enemy. Psychiatric exam-inations after the crime often reveal no evidence of a residual psychosis. Whether we may consider the span of time during which the murder was perpetrated as a fleeting psychotic episode is often a matter of opinion which can confound the most unprejudiced jury.

The life histories of those men who attempted assassina-tions appear to have much in common. The father of Lincoln's assassin died when his son was fourteen; the father of Theo-dore Roosevelt's attempted assassin died when the son was seven; the father of John F. Kennedy's assassin died before the child was born. An oppressively unhappy home, a dom-inant mother, and an actually absent or psychologically absent father seem prominent (Rothstein, 1964). The would-be assassin is similar to violence-prone persons in general, except that the assassin can be more selective in the expres-sion of his rage, planning his violence rather than acting it out in a fit of uncontrolled impulsiveness.

Delinquency, with its violent defiance of social order ex-pressed in stealing, truancy, fire setting, vandalism, cruelty, and drug abuse is related to family disturbance. There are individual delinquent children developed through faulty parent-child interactions. There is also a more general group delinquency expressive of a subculture in which antisocial gang activity is more or less the norm.

The causes of the two types of delinquency overlap to some extent: child neglect, lack of proper supervision, inadequate discipline, weak family cohesiveness, and conscious or unconscious rejection foster a child's animosity toward society as representative of a parental agency.

The overall psychological profile of the violent person begins with "poor self-identity" (Ervin, 1968). His troubled home situation has resulted in an uneven functioning, with his love, dependence, independence, and resentment "motors" running erratically. In every area of his life he has *uneven self-control*, whether it be the use of his time, energy, money, drinking, or sexuality. All his impulses tend to be acted out more readily than in the average person, and repression is relatively minimal. And of all his impulses, it is his hostility that is the least subject to reasonable control. Minor aggravations, a slight push in the subway rush hour, someone getting ahead of him in a ticket line, a request to work late some night—any of these may provoke a wild show of force. At other times he may be quiet, even retiring. There may be great remorse and depression alternating with the violent acts of rage.

In addition to the psychology of violence, there is a *sociology* of violence that influences every citizen. The continual exposure to various forms of violence will predispose a person to violence. The parent who regularly beats his child will influence that child to beat his younger sibling. Habitual styles of play form one of the elements that produces a habitual style of life. The child whose play consists in tinkering with gadgets will build that behavior into his adult life style. The TV program of shooting and killing will be imitated to some degree by children in their play. The child who identifies with the raucous violence that he sees in his parents or in his TV heroes, will tend to build that behavior into his adult life style. There is in every person an unwitting absorption of cultural tendencies. The assortment of toy ray guns, rocket weapons, and other instruments of killing that fill the counters of stores frequented by children is evidence of the pervasive aggression of our times. Since there is unquestionably more violence paraded before the eyes and ears of our population, some greater tendency to act out that same violence is an inevitable result.

The largest selling newspaper in the United States is certain, in its first three pages, seven days a week, to expose its readers to a variety of violence, ranging from misdemeanors through rape and onto murder. Despite the fact that most persons in the United States have never known a murderer or a rapist, and probably rarely met anyone who was in trouble with the law, they gain the daily impression from their newspapers that every spot on earth is a place filled with wildly violent happenings. Visitors to New York City, upon being taken for a subway ride and a walk through Central Park, are astounded to discover how casually 5,000,000 riders a day are able *safely* to get to work and back, and how many thousands delight themselves each day in the pleasures of their wonderful park.

Summary

The need is clearly for a broader and more wholesome perspective than what is now being portrayed in the news and entertainment industries. Since it is known that all people are susceptible, in varying degrees, and that violence breeds violence, it is possible for society to take those corrective steps that will make the pendulum swing away from physical attacks on other persons.

Someday, of course, there may be a lessening of the tensions in the world that are so accurately and alarmingly portrayed on TV: wars, racial violence, and starvation. If war no longer exists, it will not be daily fare on the evening news show.

It is well known that a provoking agent that leads to violence is over-congestion. Whether it is on a national scale as in Asia, or a ghetto tenement, on the experimental crowding of white rats in a laboratory, irritability and the open expression of it increase with crowding. Someday hopefully a host of reparative measures will make possible a better life for all people. Population control, freer immigration procedures, ample food production and distribution, easier mobility from city to suburb for all races, greater humanization of our city planning, adequate incomes for people so that they can buy the evidences of freedom and leisure—all of these will someday contribute to a lessening of the frustrations that breed violence.

But is there some legitimate violence? If there are a few ruling families in a given dictatorial country who have arbitrarily conducted the affairs of the country for generations, largely for their own personal gain, and who show no signs of sharing their privileged status, would it be so terrible if those families were thrown out and a more broadly based governing class took control?

And in the United States, would there have been the legislation and the social change without marches, demonstrations, and even riots? The use of force, which produced countering forces, resulted in deaths. Those very deaths, for example, the deaths of civil rights workers, brought pressures upon Congress to produce laws that will be etched in the stones of history as memorials to those slain workers.

While deploring the violence, whether it be in the Far East, the city ghetto, or the besieged office of a university president, it would be better still to be prophetic enough to

232

see where the present seeds of future violence now exist and then institute those measures that will free the human spirit to the point where violence is not necessary. The needed measures are utopian in scope at this point, but the direction of the measures needed is known. While the total task is immense, the need for each individual to do what he can, where he is, needs to be underscored. As Camus put it, "Perhaps we cannot prevent the world from being a world in which children are tortured. But we can reduce the number of children tortured. And if you don't help us, who else in the world can do this?"

18

The Social Problems of Main Street U.S.A.: The Disaffection of the Young with Our Society

My father has made a lot of money, and at the age of 60 he's finally found out that, as far as he's concerned, his life is nothing. Because he sees that in five or ten years he's going to die and he sees that he's got all his 'goal,' and he's still nowhere. Life itself was just a vehicle for him to attain these exterior goals. So now what is he going to do? How does he handle life? Because he has no goals to preoccupy his mind, what's preoccupying his mind now is life, and he can't handle that.

This cat at 60 is where I am at 20. When I'm 60, I don't want to be where he's at. Being desperate at 20, you still feel you can know yourself, but at 60—where do you go from there?   S. KELMAN

In these words a college student eloquently put his finger on the central complaint that young people have against the lives and culture of their parents: namely, the pattern of using life for a purpose other than simply living and experiencing life itself. Anything that diminishes the immediate value of the individual has become the most significant rallying point around which the young castigate their elders.

The gap between the generations has always existed. There are three factors in the present gap that give to the present situation its distinguishing features: First, this is an "acting out" generation, and rarely has the gap been so vocal and physical. Second, the knowledgeable parents against whom the young people rebel know full well that they have made many mistakes, and their own insecurity cripples them in their ability to engage in unequivocating dialog with the young. Third, the specific quality of our society's errors becomes the guide as to what the young will protest against. The main provocations of the 1960's have been the draft and the war in Vietnam.

The Acting-Out Generation

There is nothing quite so comforting as historical perspective when it comes to equilibrating oneself in the face of current events. It was in the year 383 that St. Augustine gave up college teaching because the behavior of his students was so "outrageous, licentious, and disgraceful" that even a saint wanted no more of it. Perhaps it was the memory of his own checkered past that was painfully brought back to him by his disruptive students, but at least Augustine as adult had rather typically disparaging views of young people.

There seems always to have been a conviction on the part of the old that the young are going to the dogs, that moral values are slipping away, and that respect for authority is diminishing.

Even the precise character of the way in which one generation has disapproved of the other has an historical continuity. Could not these words have been penned in any century? Aristotle wrote "Youth loves honor and victory more than money. It really cares next to nothing about money, for it has not yet learned what the lack of it means." Francis Bacon protested that "Young men, in the conduct and management of their actions, embrace more than they can hold; stir more than they can quiet; fly to the end without consideration of the means and degrees . . . Men of age object too much, consult too long, adventure too little, repent too soon, and seldom drive business home to the full period, but content themselves with a mediocrity of success." Samuel Johnson expressed his sentiments about the generation gap: "The old man trusts wholly to slow contrivance and gradual progression; the youth expects to force his way by genius, vigor, and precipitance. The old man pays regard to riches, and the youth reverences virtue . . . Age looks with anger on the temerity of youth, and youth with contempt on the scrupulosity of age."

It is possible to acclaim these differences, rather than abhor them. These differences between the generations lend to society a creative tension that gives animation to the person who dares expose himself to any citizen whose age differs by 30 years from his own. Freud, with a touch of serious levity, wrote that without the conflict between the adolescent and his parent, civilization would not go forward, because society would otherwise settle into a rut from which only the fresh vision of an adolescent now saves it.

So the basic outline of the conflict is nothing new, and, furthermore, it can be hailed for some of its salutary results. But as for the specific expression of the current conflict between the generations, more heed needs to be given to it, because of the instructive part such attention can play in the improvement of human life.

DISAFFECTION OF THE YOUNG WITH SOCIETY

If the current rebellion of the student generation were to be given a psychiatric diagnosis, it would be called "oral-aggressive behavior." That is, there is an aggressive demand for the satisfaction of one's dependency (oral) needs. While there are some frankly sadistic, pain-inflicting acts, most of it is of the nature of raising a ruckus so that one will be noticed and then be given some additional privilege or right. Thus, a sit-in will occur, and the demand will be for more liberalized dormitory hours, or for an audience with the university president who should listen to the students' pleas. While the distinction is not an exact one, there is a difference between working productively so that one earns the right for a certain reward, e.g., and increase in the number of class absences allowed, as opposed simply to refusing to leave a dean's office until such privileges are granted.

Both forms of pressure are tested means of getting things done, and our purpose is not to judge which is better or worse. It does appear that the characteristic style of this decade has been the oral-aggressive pattern. If one recognizes that such character patterns are firmed up as a consequence of early modes of child-rearing which lead to unresolved childish promptings, then the acting out quality of the generation conflict is telling us something about the way our young people were brought up. It is not, as some demagogues might say, that all of today's young people are spoiled brats. It rather signifies that their dependency needs were poorly met and now obtrude upon their young adult functioning. The satisfaction of dependency needs does not relate to whether they were given adequate allowances, enough mod clothes, and a car when they graduated from high school. Rather it has to do with whether they were given sufficient emotional support and stimulation, whether they had close relationships with parents, and whether they developed, as a result of being loved, the feeling of trust and hope in themselves and in their world. And finally it has to do with whether their parents were sufficiently interested in them, sufficiently secure themselves, and sufficiently willing to devote time to provide firm and loving discipline. For it is only through discipline, properly applied, that a child can learn to cope with the frustration and reasonable deprivation that characterizes civilized living.

The director of student psychiatry at the University of Wisconsin, Dr. Seymour Halleck, in a paper to the American Psychiatric Association in May, 1967, put it this way: "Most of the depression and chronic anxiety of the alienated student can be related to feelings of repressed anger directed at parents who have deprived him, suppressed him, or intimidated him . . . The aura of love which supposedly has surrounded the child is more often talked about than provided."

It is this oral-aggressive underlay that determines the specific manner in which the adolescent and young adult person now strives to satisfy his needs. The style is not the dependent passivity of the wall flower who fearfully cringes on the sidelines of life; rather it is the vociferous, angry, provocative, attention-getting public demonstration across the street from the White House, undertaken in the hope that the nation's "father" will be forced to take notice and attend to the needs being expressed. The current young generation characteristically acts in a way typical of the oral person, namely, in the expectation that the source of help is external to the individual. Pessimism, considerable suspiciousness, and anger mark their attitudes. By cunning activity they hope to gain some victories. Finally there is one other characteristic of the young adult generation that even their most sympathetic elders cannot help but criticize: their relative lack of anything original to put forth. They criticize but usually do not offer a workable substitute proposal. They tune out and turn off, but do not suggest another station to turn on and tune into. The lack of originality is an invariable concomitant of the oral-aggressive pattern. Characteristic of this pattern, too, is the search for magic in drugs—pot (marijuana), speed (amphetamine), and acid (LSD).

A young speaker at a demonstration and rally protesting the Chicago police tactics at the Democratic National Convention of 1968 said the following words on the corner of Telegraph Avenue and Haste Street in Berkeley, California on the night of August 30, 1968: "People over 30 are members of the fat-assed, bullshit generation. And we aren't going to go along with them. We want this corner [There had been some question about whether the police would allow the demonstration to be held on the avenue], and when they give us this corner, then we are going to want the next corner; and when they give us that corner, then we are going to get the next and the next." Those remarks, which contain the complete substance of the speech, illustrate three of the characteristics of the oral-aggressive posture: the intense anger, the implication that what is wanted should be given to them ("when they *give* us this corner"), and the utter lack of a program. Just what is the meaning and purpose of being given a corner?

To reiterate, we are not judging at this point *how* one ought to protest in life, nor whether the protests now being made are legitimate. We are examining the *style* of protest, and we find that it has been largely of the passive-aggressive, acting out quality, characteristic of certain deprivations in child-rearing, particularly in early childhood. Those deprivations consist in an improper meeting of a child's dependency and disciplinary needs, with the result that the child lacks confidence that the benificence of the world is adequate for him to reach his goals on his own. Consequently, we witness on all sides a railing against parental agencies (home, school, church, and government) which is essentially a plea for more nurture. We live in that place in history when all authority is under attack. We note with interest that the style of attack can most aptly be diagnosed as oral-aggressive.

The description of diagnosis which we have offered could be couched in other terminologies. Passive-aggressive, or hostile-dependent, or exploitative orientations imply essentially the same configurations. As we pursue the understanding of the disaffection of the young with our society, we shall see other manifestations of this character development, and how the involvement and interaction with society takes the particular form that it does.

Parental Influence

The insecurity of the parents has reduced their influence on the young. Margaret Mead has likened the difficulties of the present adult generation to the difficulties that were experienced by the foreign born when they migrated to the United States. In the case of the typical immigrant, in changing his country he was confronted with a host of cultural changes and had more or less difficulty in adapting to his new environment. Analogously, the present adult may often be a stranger now in his own land, because the culture has changed right under his own nose. While standing still geographically, he nevertheless is confronted with a host of new customs and values. He did not change his country, rather his country changed so drastically that his own childhood training and development may have prepared him for a different world than the one he now confronts as an adult. And so, like any immigrant, he may be mystified by the strange new practices that he sees around him. And adaptability is generally more difficult the older one becomes.

"Why," said one puzzled parent "my children don't even like ice cream! Have you ever heard of anything so strange?" This was a father who as a little boy, occasionally as a special treat for Sunday dinner, would experience the delight of having a pint of ice cream divided among his father, his mother, his sister, and himself. Now some 30 years later as a parent, his capacious kitchen freezer always contains several half gallon containers of ice cream of a variety of flavors— and his children, who have never been without ice cream, couldn't care less.

"Do you know that my children don't have the vaguest notion about the value of a dollar? Let me tell you, when I was a boy, and I got a dime for my weekly allowance, I appreciated it!" So speaks a man who makes $25,000 a year and who resents the fact that his children do not seem to be awed by that fact. The father of that father had made $3,000 a year, and that had been a very handsome income in those days. But "the kids now don't seem to realize how lucky they are."

"And respect for their teachers? Well, when we were young, they were held up as exemplary specimens of outstanding men and women. I don't know what the matter is now. The kids just don't look up to them any more, especially by the time they are in high school." Of course, if the truth be known, the parents no longer respect the teachers so much any more either. In many suburban towns, for example, a school teacher can't even afford to buy a house in the town where he teaches. The average suburbanite may be making twice the salary of the average teacher, and the message gets across to the children that school teaching is not the way to make it big in these times. But the parent remembers the days of his childhood, and is puzzled.

These are simple little examples of fathers who were brought up in the culture of one generation, and who now try to understand another generation that has been brought up on the basis of a different world view.

The simplistic notion that one's children should see the world the way the parent does, makes for parental disappointment, and often confusion. Returning to the analogy of the immigrant, the speed of the present cultural change has been so rapid as to leave many parents unaware that they, as well as their children, are living in a different world from the one that gave them their first impressions, i.e., their childhood impressions of what the world was like.

The result is that the advice offered by parent to child may be somewhat off target. And while children have probably always thought that their parents were somewhat old-fashioned, the present youth may have even more reason to feel that way. The two different worlds in which parent and child have been brought up have provided each with a somewhat different set of values. This makes for difficult dialog. The sensitive parent will be somewhat uneasy about offering facile generalizations to a young person on how to live his life. Many a middle class parent senses that his offspring is better educated, has had broader experiences, and is probably more mature than he himself was at the same age and stage in life. In fact, many parents are rather awed by the sophistication of their children. The consequence is that there is a certain insecurity about speaking forthrightly to one's children, and in fact, many parents tend not to stick their necks out at all, preferring the comfortable safety of silence. Unsure of themselves and of the kind of advice they might proffer, they default when it comes to offering to their children a solid background against which the children can test their own emerging ideas. To whatever extent the parents are uncertain and ambiguous in their reaction to the child, by that much the child will probe and test the parents' weaknesses. Finding a weak spot, he will both dig and manipulate, perhaps to the absolute limit of what he feels he can get away with. As the insecure parents are increasingly tested by their child, they will become all the more puzzled about how they should respond. And the child, sensing the weakness or the irrelevance of his parents' guidance, will turn more and more to his peers for his model. The cycle thus becomes exacerbated, and the provocative, acting out quality of the young person's testing behavior reaches more extreme proportions.

A second difficulty that adults experience in influencing the young is the result of their own guilt about the mess the world is in. A mother and a daughter were witnessing a television newscast which seemed to be filled with stories of violence and corruption. Finally the mother said, "Isn't it awful?" To which the daughter very casually replied, "Well, that's your generation, Mom."

The sensitive awareness that such events are a regular aspect of this era causes adults to feel more than a little self-conscious embarrassment. It is difficult today to puff up one's chest and spout red, white, and blue Americanism—much more difficult, say, than after World War I when the country had fought to make the world safe for democracy; or after World War II, a war that everyone felt had to be fought and won so that all wars forever would end. But today the rising sensitivity to injustice, the awareness of worthy causes unnoticed a generation ago, and of course, the increasing insight into the mixture of motives that prompted our intervention in a variety of other countries and continents—all this makes it nearly impossible for an adult unequivocally to say to the young "just follow my example and everything will turn out all right."

The middle class parent who reads and reacts to the day's news events is invariably confronted with a host of tragedies. Newsworthy items are unfortunately those matters which are fraught with conflict. The *New York Times*, for example, most usually writes a news story in such a way as to emphasize the disagreement between the reported event and prevailing opinion. What is *controversial* on the international, national, metropolitan, political, industrial, labor, health, science, amusement, religious, and financial scenses will be the news which somehow seems fit to print. And the result is that the reader is constantly having his own opinions called into question, and is daily reminded that his world is in a state of flux.

Everywhere is a mess. But even in the face of all this, the best father is still the one who has forthright convictions, speaks his mind without pussyfooting around, and can point to his own reasonably successful life as the model for his son. It is not an easy task for a father. Ideally, a father should be sufficiently secure so that he can let his children have a large dose of freedom, knowing all the while that his own image with his children is sufficiently heroic so that they will intuitively identify with the essential values of his life. For many a man today, the quiet confidence in his own way of life is at least moderately shaken by the events of his time, together with the barrage of criticism to which he is subject. And as we have noted, that is the atmosphere which produces more testing behavior from a child, much the same as a horse or a dog will act up with a frightened master.

The need is not for a return to being the autocrat of an earlier age, but certainly the adults need to sense that they have partially defaulted in not expressing their own opinions about certain values that have persistently stood the test of time. The need is more for dialog than control, more for discussion than for police action. It is in the vacuum of nonexistent or negligent parent-child interaction that the children become the most alienated and disillusioned. Better that more opinions be expressed, even if they are the wrong ones, than no opinions at all.

A young high school quarterback called the plays for his team. His father faithfully attended the games. After the games there was no discussion between father and son about the plays that were called. The son wondered why, because his father had played football a generation before. He would have liked some general chats about strategy and tactics. But the father, who had played during simpler days, felt inadequate about discussing the complexities of the I and T formations, cornerbacks and tight ends—jargon that was new since his own playing days. And so the father kept his silence, intimidated by what he felt was the technical sophistication of his 17 year old son. But they could have discussed more enduring factors—matters of judgment and finesse, courage, and the will to win. Both of them were the poorer for their inability to reach out to each other.

It is this talent of the older generation that seems to be muted under the stress of these times—the reasoned common sense and the maturity based on life experience. This is the contribution of the old to the young, and our present decade is one in which adults have failed to speak forcefully to young people. Liberal adults particularly have been mightily impressed that the young have been on the front lines of fighting racial and economic injustices. But it should be also remembered that the young were staunch followers during the early years of Hitler, and their performance in *The Lord of the Flies* is not entirely unbelievable. This is an outright plea for the older people to speak up, while at the same time allowing the young also to express themselves.

While a naive defense of the present state of our culture is out of the question, there are still some enduring values that can be unselfconsciously espoused. Love is still better than hate; education is better than ignorance; responsibility is better than irresponsibility; competence is better than clumsiness; and concern is better than indifference. These enduring values form the core of all ethical systems, and they desperately need to be taught by the adults, and caught by the young—regardless of how poorly our own and previous generations before us have botched the problems of war, race, and poverty.

Protest

The specific quality of our society's shortcomings becomes the guide as to what the young will protest against.

245

The quotation at the beginning of this chapter epitomizes what the young protesters have found to be missing in society today. The father did not do his own thing, and he approached the end of his life not having found himself, nor had he experienced pleasures and satisfaction that were intimately his own.

"Do your own thing" is a far cry from "Deutschland Über Alles," or "My Country 'Tis of Thee." It is the subservience to any authority but the internal one that rankles the members of the current protest movement. The shape of the protest is the direct result of the kind of home and society that cradled the turned-off generation. The turning off was from the other-directed, routinized, monotony of the parents' lives. Young people had heard their middle class parents *talk* of freedom and fulfillment, but they had watched their parents *live* restrictively and ungratifyingly. And as their parents had organized their lives around schedules and outward appearances, the young just as compulsively have now cried for the expression of immediate desires and disregard of convention.

The fantasy life of the parent may have consisted in quitting work and just going fishing. The real life of the hippie has been to do just that. It is a viable hypothesis that the hippie generation is acting out the more or less unconscious wishes of their middle class parents. In fact, the father of the leader of a university campus rebellion acknowledged that he himself had been too busy with making money, but that he was proud that his son could now concern himself with political matters. The children, perhaps sensing the emptiness of many of their parents inner lives, determined to do their own thing, which meant an earnest attempt to respond to one's inner cues, and to cry out against anything that compromised any person's freedom to do the same—whether it be a military draft, a racial pre-judging, or a ban on LSD or sex.

The present reaction against the excesses of our cultural style has distinguished forerunners. As every age has its style, the reformers of any age also have a distinctive style. We would point out four forerunners who had similar styles to those currently disaffected with our age: Socrates, Diogenes, St. Francis of Assissi, and Thoreau.

Socrates and Diogenes lived in the same century and were essentially responding to the same society. Their historical epoch was as our own. Athens was continuously at war, and the economic and military pressures necessary for the survival of the state eroded the glories of the Grecian society and spirit. Human values gave way to more narrow political ones. Justice and freedom became subservient to the cause of victory. Familiarly, the poor people had to pay the greatest price in the pursuit of an unpopular war waged on foreign soil.

Socrates saw himself as a social critic, one who lived a life of allegiance to causes beyond the utilitarian ones necessary to maintain the orderliness of a decaying society. The shallow vagueness of his countrymen's lives was his target, and walking in the park with his group was doing his own thing. His life was an offense to his society, and like other distinguished social critics, before and since, he was killed by his society.

The life of Diogenes the Cynic was an even greater offense. He tuned out and turned off from his society, became as independent of it as he could be, and then attacked ruthlessly the adulterations of the human spirit that he observed around him. Contemptuous of nearly every convention, aggressively cynical, and defiant of political authority, he pursued the criticisms begun by Socrates to such an extent that he was given the nickname of "the dog." To this day, being "one of the dogs of society" bears the same stigma.

St. Francis of Assisi started on his now famous path after he stole some of his wealthy father's property in order to repair a badly damaged church. He disowned his father, his father's way of life, and the affluence of the church, swore himself to poverty, and founded a group that survived through begging. The joyous affirmation of all the free things in life, is reminiscent of the later devotees of flower power.

Thoreau is everybody's favorite hippie. He carried it off while being able to maintain a dialog with his society, in contrast to the masochistic estrangement of many other of society's boycotters. He had the familiar stance of poverty, he was intent on the cultivation of the inner man, he was appalled by his society, and refused to pay his taxes to support laws that he felt denied human freedom. Civil disobedience was one of his styles. The thoughts of the young Harvard student whose statement began this chapter are put even more eloquently by Thoreau: "I wished to live deliberately, to front only the essential facts of life, and see if I could not learn what it had to teach, and not, when I came to die, discover that I had not lived. I did not wish to live what was not life, living is dear . . . "

These four men were all offenses to society. With the possible exception of Socrates (and even he did not leave behind any palpable contributions), they were more critical than reforming. There have been other protesters at different times who were energizers, revolutionaries, and programmers. But our present four examples were so intent on the freedom of the human spirit that they may have thought it a sacrilege to advise anyone to do other than simply live life, *his own life*.

It is in this general tradition that the present student generation finds its place. As with the societies of distinguished critics of this type in the past, the present era is one marked by war, suppression of many peoples, and by the dull, gray, monotony of great conformity. With many notable exceptions of course, there are still countless numbers of persons whose souls are not their own. They have escaped the bonds of poverty for themselves and their children, but the generation that is coming behind them is naturally intent on other goals yet unreached—pleasure, satisfaction, and fulfillment.

The nature of the rebellion generally diagnoses the condition of a society. No rebellion is without its foolish excesses, but paying heed to the central message of our youthful, outraged citizenry can instruct us. We suggest that there are three central themes that encompass the complaints of the student and young adult generation: (a) the over-emphasis on property and its accumulations; (b) the relative neglect of man's inner need for psychological freedom; (c) the hypocritical difference between what people say and what they do. To summarize all three themes: young people are saying that society has neglected the honest confrontation and acceptance of certain elemental human needs, particularly the needs for love and satisfaction. Let us explore the meaning of this.

Over-Emphasis on Property

It reflects our era that the essential meaning of the Declaration of Independence has been changed from "the pursuit of happiness" to "the pursuit of property." To quote the passage more fully: "We hold these truths to be self-evident, that all men are created equal, that they are endowed by their Creator with certain unalienable Rights, that among these are Life, Liberty, and the pursuit of Happiness."

Granted the difficulty in establishing a legal definition of the right of a person to pursue happiness for himself, psychologically it is no accident that the substitute word which was selected was "property." It is certainly a psychological sign of our time, in fact, a psychological sign of this culture for some time.

Damage to a personality has often been lightly regarded; damage to a person's property is much more easily punishable. Protection of property occupies vast resources in every level of government. One cannot set fire to a building with impunity. But one can set fire to a person's inner life, and so enrage him that he is nearly rendered irrational; and this kind of assault draws scant notice The factory workers of the 19th century were, by the conditions of their employment, damaged each day. When they inflicted damage in return upon their machines, which were the symbols of their torture, they were promptly jailed.

It has taken centuries to become aware of our moral myopia, and keen observers have at last pointed out the relative advantage that property has enjoyed over persons. It is of course, still highly offensive to many to put deferential treatment to all persons on a par with deferential treatment to all property. The day must come when the pursuit of human values is more nearly equivalent to the emphasis put on property values. Young people who, as Aristotle said, have not yet learned what the lack of money means, are in a choice position for pointing out the one-sided nature of our cultural standards.

Need for Psychological Freedom

The second major theme of the young adult dissent is encompassed in the words "Do your own thing." It is frightening to consider what share of the average American adult's time is spent in doing someone else's thing. It is rare for an adult to ask himself "What do I want to do—today, this afternoon, this very moment?" The idea of immediate joy, or responding to one's innermost feelings *right now*, is generally not a part of adult life. While many young people are alienated from the mainstream of our culture, vast numbers of adults are alienated from the flow of their inner impulses and feelings. Eventually, there is the danger of losing oneself, which means no longer being able to be in contact with the answer to the question "What do I feel and want to do right now?"

Young people have very likely seen their parents suppress many of their most intimate promptings so that they could pursue the idols of current culture. To achieve some standing in the block, the neighborhood, and the world (for oneself and one's children) would seem to be the motivation for most people, and one now rarely questions whether he *likes* to do what he is doing in order to get there. Work is not thought of as bringing its own reward, but may largely be endured for the paycheck. While many millions of parents have reached their goals through hard work, their children have observed the imprisonment of their parents by this unsatisfying, monotonous toil. Parents may be hard-pressed when they must defend their style of living on the basis of seeming external necessity, rather than inner conviction. Finally, as when Peer Gynt peeled the onion and found only layer upon layer without an inner core, the adult may have lost touch with what he really feels inside.

The price is too great, the young are saying. Gaining many of the signs of success, but losing oneself, i.e., one's inner feelings and the ability and opportunity to respond to them, is a meaningless victory.

The young then, often, know what they do *not* want, namely, the relentless, blind following of someone else's pattern. For themselves, they hope to discern for each moment that act which most fully expresses their own desire. And they would hope that no one would deny them the right—not military draft, nor Washington Square policeman, nor the scornful stare of the middle class matron. The hippie ethic implies the right of the other fellow to be free also. The "love generation" could perhaps more accurately be called the tolerance generation, because their love is not necessarily outgoing and giving. But they do wish that each man have the opportunity to respond to his own drummer, i.e., they profess tolerance.

The corrective is a needed emphasis in our society. The immediacy of experience and the joy of the moment has often been lost in the pressure for future gains and rewards. The hoarding mentality has led to the careful use of one's assets and has often been productive of capital gains. But the price has sometimes been the unlived life. Sensing the extremeness of much of the prevailing cultural style, the young people have countered with "Do your own thing."

Hypocrisy

The third target is the hypocrisy of the times. The difference between word and deed can be most clearly seen by those who are not a part of the system or the establishment. That would mean observers from another culture, or from another generation, i.e., the young.

Everyone speaks of freedom, but its limits are repressively obvious if the wrong color shirt is worn to one's office. More seriously, the limit on freedom for anyone who does not "fit" because of his appearance, his ideas, or his actions is such to make a near mockery of the words that grace the base of the Statue of Liberty.

There is no question that we espouse honesty, but our actions do not support our words on the day that we file our income tax. We are for peace, but not if it means to admit that we may have made some mistakes in our past actions with regard to other nations. We of course are for helping the weaker brethren, but not if he has a struggling delicatessen and we own the supermarket. We are against discrimination, but we rather like our country club the way it is. We say that the enhancement of humanity is the highest good, but money is spent on automobiles rather than on education or medical aid. Violence is abhorrent, but hours of it are portrayed heroically during a weekend of TV. Such habits constitute our way of life.

For anyone who is not totally caught up in the system, there is enough to be angry about, and to lash out at the incredible split that exists between what we say we believe and what we do.

Perhaps what we do is not all that bad, but then certainly something more closely approximating life as it is really lived should be taught to little children. If a certain degree of dishonesty, a certain degree of conformity, a certain degree of discrimination, a certain degree of imperialism is, after all, the way in which we have found life to work out best, etc., etc., then why not say it frankly? "Tell it the way it is," yells the young adult.

Or if we do actually believe that freedom, and peace, and nonviolence are best, then we had better admit that what we have actually been doing about these things has been terribly wrong, i.e., that we have indeed been leading hypocritical lives. This seems exactly to be what the young people have been saying about their elders; that their standards are fake and false, and insultingly deceitful. The Spartan idealism of the adolescents cannot brook such ambiguity, and they loudly are crying fraud, fraud, fraud!

Summary

The disaffection of the young with our society has, at present, at least three distinguishing features. First, we live in an acting-out era which is often more physical than vocal. The generation gap is therefore highly visible. Second, many parents are keenly aware of their shortcomings as authoritative guides, and their own insecurity hampers forthright dialog with their children. Third, the errors of our current society become the rallying points for the protests of the young. Three such errors appear to be the over-emphasis on property, the relative neglect of inner psychological freedom, and the hypocrisy of saying one thing and doing something different.

19

The Social Problems of Main Street U.S.A.: The Sexual Revolution

The great question that has never been answered, and which I have not yet been able to answer, despite my 30 years of research into the feminine soul, is "what does a woman want"?   SIGMUND FREUD

The sexual revolution, like all revolutions, has its roots in past injustices. Considering the following statements, and the men who made them, the revolution was inevitable.

"There is a principle of good which has created order, light, and man, and a principle of evil which has created chaos, darkness, and woman."

"The female is female by virtue of a certain lack of qualities."

"Woman is a temple built over a sewer . . . the devil's way in."

"It is an established fact that woman is destined to live under the rule of man and has no authority in her own right."

"Woman is man gone wrong. . . . It is not the mother who

255

begets what she calls her child; she is only the nurse of the seed planted in her womb. It is the father who begets."

"Woman is given to man so that she may produce children. She is therefore his property, as the fruit tree is the property of the gardener."

These statements are not the envenomed promptings of irresponsible women-haters. They are the considered thoughts of some of the greatest thinkers of the ages, namely, in order, Pythagoras, Aristotle, Tertullian, St. Augustine, St. Thomas Aquinas, and Napoleon. Those remarks, spanning 2,300 years, are not calculated to produce kindly feelings amongst women. Nor are they conducive of charitable generosity on the part of men for woman. Considering such a history of the relationship between the sexes, it seems reasonable that at least some of the vitriol of a Susan B. Anthony stems from that heritage. Or more recently, there is a reaping of what was earlier sown when a grimly determined Nancy Sinatra sings, "These boots are made for walking . . . they're going to walk all over *you*."

But the contemporary revolt of the female is only one part of the story. It is just as apparent that another aspect of the revolution is the outgrowth of this part of our heritage.

Historical Roots of Sexual Revolution

The utter repression of sexuality in general as a subject for public attention and concern reached ridiculous proportions during the Victorian period and is a second historical root of the sexual revolution. Research on the history of sexual expression indicates that the Victorian person saw sex as positively bestial and disgusting, not to mention sinful. The period was one in which people cherished their rationality and further distrusted sexual expression because it was not under rational control. Actions or objects in any way connected with sex were not to be named, even those words which appeared in the Bible. References to childbirth were considered indelicate. When the first advertisements of underclothing appeared in Victorian newspapers, they were shown folded so as not to reveal any bifurcation. The discussion of health matters was extremely guarded, and any complaint between the neck and the knees was referred to as a "liver ailment." Rather than mention or touch the part of her body which was causing her pain, a Victorian lady would often be given a doll by her physician, and she would point to that part of the doll which corresponded with her ailing part.

"It became indelicate to offer a lady a *leg* of chicken, hence the still surviving tradition that she is offered the breast; but even this was called the 'bosom' in the nineteenth century. . . . An American refinement was the fitting of piano legs with crinolines—though not, it seems chair legs, which presumably were too thin to inspire lascivious thoughts. To conceal the piano leg is, of course, to sexualize it. . . .In the same way Victorian clothing, so far from being aloof from sex, was obsessed with it; as all periods of repression must be" (Taylor, 1954).

With such a history of the repression of overt sexuality, the current, seething return of the repressed is everywhere at hand. The facts need not be detailed here at any length. In literature, art, drama, education, advertising, movies, child-rearing practices, television, and religion—not to mention simply walking on Main Street on a warm day or skiing on a wintry one—the presence of sex is everywhere, both latent and manifest. The following are some illustrations:

It is unheard of to write a novel now without vivid bedroom scenes. Broadway and off-Broadway plays not only allude to sexual material, but some of their themes are now

257

centrally sexual. In the educational process, what is typically called sex education is just one way in which sex is handled. The sexual sphere of life is discussed in courses in history, English, and sociology, as well as in psychology, biology, and physiology. The conscious and subliminal use of sexual stimuli is an integral part of the bulk of all advertising. The phrase "recommended for mature audiences," i.e., there is a lot of sex in it, seems to be applicable to an increasing number of the better films. There is scarcely a parent any longer who is not well-informed that a child's sex play is a natural part of every age and stage, and many dolls and toys intensify a child's sexual awareness. And finally, there has been a spate of books with titles such as "Sex and the Bible."

The sexual revolution must be understood in the historical context of the suppression of women and the repression of sexuality. There have been philosophical treatises on the superiority of maleness over femaleness. Moral and ethical strictures have been prejudicially applied to women in contrast to men. They have been denied access to political and civil opportunities. Scores of males have written about the *real* nature of females, propagandizing them to accept the stereotype and helping to boost male egos. As with minors and the mentally retarded, laws protected women against themselves.

If the pendulum is swinging a bit too far recently, the reasons for it may be found in the centuries of second class identity. It is now being persuasively argued by some that there are *no* psychological differences between man and woman. Ancient notions about women being more emotional, warm, sympathetic, receptive, submissive, passive, nurturant, mystical, concrete, etc., are being assailed. Women's rights are sought, based on the conviction that since women have all the essential qualities that men have, they should therefore also have the same rights and opportunities.

Sex in Society

The needs of society have given impetus to the drive for the equality of the sexes. Russia, with its large numbers of women physicians, engineers, and farmers, could not afford to let this brain and muscle power go unused. Israel, with its need for the constant protection of its borders, finds it more expedient than most nations of the world to use its women in the army. The United States witnessed the most dramatic increase in the emancipation of women during war times when men were scarce and labor needs were high. And conversely, in time of depression women tended to return to their more traditional roles as mothers and homemakers, while the male in the family was highly regarded for his ability to keep the family away from the bread lines. The exigencies of wartime again reversed the trend of the 1930's. And the continuing uncertainties of the cold war era, together with the necessity of maintaining a large army and huge military budgets, have provided some 20 years of the climate that fosters feminine emancipation.

The change in the status of women has resulted not only from past injustices and social needs, but is also the result of women's sensitivity to their own changing expectations. The traditional caricature of a woman barefoot and pregnant (and thus immobile) cannot easily be maintained when a woman's motivations have been energized by the actual experience of emancipation as a result of education, travel, and employment. There is a snowball effect which, once set in motion, increases its momentum from its own internal weight. The woman who once enjoyed writing critiques of Spinozoa and who is now confined to writing grocery lists, will carry within her a fantasy life that impels her toward the kind of activity that she feels is fulfilling. The woman who has seen the differing styles of life that are options available else-where in her country or in her world, will experience the kind of unrest that will produce some of the changes in her own environment. In similar fashion, once the liberating freedom of employment and resultant economic independence has been felt, a previous condition of servitude will be re-sented.

A notable aspect of women's quest for freedom has been the expectation that she should also derive the maximum satisfaction from sexual experiences. The double sexual stand-ard had been so pervasive that it even encompassed which partner should be entitled to the greater pleasure during in-tercourse, and it is not surprising that it was the woman who came second. There is a widely repeated story that the 16th century Queen Elizabeth objected to her relative inability to experience sexual pleasure and sought advice and therapy in order to gain what she was missing. The counsel which she received was frank and reportedly effective. Few women, however, until more recently, have been in a position to question their lot sexually or to take the necessary steps that would enrich and cultivate their sexual responses. What Queen Elizabeth could do 400 years ago has at last become a possibility for women of more modest station now. And a woman's resignation to being a second class functionary in sexual matters is disappearing.

There is an old World War I song "How you gonna keep 'em down on the farm, after they've seen Paree?" In the rising expectations of women, the new influences not only include Paree, but a taste of education and money as well. Once hav-ing had a piece of the action, there is no turning back, short of the cataclysmic influence of a major cultural upheaval such as a depression. Women have made more strides toward freedom in the last century than in untold centuries before this one. Is it conceivable that the trend will be reversed?

We think not. Rather, those previously untouched cultures will join the march underway in the western nations.

The second provocation of the present sexual upheaval lies in the many previous generations of sexual repression. The current reaction, or possibly over-reaction, to decades of sexual repression has a complementary effect as it combines with the pendulum swing of women releasing themselves from their fetters. While the impetus toward unrestraint is strong for everyone in our culture, there is a double propellant for women.

The most complete list of the forces operating in this direction has been detailed by Vance Packard in *The Sexual Wilderness*. He lists the influences of the life-modifying sciences, e.g., the pill; social changes produced by technological innovation, e.g., the automobile; changes in age distribution of the population, i.e., more people are younger; changes created by the expansion of higher education; changes in ideals, beliefs and national mood, e.g., the declining influence of institutionalized religion; and changes in individual life produced by wars and international tensions. To these six background forces he adds the crumbling of traditional controls, the bombardment of sexual stimuli, and the disarray in moral concepts.

These powerful forces operating in society produce a situation in which sexual influences will be more pervasive along every dimension of time and space. Sexual stimulants will be experienced earlier, later more deeply and more widely, more broadly and more intensively, more overtly and more covertly. And in an era of change, the conventions by which people generally guide themselves will have less influence. The result will be more testing and experimentation and more obvious uncertainty and insecurity. While it can be readily acknowledged that women and sex have long been under restraint, the evidence is not yet definitive on what

261

guidelines should replace the old order of things. What long term effects will result from the changing relationship of the sexes in not known. The optimum degree of sexual permissiveness has yet to be determined. All the sciences, from anthropology through zoology, know some of the questions to ask, but the answers are not in yet.

We do know that the sexual union brings fulfillment and pleasure and that for too long it has been denied its rightful place in the human economy. The sexual experience of a man and a woman together involves a more intimate communication than any other human activity. All the senses become involved. The intensity of emotional experience is rarely equalled in any other behavior. While it is true that the sexual drive is the last biological drive to mature and usually the first one to diminish, neverthless the very fact of its unique power to motivate one person to reach out to another should ensure that it will never again be subjected to the repressive treatment typical in the Victorian era.

We do know that women have too long been led to believe that sex is a duty rather than a pleasure. Only recently has it become possible for them to exert a claim to the same sexual enrichment that men have expected. It may happily be expected that a more sexually fulfilled woman will express a wider beneficence in all her daily tasks than would a sexually unfulfilled woman.

We also know, however, that in no country or culture does there exist a sexual utopia. Primitive or advanced, recent or remote, there is no known situation where all has been entirely well sexually. But that should not be so surprising; neither has there ever been a utopian atmosphere economically, politically, socially, educationally, or spiritually. The quest goes on and is perhaps impossible of ultimate attainment. It is therefore reasonable to expect that wherever we now are on the cycle, or on the pendulum, complete sexual paradise will still be elusive. And as the problems continue, further attempts to produce the optimum sexual desiderata will be pursued.

We do know that the saturation point of sexual stimulation in literature, entertainment, and advertising is fast approaching. After topless dancers made their appearance in San Francisco, it was not long before they were also bottomless. At this writing, a half hour to an hour of nude dancers is a customary nightclub act, and saturation has given way to its logical successor, i.e., boredom. There seems to be no other way to go. As we have seen *Esquire* magazine abandon its racy sexual quality in favor of other editorial content, it is also possible to watch the progression of *Playboy* magazine from sheer erotism to relative philosophical sophistication. It will undoubtedly be some time before the stark nakedness of the San Francisco entertainers makes it way all across the United States, but by that time it may be predicted that a different kind of entertainment will be *au currant* on the west coast.

The movies are presently moving from erotic sexuality into the use of sex for other purposes. No longer is the audience titillated by traditional sexuality. The point of boredom was reached. Other meanings symbolic of intense inner and interpersonal conflict, ranging from suicide to murder, must now be combined with sex in order to escape the monotony of love making alone as in, for example, *Elvira Madigan*.

The use of sex in advertising seems to be subsiding. Humor and surprise, the juxtaposition of the incongruous and a gentle laughing at oneself, now awaken the audience along with the traditional pretty girl. It is possible for some ads to sell a product these days without even a single sexy creature in the picture!

We do not know what the enduring effects of the assault of sexual stimuli on our senses may be. While the evidence of sexual influences is clear, the data regarding sexual behavior is nearly as undecipherable as it has always been. Many people will not talk at all about their sexual behavior, and the motives of those who do are often suspect. Questions remain about whether sexual intercourse, for example, is becoming more widely practiced at an earlier age, or whether sex is becoming so casual as to lose some of its meaning for the partners involved. Are there statistically more homosexuals, or are there simply more statistics? And whichever is the case, what is the meaning of the more open display of homosexual behavior?

The Blurring of the Sexes

We do know that the current blurring of the differences between the sexes is an ominous sign. Inasmuch as the unequivocal identification of oneself with his own sex is like an anchor amidst the vicissitudes of life, whatever makes it difficult for succeeding generations to identity themselves sexually will probably contribute to their emotional unrest. Maleness or femaleness, of course, does not consist in long hair, short hair, beads, or flowing robes. But there is a serious question about whether it has become oppressively difficult in the competitiveness of our society to assume the more significant marks of maleness: heterosexual participation, vocational and financial responsibility, a home, and a family. Given a vacuum of male leadership, the tendency is for females to take over for the defaulting males. While the wearing of pants and boots may be nothing more than a fad, it is not so insignificant if the relationship of adult female to adult male comes more and more to resemble that of a mother to a son. While either parent can diaper a baby, there is something more fundamental at stake when a biologically smaller and

264

weaker woman gives evidence to her children that she is psychologically bigger, stronger, and more of an adult than her husband.

The sexual revolution has been mostly a change in quantity, i.e., women are less suppressed, and sexuality in general is more expressed. Such quantitative changes in a society are usually no particular cause for alarm, and in this case the effects are generally probably salutary. Analogously, tides ebb and flow, but there is a dependable constancy in the fact that there continues to be a tide which ebbs and flows.

However, the changing identification of the sexes is a qualitative change and reflects something very different than just an ebb and flow. We suggest that in western society it has never been a simple thing for a male to become a man among men. But the present struggle that faces a young adult male as he considers the assumption of the traditional masculine life tasks is of such magnitude as to render him, in many cases, nearly immobile. The simple days are gone forever when the manly tasks were confined to adapting oneself to a routine structure of work and home—and where the expectations in each were both attainable and well defined. In contrast, consider today what a perceptive young man is called upon to know and do. He is alerted from preadolescence to the usual American dream of surpassing his father educationally and economically. He is further sensitized to his responsibilities in solving the problems of war, poverty, racial injustice, the quality of urban life, overpopulation, and education in a world where the sum total of man's knowledge can double in just a few years Such demands are not felt quite so keenly by women, because their primary duty is still seen as the bearing and raising of children, roles which have changed relatively little, being safeguarded by the biological differences of the two sexes.

The expectations of manhood now place such inordinate demands on an adolescent and young adult male that very often the result is that the young man feels woefully inadequate to the task before him. In consequence we witness large numbers of young persons who do not join the race for "success." The dropouts from middle class society have many motives, but a role that they are certainly rejecting is the one that demands that the young man pursue the kind of education that will lead to a well-paying job, and take upon himself the responsibilities of a wife, children, and a home. Perhaps it is felt that the struggle is not worth the rewards to be gained, and/or both the quest and the goal are without the kind of meaning that currently "turns on" a young person. However, we suggest that at least one of the reasons for dropping out is that the attainment of a story book type of masculine ideal, i.e., the conquering hero, is so demanding during the present time that it dissuades many young men from even making the attempt.

Every aspect of our society, even in childhood, is marked by competition. If a boy wants to have a little game of baseball after school, he most likely will have to become involved in the structure of the Little League. If he wants to go on a hike, the organization of the Boy Scouts may be his solution. If he has a yen for a college education, he has to be alerted at an early age to the realities of the college entrance examination. Whatever his interests and ambitions, he probably will have to relate himself to an organized process of pursuing his aims—which will involve him in some sort of competitive struggle. While the male tries to test himself against other males as a means of demonstrating his own self-worth, the present highly organized schemes for competitively regimenting young people is having the negative consequence of inducing many young people to give up on the whole system. "If that is what it takes to be a 'man,' who needs it" is the refrain.

There are many ways to drop out. Homosexuals have opted for the less demanding style of relating only to the members of their own sex, who are "safer," with whom involvements are more casual, and with whom the binding responsibilities of children do not result. There are the passive-aggressive methods of dropping out, notably making an attempt at something, but failing or flunking out. Here we witness the school failure who tries, but does not quite succeed at getting passing marks, or who is not quite able to live away from home for extended periods. We note also marriages which survive for only a few months and, for lack of surmounting the difficulties of the initial adjustment period, end in separation.

We note also another male escape from our culture, namely the quest for vocational security rather than adventuresome conquest. If a job was not necessarily chosen for its safety factor in the first place, often a man will experience the stress of competition within a short time and then decide that he wants no more of it. Conservative stability then becomes the style of his life, and those places that provide refuge, emotionally, socially, vocationally, and spiritually, provide surcease from the contests that he sees in life all about him.

"Making it," for many men, has become the impossible dream. When a man feels unequal to the task, the result is that he feels less of a man. He has a declining self-regard, he resents the agencies which he feels make him inadequate, and his fears about coping with life mount. The expectations of manhood that confront him place so many demands on him that there are produced intense dependency needs, resulting in the escapes that are noted above, and also in a search for strong persons on whom to lean. In many cases, it will be toward a woman that a man will turn for someone to bear him up in the face of the keenly competitive economic and social struggles that face him each day. The result is a home and family in which the husband turns to his wife for nurturance, and the wife more and more becomes a mothering figure, both to husband and children. The wife engages in the daily tasks of managing the home, and the children may observe that it is the female who is the executive director in most of the decisions that affect their lives.

From the woman's side, the retreat of the man is complemented by her own rising aspirations, and the observed weakness of the male motivates her to take over even more. The overall picture is of an increasingly assertive female and an increasingly passive male. It is this blurring of the sexual roles that carries disheartening prospects for those children yet unborn who will face the task of learning to identify themselves sexually. With a stable identification, life comes easily, and more can be made of it; lacking this central guidepost, a host of decisions become conflict-ridden and complicated.

The blurring of the sexes is the most serious aspect of an otherwise orderly sexual revolution. The demands of society, the immensity of the expectations placed upon a sensitive person, together with an undercurrent of despair resulting from the ever-present threat of nuclear destruction—all these tempt a man to withdraw rather than struggle. And unfortunately, unheroic men attract aggressive females, who together develop a succeeding generation of males who are often further deficient in their heroic qualities.

Needed is a sensitive awareness of why many men are not choosing the manly roles of courage and responsibility. There are good and sufficient reasons for the numbers of young men who are choosing not to join in pursuing the style of life of their fathers and grandfathers. What is needed is a conviction that never before in history have society's demands been so numerous and complex. It is necessarily going to take longer for a young man to find himself. It will require more effort for him to orient himself in the face of the life options open to him. While an 18 year old girl may be ready to do what is expected of her, namely, get married and have children, an 18 year old boy is probably years away from committing himself to be her partner. Educational aims, military service, and predicting his ability to negotiate an inflationary economy will give him ample cause for moving cautiously. And years later when he has matured to the point of family and vocational commitment, he may again be facing conflicts of an order of complexity far greater than what his background has equipped him to face. In many ways, there is no specific preparation for what modern man now faces, because life has never been this way before.

In offering this description, we have reference particularly to the upwardly mobile, middle class American, as he deals with the abstractions of social problems, economic stability, the betterment of his own future, as well as the meaning and purpose of life. All the options are open to him, or at least so he believes. Consequently the pressures on him are great. The possibility of mastering life beckons him during his working day, while the temptation to retreat from life when at home in the midst of his family beckons him at night. In contrast, the course of the upper class person's life is remarkably settled, and the restrictions placed upon the lower class man also serve to exempt him from the role confusion which is so evident in the middle class man.

Inasmuch as the demands on modern man are greater than before, in many ways a man will appear less manly, i.e., less able to cope easily with the challenges that confront him. He keenly senses the gap between what is expected of him and what he is able to create with his own life, and doubts about his masculinity grow rampant. He may then also feel less capable of coping with the women in his midst who, because of their changing status, may also present him with new challenges.

We suggest that it is this combination of factors which is playing a crucial role in the current blurring of sexual role identification in America. As this process develops, we may be faced with a society in which maleness and femaleness have lost much of the distinctive meaning that guides the succeeding generation in finding its way to fulness of living and loving. In understanding the process at work in our society, it will become more possible to be charitable to young persons who live in the midst of challenges that their elders never had to face. It should be possible to disengage the concept of masculinity from those habits of living that are merely cultural accretions. And it is conceivable that our society will recognize a variety of ways in which one can be manly and responsibly productive apart from the puritan model.

At the same time the fear that men harbor within themselves of domineering women must be recognized and dealt with. And the contempt on the part of women for what they perceive as a "weak man" must be understood and changed. The responsibility lies on both sides, and the issue at stake has immense consequences, among which are the stability of the family and therefore, also, the stability of society.

Men at every age need the kind of ongoing education which will equip them to cope with the quandaries of living with themselves and others in this kind of society. This will, it is hoped, encourage human beings to engineer the removal of social evils that breed poverty, prejudice, and violence on national and international levels. Such objectives call for a kind of therapeutic-educational milieu in which men's efforts are spent in retooling their interpersonal and vocational skills in the light of changing social conditions. The notion of completing one's education at age 25 will be abandoned. Part of working will be intrinsically educational. There will be less emphasis on a book-learning model, and more emphasis on an experiential model, guided by "trainers" whose skills will include their ability to be generalists in helping persons to become more accessible to their fellow men and also more accessible to their own inner creative and spiritual promptings. Education for living will be as much of the daily process of living as eating one's daily bread. The relationships between the sexes will be part of the ongoing training. Circumstances, and the cycles of history will no longer be so fully in control of how a man is to be manly and a woman to be womanly. The conscious appraisal and re-appraisal of how best to draw upon both the similarity and the differences between the sexes will create an atmosphere in which both can be most fully human, while he is most fully masculine and she is most fully feminine.

Summary

It has seemed natural to center our attention on young people while examining in these last three chapters several of the current problems of our society. This is not to say that young people are the problem, but only that their behavior—their reaction to society—illustrates the problems that exist. It was Woodrow Wilson who said that the use of a university was to make young gentlemen as unlike their fathers as possible. By that standard, universities of today are admirably fulfilling their function! In these chapters we have explored the how and the why of the young adults' violence, sexual behavior, and cultural discontent.

It is impossible not to have some considerable sympathy for both the young critic and for his criticisms. It is well to recall the Hindu fable of the six blind men and the elephant. Each of the blind men felt a different part of the elephant: The one who touched the elephant's side thought the elephant was like a wall; another in feeling the tusk reported that the elephant was like a spear. The trunk was like a snake, the ear like a fan, the knee like a tree, and the tail like a rope. The fable concludes "though each was partly in the right, all were in the wrong."

Now the elephant is our universe. We each, even in our wisest moments, have a grasp of only a piece of the elephant—a piece of the universe. That is, we do not understand all of reality. We need the eyes and ears and touch of the other fellow. It is the part of wisdom to listen to the young for their description of their piece of the universe, for they have often had the fresh vision that has enabled them to see the crucial issues of the era. Since they are the heirs of their parents, it is no wonder that they often need not fight the same battles that preoccupied their parents. The young stand on our shoulders, and therefore they can often see further—or into different corners.

We conclude with these words of Sir Winston Churchill: "Come on now all you young men, all over the world . . . Twenty to twenty-five! These are the years! Don't be content with things as they are. 'The earth is yours and the fulness thereof' Enter upon your inheritance, accept your responsibilities. Raise the glorious flags again, advance them upon the new enemies, who constantly gather upon the front of the human army, and have only to be assaulted to be overthrown. . . . You will make all kinds of mistakes; but as long as you are generous and true, and also fierce, you cannot hurt the world or even seriously distress her. She was made to be wooed and won by youth. She has lived and thrived only by repeated subjugations."

20

Exercises in Maturity: Twelve Healthy Values One May Profitably Pursue

One's own self is well hidden from one's self: of all mines of treasure, one's own is the last to be dug up.
FRIEDRICH WILHELM NIETZSCHE

All of human behavior is purposeful and determined: getting an ice cream cone, a preference for the color red, kicking oneself in the shins when walking past the footstool, choosing to become a psychoanalyst, voting the Republican ticket, wearing rumpled suits, humming "We Shall Overcome." This is a simple way of saying human behavior is motivated by impulses and needs.

It is the ideal to understand that any one act or feeling or thought is a parcel of a much broader design. In this book we have chosen to call this broad design by the name "personality structure." In human life, personality patterns are constantly operating; they are the structure out of which issue the individual acts of making love, buying a loaf of bread, or getting a traffic ticket.

It is part of the wisdom of living to gain understanding about how the events of one's life are not capricious, but rather related to definite causes. Such wisdom enables a person to perceive in the ventures of his life a pattern with a design. The significant forces of his life can be seen in relation to his isolated deeds. This wisdom forms the most reliable basis for changing the conduct of one's life.

We are currently witnessing a depreciation of insight as a moving force toward personality change. It is true that many people *know* more than they *do*. A person may "understand" why he is the way he is, but be unable to change. Because some people cannot always use their insight constructively, some authorities negate its value and substitute other, more forceful measures in the form of behavioral reinforcements. These behavioral therapies attempt to bypass the history and development of a complaint and minimize the awareness of the motives for "choosing" a neurotic symptom. Direct intervention designed to change the overt behavior becomes the focus of the treatment. These new therapeutic ventures are showing promise, but they should be seen as complementary, rather than substitutes for understanding the bases of personality development.

It is not impossible that the nature of personality development, structure, pathology, and adaptation will some day become the daily fare of school children, in addition to learning the dates of English kings and the Pythagorean theorem. The content of this book, for example, was as unknown as nuclear science when the basic curriculum of our schools was established. But as nuclear science has made its way into the elementary schools, so too, someday will the subject of psychodynamics.

This is all by way of saying that *insight* about personality functioning is the basis on which rests one of the major devices for the eventual betterment of man's condition—intrapersonal, interpersonal, intercommunity, interracial, and international. At some future time there will be a common body of psychodynamic understanding that will permit a person, and groups of persons, to apply themselves more effectively to the task of self-understanding. While understanding alone is not sufficient, it forms a foundation for a person to repudiate those habits that are in need of change. We, therefore, present below five themes around which self-understanding can systematically be pursued. It goes without saying that the most effective search for this insight will be based on a broad appreciation of all the major principles of personality functioning.

An Organized Outline
for Self-Observation

There are five conditions of life that are especially rich sources of information about the nature of one's personality composition.

1. *Observing the relationship between the onset of some emotional distress and provocative incidents in one's milieu.* A young man noticed that for the previous two weeks he had been very nervous when driving his car. Proceeding from a side street into a busy avenue made him tense, and he feared that he would fail to see an approaching car or truck bearing down on him. The logical questions for him to ask himself would be: "What was happening in my life about two weeks ago? What was going on? Why right *then* did I get nervous while driving, whereas before I was relaxed?" Persistent effort would reveal something in his life that produced his

fears of being attacked and hurt. If his self-questioning rests on a good sense of his basic life style, he will be able to relate the current fears of being hurt to previous occasions when he had similar excessive fears—perhaps of being beaten up on the street, or having his wallet stolen. Perhaps he will not understand the full meaning of his fear, but if he recognizes that his fear began after he had received a promotion at work, just as once before he had had an upsurge of fears after buying a house, then at least he will not feel that he is the victim of entirely adventitious events.

2. *Observing circumstances that boost or lower feelings about oneself.* A person may be aware that he feels better as soon as he gets alone in his basement workshop, where he has all his tools neatly ordered and where no one will bother or make demands on him. He may then interpret detachment as a device that brings him some peace. He may also realize that he can only stay in his shop for an hour or so, after which he begins to feel depressed and eager to try once more to establish contact with others. Someone else may find that he experiences great release in arguing with someone and establishing his own superiority, but that this leads eventually to a sense of isolation. A third person experiences a boost in his own good feelings when he has a mutually engaging conversation with a friend. He realizes that such contacts are constructive for him, so that he pursues the kind of dialog that brings satisfaction to others and to himself.

3. *Observing the form of one's relationship with people.* It is a rule of thumb that people usually become more upset in relation to people than they do in relation to things. Therefore it is particularly fruitful to ask a host of questions about the quality of one's interpersonal activities. "What tensions do I get with people? What kind of people do I like and dislike? Are these tensions with all people or only with certain kinds of people? What do people do to upset me, and in what

ways do I get upset? What do I do to upset them, or to get myself upset when I am with them? What do I do and what do they do that tends to make me angry? What problems do I have with my parents, my mate, my children, my boss, associates at work, authorities, people in general? Do I tend to treat anyone in a way similar to the pattern that I established with my father, mother, siblings? How is my reaction to people above me, below me, equal to me? What are my expectations when I meet a very attractive person of the opposite sex? What are my expectations when the boss calls me, or when I get a telegram, or when I get a Christmas present?

One man discovered that he thought of himself as a dirty old man when he tried to strike up a conversation with a girl. A salesman sensed that he regarded himself as an unwanted intruder whenever he walked into an office. A husband expected to be rejected if he approached his wife sexually. A woman looking for a fur coat anticipated that the salesman would try to deceive her into buying last year's model which actually did not happen. It takes little imagination to see how these negative expectations would sabotage a person in his quest for successful interpersonal relations if he acted on them. When a person gains understanding of how habitually he uses the same self-defeating patterns, even against his own better judgment, he realizes that any change in himself will require disciplined concentration and action.

4. *Observing daydreams or night dreams.* A useful outline for observing the meaning of one's day or night dreams includes these three questions: What is my feeling about myself in the dream? What problem am I wrestling with in the dream? By what means do I reach, or fail to reach, a solution to the problem of the dream?

Recurring dreams are particularly significant because they represent a continuing core problem of one's life. Again, whenever possible the dreamer should attempt, if he can, to relate the content of his dreams to what is happening in his life at that time. One man found that he had recurring dreams of bloodshed but that those dreams only recurred after he had made an attempt to assert himself by asking for a raise in pay or by going out with a girl that he liked. He was much reassured to discover that his frightful dreams were actually evidence that he was indeed being himself, but that he still had some old childish fears about standing up for himself.

Although everyone dreams every night, the ability to re-member dreams varies from person to person. And with all self-analyzing techniques, the ability to profit from observing one's remembered dreams will also vary markedly, because in many instances dreams are so highly symbolized and dis-torted that only a trained professional person can make sense out of them.

5. *Observing resistances to putting one's insights into action.* A person who continually lied to cover up his short-comings knew that he lied because he felt inadequate about his accomplishments. He knew that he was passive and that it was easier for him to say to his boys that the baseball game was sold out, rather than to go to the ticket office, buy tickets, and attend the game. But his lies further served to devalue his self-esteem, and with lowered self-esteem he took less initiative in life, and hence lied even more to cover his omissions. And the cycle repeatedly reinforced itself. The recent increase in the use of conditioning and behavior therapies for the alleviation of such disastrous cycles is based on the correct premise that every time the person changes any aspect of his cycle, he will be strengthened. Returning to our example, if he can actually go to the ticket office, or refrain from lying about it, he will feel better about himself, which in turn will breed more positive actions. But there will be

inevitable resistance when one tries to stop neurotic patterns. And there will be tension and fear when one faces a challenge that formerly has been evaded. When delaying and avoidance continue to occur, it is well to question the reasons for the delay and ask why one is afraid—and then to take heart and deliberately challenge the fear to see if it can be overcome.

The disciplined practice of these principles of self-observation can lead to progressive growth. Patterns have to be recognized and revised if one is to achieve more satisfying goals in life. But as everyone knows, the habits of the years give ground grudgingly and slowly. Ideally, however, the process of personality understanding and growth is marked by several discrete features: There is the awareness that one's problems do not occur fortuitously but are intimately connected with the events, and especially the human interactions of one's life. For a given individual, there is a certain quality of human event that generates anxiety, conflict, and stress. These phenomena lead next to a searching for the genesis and history of these patterns. It is not impossible to see how these patterns operated as far back as a person can remember in his life—perhaps even his very earliest memory contains something of the same thing. Seeing the conditions under which his fears originated, and under which they are now retriggered, he may next determine whether he can be more the master of his life, rather than a victim of it. Could he be different from the way he has always known himself to be? And ever so slowly, he challenges one habitual, childish fear at a time, pushing himself to break out of the prison of his neurotic, self-defeating patterns. Success breeds success, and victory leads to victory. Defeats are re-analyzed in accord with their place in his psychic structure. Seeing himself defeated by the same old enemies, he is buoyed up in knowing that his formulations about his personality are correct, and he is encouraged to fight on. He increasingly expresses a claim to a new life, he finds himself able to be more expressive, and his self-recriminations diminish. The executive capacity of his ego expands and he gratifies more of his needs. Feeling less frustrated in life, and therefore less angry, he can enter into relationships with people with more openness, and a greater ability to share.

These are idealistic goals, but they represent a guide along the way toward greater self-understanding and richer living. Fidelity to the practice of self-observation, as pursued along the five channels noted above, together with the actual translation of insight into action, can be a lifelong quest marked by high adventure, and notable results.

The knowledge of one's psychodynamics (which literally means psychic motivations) continues to constitute the surest path to self-understanding, and hopefully, to mature behavior. The maturity engendered by self-understanding can be augmented by the conscious adoption of a set of human values that are conducive to life, and not to personality morbidity. Everyone lives by a set of values that support his actions and give meaning to his conduct. As we have seen in Chapters Three and Four, these values are gleaned from interactions with significant parental agencies, from group identifications, and from cultural standards. The examination of one's value system constitutes another of the tasks productive of personal maturity.

Twelve Healthy Values
One May Profitably Pursue

We present here a dozen propositions that encompass many of the marks of a healthy value system. These are values that are rooted in a realistic conception of one's inner world and one's outer environment—based particularly on the findings resultant from dynamic thought and practice. These values have a certain empirical validity, based on what has proven to be conducive to the growth of personal maturity, i.e., the ability to love and do productive work. It would be presumptuous to call the following propositions a philosophy of life, but they are at least operational guidelines for many of the events of one's daily existence. Obviously they are no substitute for professional help where this is required. But even where a person seeks such help, or has already obtained it, these values may supplement what he has learned about himself and enable him to hasten his progress.

1. *One's past can be isolated from the present.* The picture of the self-pitying adult who bewails the untoward influences inflicted upon him as a child is a common scene among those who have a smattering of psychological acumen. It is true that every person is victimized by his past which operates as a mischief monger in the present. But a good adjustment presupposes modulating one's activities to present-day considerations rather than resigning to promptings inspired by the blind repetition of the sort of experiences that were commonplace in childhood. One may have been beaten down in childhood. There may not have been enough of any good thing then. But the world is full of resources for any adult who has the opportunity to learn how to avail himself of those riches.

The self-defeating patterns that persist in adulthood can be seen as an intrinsic part of an honest childhood attempt to survive psychologically. This perception should form one of the incentives for change. But among some individuals it provides an excuse for rationalizing his errors on the basis of the irreparable damage that was done to him by his parents who are responsible for all his trouble. This is self-pity, and there is scarcely any emotional state which has fewer virtuous consequences than does self-pity.

While early deprivations certainly contribute to adult insecurity and devalued self-esteem, they continue to contaminate adult adjustment and hence must be overcome. Ruminations on unfortunate childhood experiences are indulgences that one cannot afford. They poison one's present life. While countless self-pitying persons can be cited, so also are there countless examples of persons who have risen above early misfortunes. It is possible to restrain oneself when one begins to dwell on past events over which one had no control. While one was not responsible for what happened to him as a child, he is responsible for perpetuating these patterns in the present. Through working at it, one can be released from the bonds of the past.

This explanation is not a simplistic statement to the effect that every person can simply pull himself up by bootstraps if he would only make an effort. Great potential for change is indeed present in every person. And while the importance of individualized effort is being made here, some conditions of personality impoverishment will require the help of outside persons and agencies. To say to the chronically beaten man "snap out of it" is as useless as telling a man with appendicitis to perform surgery upon himself.

2. *Tension and anxiety can be regulated.* Something positive can be done about feelings of emotional distress. The first device is to know why the tension arises. Is it the immediate situation? Is it something that happened before? Is it something that will be happening? Knowledge of the source of the tension focuses the approach in dealing with the tension, which enables one to feel that he is not helpless. He gets a greater sense of mastery, which is the direct opposite of anxiety. Knowing that this was the first approach to dealing with any untoward feeling, a young woman became aware

that she was immediately depressed and tense after meeting the wife of her husband's new boss. Asking herself why, she sensed that the boss's wife was a woman who was plagued by many vague physical and psychological complaints—bitter about life, resentful of the demands on her—and who wanted only to retreat from contacts with people. Her goal was for her husband to retire, which she imagined would solve all her problems. The younger woman sensed that she was dealing with the image of her mother, a woman who felt that the lot of a female was to be a beast of burden from which there was no escape short of death. She had tried to convince her daughter that this was the kind of life to which she must also resign herself. The daughter had fought to escape this image, but upon being confronted suddenly with another mother figure in the person of the boss's wife, she was thrown back into the same repressive atmosphere of her childhood. As she understood what was going on in her, she was able to revive her spirits through realizing that her own life was hers to do with as she pleased, and that the life that her mother had chosen for her had no power over her as an adult.

While many anxieties can be handled by this kind of on-the-spot insight, it is realistic to remember that tension and anxiety are inherent parts of living. There is no escape from them. Everyone must accept the fact that not all anxiety can be dissipated, regardless of how mature or insightful one may be. The fact is that some anxiety *must* be tolerated—that one will have to live with *some* anxiety. This anxiety, from time to time, will give rise to various emotional and physical symptoms. A person may begin to perspire suddenly, he may get butterflies in his stomach, or he may find himself with an aching back. He may intermittently be plagued by unwanted thoughts, or needless fears, or feel unduly blue on Monday mornings. But it is well to remember that these feelings are common to most of the human race, and they do not mean that life is caving in. One can remind oneself that this, too, shall pass away. When one is unable to put a finger on the cause of the anxiety, one will nonetheless be able to recall previous incidents of having safely passed through conditions that, at the time, seemed terribly upsetting.

While in the midst of an anxious spell, the soothing effects of temporary escape should be borne in mind. Outside activities that take one's mind off oneself are effective, whether they are undertaken for the purpose of forgetting a toothache, or dealing with the anxiety about tomorrow's job interviews. Many minor emotional upsets are self-healing, and an hour in front of the television, for example, may relieve the sense of distress while the underlying emotional equilibrium is being restored.

3. *A certain amount of hostility can be tolerated.* There has never been a person who did not become angry. It is understandable then, that one will occasionally become irritated and annoyed and resentful. If this can be understood, the anger need not lead to unwarranted behavior nor emotional symptoms. Exploring the reasons for one's anger will in itself serve as a release valve for these powerful feelings. One can learn to permit oneself to feel angry as the occasion justifies it. *Unrecognized* anger, however, is potentially damaging to oneself and to others. The outward expression of anger will depend on what the situation will tolerate. A useful guideline to follow is that anger can be expressed in such a way that it does not hurt oneself nor damage others. There are many constructive uses for the expression of anger, but generally such expression should be proportionate to the exacerbating condition of injustice. The release of anger can be accomplished directly, or simply through loud talking when one is alone, or through muscular exertion. Singing in the bathtub, yelling that the ump is blind, or cursing at snarled traffic are releases that are readily available. In spite

of such discharges, one will still remain angry, particularly in situations where the exercise of one's freedom is limited. But so long as the anger is kept in hand, while recognizing that it exists, it will not be harmful to oneself. Everyone has to live with a certain amount of anger.

4. *Some frustration and deprivation are essential parts of life.* No person can ever have all his needs met. There is no such thing as a continuously completely gratified person. The analogy of the ball player's batting average has been helpful to many people: no player hits the ball every time at bat. But a decent average is enough to make one content. Whether it is completing a successful business deal, enjoying a movie, having a train arrive on time, or experiencing simultaneous orgasms, there is a certain batting average with which one can be pleased. In no venture of life, worthy to be called challenging, is there apt to be an average of 100 percent. That kind of a record existed only back in the days of simple spelling tests in grammar school. One learns to be frustrated to some extent, and can live with it. The philosophical baseball player was utterly correct about life as well as his schedule when he said "You win some, you lose some, and some are rained out."

5. *Many elements in one's environment can be corrected; one can adjust to other irremediable situations.* Years of psychotherapeutic practice have led to the unequivocal conviction that a given individual's life and environment are far more malleable than he has believed. One needs to be reminded of his responsibility to remedy any alterable factors in his life situation. Once the area of trouble is defined, the next thing is to figure out what can be done about it. A plan of action is to be developed. The steady application of this plan for a day, a week, sometimes for years, will almost invariably bring measurable results. Hopelessness is in the eye of the beholder, especially when it comes to one's interper-

sonal environment. No matter how hopeless things appear to the individual himself, the outside appraiser will often have a supplementary view that is worth hearing. To keep working away is often the key to success. Simply because a certain task requires 100 distinct operations does not mean that it is impossible; it only takes longer. Ingrained in everyone should be the firm belief in the changeability of both man and nature. The patient's words "Such an accomplishment would be impossible for me" have proven to be wrong so many times in a therapist's office that those words now bring a smile to the face of any psychotherapist.

The other side of the coin is that no matter how one may wish to correct certain conditions, practical considerations may prevent doing much about them. For example, one may have to learn to live with a handicapped child or a sick husband or wife. One's financial condition may be irreparably marginal. There are certain situations, proverbially like death and taxes, with which all people have to cope, and from which there is no escape. If a person engages in unrealistic dreaming, or hopes for magic (i.e., a pill will be discovered, or "someone will leave me a million dollars") the realities of his life will be even more frustrating. The appreciation of the ambiguities, the ironies, even the accidental injustices of life, can lead to a balanced view of the necessity for changing some things, and of the necessity for accepting other things. When the frustrating conditions of life persist, it is well consciously to remind oneself that one must and can live with them, and to resolve not to let those things destroy oneself. Everyone has the responsibility to carry certain indissoluble troubles. Part of the solution lies in not responding to trouble like a weathervane. One can concentrate on the fulfilling aspects of his life and minimize the troublesome.

6. *Will power helps one to stop engaging in destructive activities.* Again we meet one of the unfortunate side effects

of psychological sophistication: a person may have the idea that he is under the influence of unconscious monsters that he cannot control. He will then rationalize that he was inexorably acting out his "automatic repetition-compulsions." Actually, the more that he knows about those repetition compulsions, the easier it is to stop them. He can enlist the cooperation of his will power to help inhibit himself. When one knows that a situation will be bad for him, it is well to muster one's forces of self-control in order to prevent the unfortunate deed from taking place. There are substitute solutions that are less destructive, even though they may not be so immediately gratifying. Since a certain amount of deprivation and frustration is normal in everyone's life, it is a complimentary sign when one can bear one's frustrations without being victimized by them. Further, the understanding of any self-destructive act involves knowing why and how one needs and wants to punish himself. This hair-shirt approach to life can often be deliberately halted. Anytime that a person observes himself acting masochistically, it should be a signal to stop right there in his tracks and figure out what he is doing to himself.

A woman found herself becoming so enraged at her children that she would spank them until she was so fatigued that she could no longer lift her arm. Only then would she stop the spanking. At times she counted the continuous hits, and the number would often run up to over a hundred. While she felt a sense of release when she started to spank a child, afterwards she felt terrible remorse and was fully aware of what damage she was doing to her young, impressionable children. But she said that she could not stop the spankings: the children misbehaved fiendishly, she felt they needed to be punished, and no other outlet for her anger could possibly relieve her of what she was feeling inside. Her therapist asked her to stop the spanking, because they both knew that in her best judgment she wanted to stop. In

287

the meantime they would work on the factors that caused her to feel so angry. She insisted that it would be impossible to stop, and refused even to try. But eventually she gained strength from the fact that there was another person beside herself who wanted to help her stop. By the exercise of her will power she first reduced the number of times that she hit each child, and later found substitute releases for her anger. At the same time she began to see how she identified her children with her own sister with whom she had had a spiteful and unsuccessful rivalry during her childhood. She was then able to provide her children with loving attention instead of going to them only when they were "bad."

7. *Unreasonable demands on oneself can be stopped.* What prompts one to push himself beyond the limits of his capacities, or to set too high standards for himself? The cause of such behavior is not usually an ordinary desire to do a good job or to test one's abilities. It is more likely to be some parental pressure that he is trying to meet, or to be a compulsive effort to make up for some deeply felt inadequacy. Perfectionistic standards are impossible to attain and are ultimately self-defeating. The appraisal of oneself may be carried out with impossibly superior models as comparisons. If one chooses to do so, one can always find a Bach or an Einstein or a Schweitzer as a rival, and of course he must then feel woefully inadequate about oneself. It is more realistic to recall that persons have a variety of gifts, that all people have their assets and liabilities, that each person is unique in his ability to do something that no one else can do, but so also is he less able to do something that someone else can do. It is possible, of course, through inordinate efforts to accomplish the nearly impossible. But such efforts are more than likely neurotically based, and therefore will be accomplished at enormous personal cost, and bring an illusory victory when once reached. The well-functioning machine or

organism has a natural rhythm of its own which, while being productive, does not tear itself to pieces. Efforts that result in tearing oneself to pieces are unreasonable demands on the self. In gradual or sudden martyrdom, the burden of proof is on the subject to demonstrate that he is not destroying himself because of his own neurotic needs, rather than for the accomplishment of some great and noble purpose, as he may rationalize. There should be the pursuit of one's goals, but without going to self-destructive extremes.

8. *A devalued self-image must be challenged.* Often an individual retires on the investment of his conviction of self-devaluation. What need is there for him to make any effort if he is so constitutionally inferior that all of his best intentions and well-directed activities will lead to naught? Such attitudes indicate that one is utilizing his self-devaluation as a destructive implement to bolster his helplessness and perhaps to sponsor dependency. In this way he makes capital out of a handicap.

The awareness of what one is getting out of running himself down can be the beginning of a more realistic self-appraisal. It helps a person to believe that his low opinion of himself is not necessarily objectively true, but exists in order to accomplish these other goals. Pointing up one's realistic assets will not succeed in destroying the negative view, but it may begin to help oneself avoid the despair of feeling completely hopeless. One may focus on instances of his successes. Most people can succeed at an activity when they are vitally interested in it. The converse is also true, and the realization of this fact may give one a different basis for evaluating his past record.

A woman with a deep sense of inferiority and lack of self-confidence was exhorted to add to her knowledge of the history of her own neighborhood, with which she was fascinated. At gatherings she was emboldened to talk about her speciality when an appropriate occasion presented itself. She found herself the center of attention among her neighbors who were eager to learn what armies had marched at one time in their own back yards. This led to membership in historical societies and museums and provided her with social contact and with a way of doing things for others which built up a more generous estimate of herself.

Another woman, keenly embarrassed about her nearly total lack of formal education resulting from a long series of childhood illnesses, desperately wanted more schooling and the feeling of success that would accompany it. To pursue even a high school equivalency test seemed intolerably gauche to her. But her interest and ability in dancing led her to attend dancing classes and schools, which fortunately had no academic prerequisites. Her self-regard increased to the point that this unschooled girl eventually started her own school of the dance.

Logic obviously cannot convince a person with significant inferiority feelings that he has merit. But unless a proper assessment is made of his existing virtues, the person will be retarded in correcting his distorted self-image. Persons devalue themselves because they were "taught" to do so, most likely by insecure parents or siblings who needed to belittle those around them in order to enhance their own status. With this understanding of how a person began to have a distorted self-image, he can often question whether or not he still has valid reasons for feeling inferior. His objective qualities may be at least equal to the norm, but he persists in his self-devaluation as a means of punishing himself because of guilt, or as a way of making people feel sorry for him, or of rendering himself helpless and dependent. As neurotic, self-destructive acts can be stopped as they began, so also the use of will power can lead to the halting of self-abasing evaluations. There is no one best nor worst person. All persons are different, and each person has been provided with enough talents to provide a basis for a reasonable self-affirmation.

9. *Deriving enjoyment from life should be a daily pursuit.* In the story of The Great Stone Face, the young village lad who habitually directed his attention to the heroic, mountainous visage, eventually developed a resemblance to the model he had so long contemplated. The psychological truth of this story also has a corollary, namely, that one can also reinforce negative qualities through habitually dwelling on them. The boy who believes that he is clumsy, and who thinks about it a lot, will be more apt to act clumsily. The constant memory of past embarrassments and the reliving of unfortunate experiences can predispose one toward a mental set that will induce that same behavior again. If we identify ourselves with our failures, we enhance our failing proclivities.

Focusing on troubles and displeasures in one's existence can deprive a person of joys that are his right as a human being. Rather, it is important to reap out of each day the maximum possible joys. There is a need to get the grimness out of one's daily life, and to see the humor, even the folly of many things. Humor has been described as the juxtaposition of the incongruous, e.g., the pompous, top-hatted man slips on a banana peel. Surely there are enough humorous incongruities in everyone's life to lighten the terrible sobriety with which many persons pursue their existence. For example, it takes but a moment of thought to enjoy the basic silliness of the way that a man's suitcoat and vest are made. Women's fashions, of course, are nothing if they are not incongruous.

Each day can be seen as an event filled with major and minor bounties to be appreciated and savoured. An unhappy remnant of the puritan ethos is that the focus of pleasure has often been placed in the future. Get ready for some future event, prepare for the morrow, save for the rainy day—these maxims are often pursued to such an extent that the joys of this very moment are disregarded. The one-sided struggle to reach future goals will leave one unfit to enjoy the goals once they are reached, if indeed they ever are. This is the day we have been given, let us rejoice and be glad *this day*. There are more than ample resources in one's current situation which make possible considerable enjoyment, if one will determine to focus upon them, and to avoid negative recriminations and forebodings.

10. *One's social role can be accepted.* Every adult has a varying role to play: male or female, husband or wife, parent, taxpayer, home owner. He must on occasion relate to authorities, and at other times be the authority himself. He has obligations in every sphere of his life. Though he may feel immature, dependent, hostile, or hypocritical, he must still try to fill his expected role as completely as he can. A mother may feel uncertain about her own ability to guide her daughters; a member of the church's building committee may find it hard to believe that he is being asked to play an influential part in determining whether the church should build a new $100,000 education building; a woman may wonder what right she has to stand up and tell others at P.T.A. about pornography at the corner newsstand; an employee may bridle at having to compliment his boss at a testimonial dinner, when he would rather tell him to go jump in the lake.

There are certain obligations attendant upon being adult, and these can be carried out in a way that convention dictates, generally without destroying one's own integrity, nor doing anything that is destructive to one's security. Even when the boss is disliked, there are certain amenities that can honestly be observed. Even if one can't stand his job, it is possible to bear it until such time that a change can constructively be made.

It is crucial that one explore and understand the forces that serve to disturb one in his relationship to a boss, a job or a committee responsibility. One way to achieve harmony is to try and put oneself in the position of the other person, and to see how things would look from his vantage point. What is going on in the other person right now, that causes him to feel and act the way he does? What is on his mind? How does he see me? How would I feel if I were in his shoes? If both sides of a situation can be recognized, then this very recognition gives one a needed sense of mastery which often will restore equilibrium—even when the objective situation remains unchanged. If, then, one can react to the good rather than the bad in people, one can get along without too much difficulty.

No one feels ideally mature. Inner doubts often will arise when one is called upon to assume some of the roles that are a part of adult living. It is helpful to remember that neither does anyone else feel perfectly secure in all situations. When Eisenhower chose to invade on D-Day, when Pope Paul pronounced on birth control, or when Shakespeare finished writing a play—there must have been doubts in all of them. When the master of ceremonies tells his jokes at the high school football banquet, when the neighbor complains about the volume of the rock and roll on your stereo, and when someone speaks up for racially integrating one's own block, there are fears and insecurities operating then, too.

But the point is that these tasks can be accomplished, the roles can be fulfilled, even in the face of anxiety. Nothing worth doing was ever accomplished without some risk, and hence also some insecurity.

11. *Part of living is being of help to others.* There is an oft-told story about the difference between the Sea of Galilee and the Dead Sea. Around the Sea of Galilee, the countryside is beautiful, and the vegetation is luxuriant. Around the Dead

Sea the environment is harsh and bare, and no life flourishes. The waters of Galilee support the growth of fish, and people enjoy the use of the lake. No animal life survives in the Dead Sea, and people do not enjoy recreation in or around it.

The difference between the two bodies of water illustrates something about human life. The Sea of Galilee is fed by other waters, and also has an outlet where its water flows on to feed other waters. In contrast, the Dead Sea only receives water from other sources, it has no outlets, and does not give up any of its water. This difference accounts for the freshness and vitality of the one water, and the utter saline deadness of the other.

Life has a balance to be maintained between receiving and giving. The solitary pursuit of one's individual needs, without reference to others, ends in emptiness. Giving to others brings returns beyond measure. At a testimonial dinner, when several hundred of the honored man's friends came in order to show their regard, the feted man began his thank you speech with the words, "I did not know I had sown so wisely, nor so well." It was his giving that increased his receiving.

Aside from the return on one's emotional investment in others, there is an inward recognition that the very act of helping others is in itself rewarding. We speak now not to those persons who are able only to be abjectly slavish toward others in their demeanor, which is a pattern also apt to end in hollow bitterness. But rather, we underscore the need to see living as a balance—and that part of living is in being of service to others.

12. *Self-fulfillment is a goal for every stage of life.* The infant is fulfilled as he sucks, the one year old is fulfilled as he walks, the two year old as he shouts "no," the eight year old as he finds a buddy, the 16 year old as he gets a date for the prom, the 20 year old as he moves out of the house. At

every age and stage there is a meaningful relation to others to be undertaken and a fulfilling task to perform. In adult life those self-fulfilling tasks are more subtle, not so biologically oriented as in a one year old, and call for greater perceptiveness.

A person becomes restive unless he is doing what he is fitted for. An activist must be active, a contemplative must meditate, an extrovert must find people. If a man is to be at peace with himself, he needs to join together the wee, small voice of his inner promptings and the external activity that will allow the inner prompting to bear fruit. Leonardo da Vinci drew on anything, Leonard Bernstein must make music, Demosthenes had to orate, James Baldwin needs to pen his outrage.

What a man can be, he must be. This is what self-fulfillment means.

The subtle process of finding oneself in adult life is often seriously hindered by the habits of the years and the exigencies of everyday desiderata. Important decisions made early in life, on the basis of necessity, opportunity, or accident, often do not form the basis for life long fulfillment. Certain needs become gratified, others arise, different opportunities present themselves, and the person who is maturing will adapt himself to a new set of circumstances. Picking up the pieces of one's identity that earlier had to be subdued, the man in middle age may find it possible to express his penchant for machinery, or water, or water colors.

One has the obligation as a member of the human community to be faithful to himself, as well as to others; to be a wise steward of his own inner life, as well as of his money, or his family. It has been found that placing the proper value on responding to one's inner calling, is one of the essentials among a healthy set of values.

Summary

These twelve values, and the five criteria for self-observation that preceded them, are presented as an ongoing program through which personality growth can be promulgated.

Values that people live by are often subliminal. As such they are less subject to scrutiny for the purpose of exploring their effects on living. We have presented here values that are able to bear up under scrutiny, at least the scrutiny of the home and the marketplace. They are on the side of life.

Exercises in self-observation and the practicing of a more constructive life adaptation can be helpful to all persons— to those whose problems do not require formal psychotherapy and those who have had psychotherapy and need to practice patterns essential for their adjustment. They should be utilized selectively but consistently. A thorough reading will enable one to choose areas most pertinent for one's special needs. These may be reviewed daily until they have become fully incorporated. Difficulty in executing essential precepts may be mastered with patience and persistence. Of course, they cannot substitute for competent, professional help where this is required, but they may provide useful supplementation.

21

Guidelines for Parents

Life is like playing a violin solo in public and learning the instrument as one goes on. SAMUEL BUTLER

Parents have developmental stages, too. By the time their oldest child is 16, parents have been parents for only 16 years. And they will have passed through a variety of tribulations and challenges. A mother's talents, for example, must range from nursemaid to den mother to sex educator to fashion consultant. It is reasonable to suppose that she can adapt herself naturally to some stages, but not to others. A father may have an intuitive sense of what is the best thing to do at some strategic times. At others he may show a confounding inability to empathize. Many parents experience an intense feeling of disquietude, for example, at the early signs of a two year old's burgeoning hostility. Parents must move from an experience of omnipotence, resulting from their almost complete sense of mastery over their helpless infant, and grow into a stage of more democratic leadership. Mothers must modify from holding close to letting go, from protecting against all hurt to letting a child have an opportunity to fail on his own. Many parents find it easy to be charitable toward the soft, round, helpless bundle that is a six-month-old child, but may resent the irascible character with a negativistic mind of his own who emerges a year later.

The different qualities required necessitate that parents grow from one stage into another, just as surely as the child grows out of one stage and into another. As a teacher of high school students needs a different approach than a kindergarten teacher, the same is true for a parent.

Many things have been written about stages in childhood and the stages of personality development. To complement that material, we present herewith the *stages in parental development,* in the conviction that the parents who are aware of the stages that they must grow through, and who are aware of the particular demands upon them as they respond to their children, will best be able to develop the kind of family living that promotes robust personality growth.

We begin this exposition now with a single crucial parental variable of great relevance throughout all the parental years. We conclude the chapter with a second key component in parental responsibility. Between these two major principles are specific guidelines for each of what we shall call the five stages of parenthood.

Parental Attitudes

Parental attitudes are more crucial than techniques. A generous spirit and a warm heart are worth more than a hundred rules about child-rearing practices. Feeling tone is difficult to disguise, and the best conscious intentions can go astray under the presence of underlying depression or hostility or detachment. The best gift a child can have is two happy and mature parents. Time spent by parents working on their own frustrations usually helps a child far more than simply an intellectual awareness of good child-rearing methods, apart from any change in attitudes. The most significant requirement for parents at any age is to strive toward personal emotional health, or at least to express emotionally healthy attitudes, which means that the parents will demonstrate love toward their children in a mature fashion. As strong people, they will function as strong parents, able to guide and influence the children. On the other hand, weak, immature, or insecure parents are less able to provide leadership, particularly at those times when parent-child conflict becomes intense and parental firmness is most important.

No parent has an ideal understanding of the nature of his attitudes toward an interaction with this child. Everyone is too close to himself to see precisely what he is doing. As Kierkegaard once wrote, the majority of men are subjective toward themselves, and objective toward others. He felt that what is needed is that persons be objective toward themselves and subjective toward others. Good interpersonal relationships involve the problem of basic attitude and stance in life, not of methods and techniques. Competitiveness, detachment, a hostile need to put people down, disinterestedness caused by preoccupation with one's own inner insecurity, excessive talking prompted by nervous tension, etc., are the kinds of habits that often go on without one being fully aware of how consistently and pervasively they are being employed—although such traits are glaringly obvious to any observer. For this reason, the careful examination of one's attitudes toward others, including one's children, is essential because those underlying attitudes constitute the basis of a person's behavior.

What attitudes are important in a parent? Given a parent with breadth of mind, reasonable maturity, a high estimate of the worth of the youthful personality, a resolve to be of help in every feasible way, and a sense of modesty resulting from self-understanding, we can have some considerable hope that the parent has those attitudes that promote healthy personality growth.

Stages in Parental Development

Parents During the First Year

Parents cannot spoil a child during the first few months of the child's life. A child's experience that all is well comes not from being born with a silver spoon in his mouth, but from the things that money do not buy, namely, parents with unequivocal compassion and relaxed and playful joyfulness in the company of their infant. Tender stimulation, concomitant with the prompt overcoming of the infantile frustrations to which the newborn child is prey, promotes the *joie de vivre* that is one of man's most precious assets.

At six months, nearly all children are utterly delightful. Up to that point, the odds are great that a mother has been generous in her giving to her little offspring, who though obviously selfish, was not in the least malicious. And for most parents, it is not difficult to be generous and giving to someone who is virtually helpless. In fact, many mothers whose children have grown older, remark that they miss having a baby around the house. They miss having an adorable bundle of helplessness who is totally dependent and responsive to ministrations. Subtle satisfaction permeates most mothers at this stage, because they identify themselves with the infant who is being tenderly mothered, as well as enjoy the role of being tender to an infant. They get some sense of gratification at being both child and a mother.

The parental stage of having to give, give, give is one that requires vibrant good health, loads of energy, and plenty of sleep. A large measure of aid from others is enormously helpful at this stage, because this subsidy lightens the load. And in receiving assistance from others, a mother has more to give to her child. Loneliness, insecurity, and fatigue are the great saboteurs of a healthy first stage of being a parent.

The stage of fathering intensifies at six months. Father's task is to demonstrate that there is more than one person in the infant's life who cares for, plays with, and enjoys the child. Most fathers do this admirably. They are just "fun guys" at this point, nearly all play and no work, and the living is easy. The little fellow can smile, and distinguish father from mother, and that is reward enough for all but the angriest of fathers. Most fathers at this stage can help give the little one a sense that he is liked and wanted. They thus play a role similar to that of grandparents with grandchildren: they have all the privileges and few of the responsibilities. Their task is simply to enjoy their offspring. Discipline is not involved, and a father can convey total acceptance.

The beginning signs of a child's discriminations usually constitute a crisis for the parents. When the eight month old begins to lose that innocence that had previously made him so charming, the parents often have some troubles. The first signs of battle begin to appear. The child no longer wants just anybody; he wants his mother. He demands and needs constancy, even as he did before the age of six months, but now he can express a particularized demand better than he could before. Many parents do not do quite as well when a child begins to object to being left alone in another room or with a baby-sitter. This is the first testing period when the parents find out whether they can tolerate letting their child have a mind of his own. This "eight month anxiety" resembles selfishness; however, it actually is the beginning of a child's capacity to love—that is, to form a conscious emotional relationship with a specific person. The parental task is to assure a child that his early efforts to be loving are worth the risk, that his desire for constancy and faithfulness will be met, though within the bounds of what is humanly possible, i.e., a parent cannot and need not attend to him every moment. The child's anxiety about forming individual human attachments during this stage usually lasts only a couple of months, pro-

301

vided that the parents are able to be democratically available, which means that they respond both to the child's needs and to their own needs in interacting with their child.

Parents During the Second Year

Growth as parents calls for athletic participation. The toddler at age one needs parents who can dirty their hands, relax their inhibitions, and involve their bodies in the action. This is a stage for parent to roll and rough house on the floor. Around his first birthday, a child becomes suffused with boundless energy and begins to test his strength and resistance against the world around him. At the same time he begins to experiment with independence and to seek for and to find mastery. With this comes a searching curiosity and desire to explore. It is the task of the parents to be deeply involved, but not so restrictively that the child becomes unduly rebellious or gives up and becomes excessively submissive. The growing parent shares the joy of physical activity and experiences with his child the thrill of conquering new territory. Some parents, of course, have difficulty exploring their own space, and they will experience trouble in letting a child become physically involved with his environment. And then the child will somehow inhibit a part of his venturesome and courageous spirit.

The conflict between love and justice must be confronted. Does justice demand punishment when the two year old smashes a lovely vase to the floor, or does love demand forbearance for the act? Solomon in all his wisdom would be hard-pressed to adjudicate the everyday stresses of the two year old's parent. To protest the child against the tyranny of his untrained judgment calls for firm discipline. To encourage the child in his quest for autonomy calls for great faith. This is clearly one of the most difficult of all stages for parents.

302

When cuddling with their infant, they did not reckon with the constant harassment that they would be facing 18 months later. This is the stage when parents must be secure enough to face constant threats to their authority. At such a time some parents, perhaps out of fear, will over-emphasize justice; others, perhaps out of weakness, will over-emphasize love. The choice often seems to be between tyranny and chaos. The mature parent can speak the truth in love, calling the child to responsibility while still providing the assurance of unconditional love. If parents cannot discipline their child firmly, it is they who need to grow; or if they cannot generously allow autonomy, then it is also the parents who need to grow.

The problem of parental anger and hostility must be faced. Anger is caused by frustration. If there is a crack in the sidewalk and a person trips over a raised slab of cement, he angrily wants to kick the sidewalk, because it has frustrated him in his attempt to hurry down the street. This is the model for nearly all anger. Adults can quickly reason that the sidewalk is really not at fault, and the anger dissipates. Two year olds have no such ability to reconcile cause and effect, but they do have an exquisite sensitivity to frustration, and rage is the result. A parent who himself has a low frustration tolerance will also experience inordinate rage. If both parent and child are "two year olds" emotionally, near bedlam will result. Some parents regard a child as an immense frustration—an infringement upon their own autonomy—and roar accordingly. Other parents feel the same way, but veil their feelings, and the result is a pervasively hostile attitude. And still other parents can be more accepting of the realistic hardships of parenthood and be appropriately angry as the situation demands. The legitimate, open expression of both parents' and children's anger aids a child in understanding what the real world is all about. Facing the justified anger of another person can be reassuring for both parties. Proper

303

habits in the expression of strong feelings are best taught by parents who are comfortable being angry, resorting neither to breaking furniture nor hostile sweetness. However, the parent who either cannot control, or cannot accept his own angry feelings will have undue difficulty adjusting to a two year old's impulses. By exploding and paying undue attention to truculent or obstinate behavior, he may encourage and reinforce it.

Parents at Ages Three Through Five

A parent must be secure with his own sexuality. After a child subjects his parents to that phase called the terrible twos, he soon begins the next phase, marked by more than casual sexual preoccupation. To cope with this phase successfully, parents will need to be quite free of prudish attitudes and free of the problems that result from their own ungratified sexual needs. At this age, three through five, the little fellow or girl becomes frankly seductive, and a parent can often tend to substitute the affection of a child for that of a spouse who is emotionally or sexually distant. The need is for parents who are, on the one hand, comfortable with the open display of their child's sexual curiosity, but, on the other hand, do not need to gratify their own needs for physical attention and affection through their children.

Parents must understand their sexual identity. Part of parents' sexual security is a firm understanding of their own sexual identity. That includes deriving generous pleasures from a mature sexual life, and it also means deriving pleasures from a myriad of other activities appropriate to one's sexual role. Thus, for example, a man finds it natural to be a woman's protector, and a woman delights in making a man comfortable. This interplay is one of cooperative receiving and giving. Parents like these are able to provide the models for their children wherein the youngsters readily develop their own sexual identity. On the other hand, grumbling acceptance, or boredom or fatigue resulting from the activities appropriate for one's sex provide poor models to emulate. Infectious enthusiasm is the mark of the adult who enjoys himself or herself, and it is this very infectiousness that is passed on to the child.

A frank revelation of the facts goes farther than their concealment. Parents understandably feel uncomfortable when their children go through the exploratory stage of handling their genitals and inquiring about the processes of conception and birth. Such curiosity is a healthy and essential part of their development. A frank, truthful approach to these questions, couched in non-threatening, non-frightening language the child can understand, will do what evasion can never accomplish. There are many excellent books available for parents. One may begin with Spock's *Baby and Child Care* (1968). Even more specifically helpful is Hegeler's *Peter and Caroline* (1960), which is a picture book to be used by the children themselves.

A parent must expect to endure the rigors of sibling rivalry. Parents simply must plan to "fasten their seat belts" because there is little they can do to reduce the anger of a child being displaced by a newcomer. No matter how thoroughly prepared a child is for the contingency of a baby, he may be expected in thought or action to want to dispose of his rival. The parents must steer a course between sharing affection and firm, loving discipline, frankly expressing disapproval if the new baby is mishandled. They must convey the fact that the baby is here to stay, but this need not result in withholding love from the older child.

Letting go of a child at age five is most possible when parents have faced their own dependency problems. Chil-

305

dren achieve the most when parents have expected them to pursue independent activities and to make friends outside the home. Such a climate of growth means that the parents are not unduly frightened by the terrors lurking in the neighbor's yard, or across the street, or even in the next block. Parents must have reckoned with their own ambivalence about wishing a child to be out of the way. They must have matured enough so that they can relinquish their desire to over-protect, and thus permit teachers and a child's peers to contribute to the growth of offspring. But if a parent is not able himself to be independent, if he feels that he must protect himself against outside environmental influences, then he will not freely allow a child to go to school and be a part of the crowd. And absence from the parent may then give the child a variety of dreadful terrors. This juncture for parents is a continuation of the earlier epoch when they had to allow their two year old to navigate the hazards of a stairway; it is a forerunner of the regimen when they will have to allow their teen ager to traverse the hazards of a heterosexual social life.

Parents During the Early School Years

School years introduce the stage when parents must ignore many things. It comes natural for parents to want to superintend every little activity of their children. And if they keep doing that on into childhood, they will find *themselves* manipulated by their child. For example, whenever a child finds that a certain act will get attention from a parent, he will automatically repeat that activity. This applies to rewarding as well as punishing attention from the parent. P. T. Barnum once colorfully indicated a great truth about human nature when he said "Say anything you want about me; if you like, say that I stole the money from the church's collection plate, just be sure to *mention my name.*" The truth is that any enterprise that regularly gets a response out of the parent will become an automatic habit—both for the child and for the parent. This is why a child who chatters incessantly will increase his chattering if it always gets his mother to respond to him by saying "you aren't making sense. You are just making noise." An argument then follows, and obviously both mother and child are getting some of their needs satisfied through quarreling. *It is difficult for parents to learn that it is wiser to keep their mouths shut about a great many little things, because the best way to extinguish a habit which the child already knows to be obnoxious is utterly to ignore it, while responding generously to those positive activities which are mature and praiseworthy.* A child should not be allowed to get any "mileage" out of misbehavior. The fun disappears from any activity where there is no pay-off. "Don't sweat the little things" is a maxim that is particularly appropriate to the school years, a maxim that may permit parents to enjoy their children once they realize that only bad results accrue from continually nagging their offspring.

The enjoyment of learning is a positive force in parents of school children. Good school attitudes can be absorbed at home from parents who love books, who relish intellectual discussions, who are curious about new ideas, and who are not dismayed if their children are being taught differently from the traditional methods of the previous generation. Some parents who push their children to read are rarely themselves seen reading for pleasure. Some parents speak of the necessity for learning, but do not exhibit at the dinner table that they have pursued the quest themselves. Joy is usually infectious, and parents who can genuinely express the delight of intellectual mastery can transmit this to their child and convert what is so often a dismaying succession of coercions to a delightful time of sharing.

307

Parents During the Teen Years

The successful parent needs four essential qualities during the child's 13 through 19 year span.

A sense of freedom and spontaneity. A parent is fulfilling his responsibilities when he allows his child to be as original as he himself is original. The more a parent can "do his own thing," the more he will be able to trust his child to become responsibly independent. Parents should be free to speak their own minds, to knock heads verbally with their offspring, to be blunt, direct, and, if necessary, forceful. This kind of security provides the atmosphere with which children can safely argue and disagree with their parents, thereby testing their own strengths and experiencing a growing ability to hold their own. The adolescent needs this conflict, and parents should not retreat from it. When the parent feels positively about his own values, and has resolved his own ambivalence about living responsibly in society, he has become the kind of parent that a teen ager needs. And the teen ager will then become "his own man"—not his father's man to be sure, but probably as independent as his father before him was able to become independent. All indications are that reasonable and independent parents enable their children to emerge from adolescence as reasonable and independent young adults.

Rich social and sexual relationships. Teen agers will vary from alarming seclusiveness to profligate personal involvement with others. Parents will often be hard pressed to weather the vagaries of their child's social and sexual experimentation. The social intercourse of the adolescent ranges from the earliest intimate contacts which take the form of boys and girls physically pushing and shoving each other around the age 13, on through serious courtship and sexual closeness. It takes mature parents who themselves are capable of accepting others to provide a teen ager with a model on how to perform socially. Conversations about social and sexual matters may advantageously become as much a part of the interaction in the family circle as discussions about money, education, religion, and politics. The individual climbs from a social involvement exclusively with his mother, such as prevails at birth, through a variety of steps leading eventually to the most intimate of all social involvements, namely adult heterosexual intercourse. Parents who themselves have reached the stage of enjoying their sexuality will, without any special fanfare, help prepare their children for an equally satisfying stage. Best prepared for the task of helping their adolescent become sexually secure are those parents who satisfy their own needs without guilt and fear.

Recognition of proper vocational aims. How does a teen ager decide that work is fulfilling? It is first through observing others and realizing that work brings self-respect as well as a good income; thus he senses that a vocation can be rewarding. During these years a young person sets some of the directions for his career, and the parents who can speak frankly about their own goals (whether they have been realized or not) will encourage the dialog that leads to responsible vocational choices. Bitter disillusionments, unrealistic scheming, or silent resignation indicate that the parent has not yet reached the stage where he can be the most helpful to a teen ager who is anticipating his own occupational future. Mothers at this stage often fail to demonstrate that they have made peace with their staying at home situations. This complicates a daughter's expectations by casting doubt on a woman's ability to make satisfying career choices. On the other hand, a woman who has "found herself" by this age will exude a confidence that proclaims to her daughter "if I can do it, you can do it." In a changing society, it is not easy for both parents to have surmounted successfully the goal of vocational fulfillment, but it is nonetheless true that their own readiness to wrestle with the problems involved will materially affect their offspring as he faces one of his crucial life tasks as an adolescent.

A firm establishment of identity. It is understandable that it may take some people a long time, even beyond 40, to know fully their capabilities, their values, and their overall stance in life. We set a minimum age of 35 for the United States President, and our opinion is actually that he should be considerably older before he is entrusted with the supreme office. In like manner, we do not expect the average citizen to be fully mature until he has advanced beyond the 30's. Fortunate is the teen ager who firms his identity in late adolescence, in the mold of his parents who have securely found theirs.

Identity is an inward sense of one's uniqueness, coupled with the ability to assert that uniqueness in everyday life. Having an identity of his own lifts a person above commonplace conformity. Lacking a sense of his own identity, a parent will tend to be more competitive with his child. If he needs to gain a feeling of superiority by being critical of others, even his children will be subject to the rivalry that stems from his insecurity.

One of the greatest gifts bestowed on a young person are parents who have attained a sense of their own identity, and who can rather unself-consciously and undefensively express it. Freedom fosters the growth of freedom, and a child experiences that he, too, has the right to become himself.

Parental Involvement

The final parental component, crucial for every age and stage, has the same effect as yeast in dough—it makes for growth in every particle of the mixture. The principle may be stated as follows: *Concentrated parental involvement and stimulation vis a vis a child leads to optimum intellectual, emotional, and social growth.*

There is naturally, an appropriate type of stimulation for different ages. As infants demand all the cuddling possible, two year olds require parental playfulness, eight year olds relish learning experiences, and adolescents need debates to mention only a few of the stimulants on which growing personalities thrive. The emotional and intellectual accessibility of parents make possible the continuing interaction between parent and child. This is the yeast in the growth process. The more of the world a child experiences, the more he wants to experience, given a firm security base. And the more he experiences, the greater becomes his capacity to amalgamate his inner world with his external environment. This leads to the development of personal wisdom and social intelligence.

Wise parents have noticed how a baby in a carriage is fascinated by leaves overhead shimmering in the sunlight. Now, artistic mobiles are attached to cribs to exert the same stimulating effect. Similarly, bombarding a child with appropriate *interpersonal* stimuli is one of the most crucial of parental tasks. Responsiveness and depth of feeling are learned by example and consolidated through practice. As a muscle grows with exercise, emotionality and intellectuality expand with the interactions accessible parents provide.

Twentieth century man, it is acknowledged by all, is having great problems in communication. Whether it be between parent and child, or between East and West, there is difficulty in hearing and understanding one another.

It is little wonder that our contemporary homes harbor insufficient personal involvement of parent with child. Television has greatly reduced the numbers of words spoken per day between members of a family. Differing daily schedules have reduced the percentage of meals eaten together. Smaller

311

apartments and houses have lowered the quota of grand-parents and aunts and uncles in the home. Geographical mobility has increased the distances between members of the extended family. The summation of activities participated in by the entire family together is without question less than in previous generations. Concentrated parental involvement with a child must be conscientiously pursued. To become most fully human, persons need intimate human involvement on intellectual, emotional, and social levels. The current problems of mankind, especially the calamities of war, prejudice, poverty, and the battle between generations, are related to man's understanding and appreciation of his fellow man, and to his ability to enter into the other person's communicative world. We suggest that one early, influential step toward the relief of the dilemma of our time is for prudent parents to spend more time with their children in their growing up period, fully participating in dialog and helping them to face and resolve the problems that constitute the essential tasks in personality development.

Summary

With a large measure of optimism, we conclude with the powerful words of Dr. Martin Luther King when he received the Nobel Peace Prize on December 10, 1964. His thoughts are also our thoughts:

"I accept this award today with . . . an audacious faith in the future of mankind. I refuse to accept the idea that the 'isness' of man's present nature makes him morally incapable of reaching up for the eternal 'oughtness' that forever confronts him."

References

ARDREY, R.: The Territorial Imperative. London, Collins, 1967.

BENJAMIN, S.: The innate and the experiential in child development. In: Lectures in Experimental Psychiatry. (Brosin, H. Ed.) Pittsburgh, Univ. of Pittsburgh Press, 1961.

BERGMAN, P. and ESCALONA, S.: Unusual sensitivities in very young children. Psychoanal. Stud. Child. 3/4:333-352, 1949.

BOWLBY, J.: Maternal Care and Mental Health. Geneva, World Health Organization, 1952.

BRUCH, H.: Psychotherapy with schizophrenics. In: International Clinics—Schizophrenia. (Kolb, L., Kallman, F. and Polatin, P., (Eds.) Boston, Little, Brown and Co., 1964.

CAMUS, A.: The Myth of Sisyphus. N. Y., Knopf, 1955.

CAPOTE, T.: In Cold Blood. N. Y., Random House, 1965.

DOBZHANSKY, T.: Mankind Evolving. New Haven, Yale Univ. Press, 1962.

DOUVAN, E. and ADELSON, J.: The Adolescent Experience. N. Y., Wiley, 1966.

EIDUSON, B.: Brain mechanisms and psychotherapy. Am. J. Psychiat. 115:203-210, 1958.

ERIKSON, E. H.: Childhood and Society. N. Y., Norton, Pp. 247-274, 1963.

ERVIN, F., LION, J. and BACH-Y-RITA, G.: The self-referred violent patient. J. Amer. Medical Ass'n. August 12, 1968, Vol. 205, Pp. 503-505.

———: Violent patients in the emergency room. Am. J. Psychi. In Press, 1969.

ESCALONA, S. and HEIDER, G.: Prediction and Outcome. N. Y., Basic Books, 1959.

ESCALONA, S. and LATCH, M.: Early Phases of Personality Development: a Non-Normative Study of Infant Behavior. Evanston, Child Development Publications, 1953.

FITZGERALD, F.: Tender Is the Night. N. Y., Scribners, 1934.

FREUD, S.: Instincts and their vicissitudes. In Collected Papers. Vol. IV, Pp. 60-83. London, Hogarth Press, 1946.

———: The Origins of Psychoanalysis; Letters to Wilhelm Fliess, Drafts and Notes, 1887-1902. N. Y., Basic Books, 1954.

GESELL, A.: The Embryology of Behavior. N. Y., Harper, 1945.

GOLDING, W.: Lord of the Flies. N. Y., Coward-McCann, 1962.

GREENACRE, P.: Early physical determinants in the development of the sense of identity. J. Amer. Psychoanal. Ass'n. 6:612-627, 1958.

GURR, T.: A causal model of civil strife: a comparative analysis using new indices. American Political Science Review. 62:1104-1124, December 1968.

————: Psychological factors in civil violence. World Politics 20, 245-278, January 1968.

HARLOW, H. F.: The Development of Learning in the Rhesus Monkey. Sci. Progr. 12:239-69, 1962.

————: Primary Affectional Patterns in Primates. Am. J. Orthopsychiat. 30:676-84, 1960.

HARLOW, H. F. and HARLOW, M. K.: The Effect of Rearing Conditions on Behavior. Bull. Menninger Clin. 26:213-24, September, 1962.

HARTMANN, H.: Comments on the psychoanalytic theory of the ego. The Psychoanalytic Study of the Child, 5:74-96. N. Y., Inter. Univ. Press, 1950.

HARTMANN, H., KRIS, E., and LOWENSTEIN, R. M.: Comments on the formation of psychic structure. The Psychoanalytic Study of the Child. 2:11-38. N. Y., Inter. Univ. Press, 1946.

HASTINGS, D.: Psychiatry of presidential assassination. Journal-Lancet 85. March, April, May, July, 1965.

HEGELER, S.: Peter and Caroline. N. Y., Abelard, 1960.

HOFFMAN, L. and HOFFMAN, M. (Eds.): Review of Child Development Research. 2 Vols. N. Y., Russell Sage Fdtn., 1964 and 1966.

JACOBSON, E.: The Self and the Object World. N. Y., Inter. Univ. Press, 1964.

JAHODA, M.: Current Concepts of Positive Mental Health. N. Y., Basic Books, 1958.

KAGAN, J., and MOSS, H.: Birth to Maturity. N. Y., Wiley, 1962.

KARDINER, A.: The Individual and His Society. N. Y., Columbia Univ. Press, 1939.

KELMAN, S.: These are three of the alienated. The N. Y. Times Magazine. October 22, 1967.

KNIGHT, R.: Introjection, projection and identification. Psychoanal. Quart. 9:334-341, 1940.

LORENZ, K.: King Solomon's Ring. London, Methuen, 1952.

————: Man Meets Dog. Baltimore, Penguin, 1965.

————: On Aggression. London, Methuen, 1966.

MAHLER, M.: Problems of identity. J. Amer. Psychoanal. Ass'n. 6: 131-142, 1958.

MASSERMAN, J.: Principles of Dynamic Psychiatry. Philadelphia, W. B. Saunders, 1961.

McCAGUE, J.: The Second Rebellion. N. Y., Dial, 1968

McCLELLAND, D.: Talent and Society. N. Y., Van Nostrand, 1964.

————: Roots of Consciousness. N. Y., Van Nostrand, 1964.

————: Achieving Society. N. Y., Van Nostrand, 1961.

———: Personality. N. Y., Holt, Rinehart & Winston, 1951.
———: Achievement Motive. N. Y., Appleton, 1953.
———: Studies in Motivation. N. Y., Appleton, 1955.
MURPHY, L.: The Widening World of Childhood, the Paths Toward Mastery. N. Y., Basic Books, 1962.
MUSSEN, P.: Some antecedents and consequents of masculine sex-typing in adolescent boys. Psychol. Mongr. 75, No. 2, 1961.
PACKARD, V.: The Sexual Wilderness. N. Y., David McKay, 1968.
PIAGET, J.: Origins of Intelligence in Children. N. Y., Inter. Univ. Press, 1952.
REICH, A.: Pathological forms of self-esteem regulation. The Psychoanalytic Study of the Child. 15:215-232. N. Y., Inter. Univ. Press, 1960.
RIBBLE, M.: The Rights of Infants. N. Y., N. Y. Univ. Press, 1943.
ROCHE REPORT: Varied temperamental patterns described in neonates. Vol. 1, No. 5, Pp. 1-2, June 1, 1964.
ROTHSTEIN, D.: Presidential assassination syndrome. Arch. of Neur. of Psych. 2, 245-254, September 1964.
SCAMMON, R., The measurement of the body in childhood. In The Measurement of Man (J. Harris, et al.) Minneapolis, Univ. of Minn. Press, 1938.
SCHLESINGER, A.: Kennedy or Nixon. N. Y., Macmillan, 1960.
SCHUR, M.: Phylogenesis and ontogenesis of affect—and structure-formation and the phenomenon of repetition compulsion. Int. J. Psycho-Anal. 41:375-287, 1960.
SCIENCE NEWS LETTER: Infants need companions. December 12, 1959.
SCOTT, J.: Aggression. Chicago, Univ. of Chicago Press, 1958.
SELYE, H.: Stress, The Physiology and Pathology of Exposure to Stress. Montreal, Acta, 1950.
SOFOKIDIS, J. and SULLIVAN, E.: A New Look at School Dropouts. U. S. Dept. of Health, Education and Welfare Indicators, April, 1964.
SPITZ, R.: Anaclitic depression. In: Psychoanalytic Study of the Child. Vol. 2, N. Y., Inter. Univ. Press, 1946.
SPOCK, B.: Baby and Child Care. N. Y., Pocket Books, 1968.
SROLL, L., OPLER, M., and LANGNER, T.: Mental Health in the Metropolis. N. Y., McGraw-Hill, 1962.
STORR, A.: Human Aggression. N. Y., Atheneum, 1968.
TAYLOR, G.: Sex in History. N. Y., Vanguard, 1954.
TILLICH, P.: The Courage to Be. New Haven, Yale Univ. Press, 1952.
TINBERGEN, N.: Bird Life. London & N. Y., Oxford Univ. Press, 1954.
———: Curious Naturalists. N. Y., Basic Books, 1959.
———: Herring Gull's World. rev. edit. Basic Books, 1961.

REFERENCES

———: Social Behavior in Animals. N. Y., Wiley, 1953.
———: The Study of Instinct. London & N. Y., Oxford Univ. Press, 1951.
WHITING, B. (Ed.): Six Cultures: Studies of Child Rearing. N. Y., John Wiley and Sons, 1963.
WINNICOTT, D. W.: The theory of the parent-infant relationship. Int. J. Psycho-Anal. 41:585-595, 1960.
WOLBERG, L.: Psychotherapy and The Behavioral Sciences. N. Y., Grune and Stratton, 1966.
WRIGHT, H. F.: Observational Child Study. In Handbook of Research Methods in Child Development. (Mussen, P. E., Ed.) N. Y., John Wiley and Sons, 1960.
YARROW, L. J. and GOODWIN, M. S.: Some conceptual issues in the study of mother-infant interaction. Am. J. Orthopsychiat. 35: 473-481, 1965.

Index